WITHDRAWN

A CRITICAL SURVEY OF ETHICS

A CRITICAL SURVEY OF ETHICS

Howard A. Slaatte

UNIVERSITY
PRESS OF
AMERICA

Lanham • New York • London

Copyright © **1988** by

University Press of America,® Inc.

4720 Boston Way
Lanham, MD 20706

3 Henrietta Street
London WC2E 8LU England

All rights reserved

Printed in the United States of America

British Cataloging in Publication Information Available

Library of Congress Cataloging-in-Publication Data

Slaatte, Howard Alexander.
A critical survey of ethics.
Bibliography: p.
Includes index.
1. Ethics—History. I. Title.
BJ71.S58   1988   170   88-20678
ISBN 0-8191-7165-4 (pbk. : alk. paper)

All University Press of America books are produced on acid-free paper.
The paper used in this publication meets the minimum requirements of
American National Standard for Information Sciences—Permanence of Paper
for Printed Library Materials, ANSI Z39.48-1984.

LISLE LIBRARY DISTRICT
LISLE, ILLINOIS 60532

Preface

One of the great needs of the present generation is for a recovery of moral principles among the people of Western culture. It goes almost without saying that an ethical decline has set in leading to what the noted Harvard sociologist Peterim Sorokin has called "a sensate culture." To offset this decline and to prevent the collapse of our civilization we must recognize "the crisis of the age" and reintroduce principles that make for an "ideological culture" to balance up the trends of our civilization today.

An important aspect of such a moral recovery is the study of ethics. Far too few of our college students today are exposed to ethics as a field of inquiry. Though a slow growing number of students are being exposed to specialized fields of ethics such as business ethics and medical ethics, too few are being exposed to the cross-section of the greatest ethical theories to have appeared in the West. The present project is designed to help meet such a need both as a survey and as a critique of such theories. Though not a totally new approach to ethics, this one is a series of precise essays on the leading ethicists of our history. In general it combines a historical perspective with classifications of theories and theorists. Towards the close of each discussion criticisms both pro and con are offered. The critique which this embraces is in the main the writer's own views while for the most part of a practical and existentialist perspective of a balanced type. By the latter is meant a holistic view of selfhood combined with a temperate empirical approach making for a touch of critical realism interrelated with a phenomenlogical respect for the primacy of human consciousness. At the same time the individualism implied is related to a strong social concern, thus the kind of personalistic existentialism expressed by Nicholas Berdyaev in his many works. Not that this position is expressly expounded but that the author concedes its influence upon his views.

Stylistically, the project begins the respective essays with a broad summation of the thinker's position followed by documented explications and critiques. Though the general reader is kept in mind, the work lends itself to a textbook in the field of ethical studies. As such it is a survey from Plato to Fletcher. Classical, medieval, modern and contemporary schools of thought are all represented by leading thinkers of the periods. The Introduction is meant to provoke the reader's concern for ethical issues relevant to life in today's world and to stimulate interest in such matters to whet the appetite for the studies that follow.

I cannot overstate what I owe to my good wife, Mildred, for typing the manuscript, and I am grateful to my editorial advisors.

Also to U.P.A. for permission to include the essay on Bertrand Russell. "I am a debtor."

Howard A. Slaatte, Ph.D.
Department of Philosophy
Marshall University
Huntington, West Virginia 25701

TABLE OF CONTENTS

Introduction — xi

Chapter I

Ethics and Classical Thought — 1

1. The Ethics of Plato — 5
2. The Ethics of Aristotle — 15
3. The Ethics of Epicurus — 27
4. The Ethics of Epictetus — 35

Chapter II

Ethics and Early Christian Thought — 43

5. The Ethics of Augustine — 47
6. The Ethics of Thomas Aquinas — 55

Chapter III

Ethics and Social Theory — 61

7. The Ethics of Thomas Hobbes — 65
8. The Ethics of the Earl of Shaftesbury — 73
9. The Ethics of David Hume — 79

Chapter IV

Ethics and Rationalism — 83

10. The Ethics of Benedict de Spinoza — 87
11. The Ethics of Joseph Butler — 95
12. The Ethics of Immanuel Kant — 103

Chapter V

Ethics and Utilitarianism   111

    13. The Ethics of Jeremy Bentham   115

    14. The Ethics of John Stuart Mill   121

Chapter VI

Ethics and Ideal Utilitarianism   125

    15. The Ethics of G. E. Moore   129

    16. The Ethics of John Rawls   139

Chapter VII

Ethics and Positivism   145

    17. The Ethics of A. J. Ayer and Charles Stevenson   149

    18. The Ethics of Bertrand Russell   157

Chapter VIII

Ethics and Pragmatism   165

    19. The Ethics of John Dewey   169

    20. The Ethics of Erich Fromm   179

Chapter IX

Ethics and Existentialism   187

    21. The Ethics of Søren Kierkegaard   191

    22. The Ethics of Friedrich Nietzsche   203

    23. The Ethics of Jean-Paul Sartre   213

    24. The Ethics of Joseph Fletcher   221

Introduction:

Ethics is the branch of philosophy that may be briefly defined as the science of morals. As such it is the study of the moral principles and problems involved in what to the Greeks was man's pursuit of "the good life" or what later thinkers viewed to be "right conduct." Among philosophers it is the principles of ethics which are basic to the study, yet at times ethics refers to an accepted code; at other times to a specialized field such as medical ethics or legal ethics. In general there are two broad types of ethics, the theoretical and the practical. This distinction goes back to Aristotle's view of truth as both <u>theoretikos</u> and <u>praktikos</u>. In this book theoretical ethics will be kept uppermost with occasional movements into practical areas for illuminating and comparative purposes.

Usually philosophers refer to ethics as theoretical study of moral principles, there being a variety of perspectives, classifications and historical developments. Beneath these concerns lie the underlying questions: What is the basis of the good life and right conduct? How ought men to behave? Theoretical ethics is basic in the sense that it provides us with fundamental theories that give intellectual integrity or "backbone" to applied ethics. It gives principles to the various areas and problems of practical ethics. Without ethical theory there would be no foundation for the moral choices or decisions we must make in everyday life. In other words, theoretical ethics is what makes sense out of practical ethics. Though it may not always be absolutely convincing it represents the best thinkers have managed to develop upon suggesting intellectually how to attain the so-called good life.

As already intimated, there are different types of philosophical approaches to ethics. The varied types of theories have different effects on human existence. Some appear plausible at a glance but upon further inquire do not pass the tests of either reason or experience. One of the oldest such theories is that of hedonism, the doctrine and appeal to maximum pleasure and minimum pain. It was first proposed systematically by Epicurus (341-370 B.C.), whose chief philosophical contribution was to appeal to long-range pleasures as good together with the suspension of lesser pleasures. Though a popular view at times, hedonism is to be called in question, for often there are bad pleasures that lead men into a kind of self-enslavement. Often momentary pleasures have long range displeasures or subsequent pain and travail, drugs being a case in point. It can be questioned, then, whether pleasure is basic to the ethical life. But what is the basis if it is not pleasure? Philosophers have pondered long and hard over this questions studying and developing many ethical theories to answer it.

An alternative to hedonism in ancient Greece was cynicism. Whereas hedonism was used often as a kind of escapism in times of catastrophe, cynicism was different. It arose at the time of the collapse of the Greek city states under the influence of the wars between Sparta, Corinth and Athens as well as the collapse of the Alexandrian Empire. As society broke down a personal salvation was sought through withdrawal. As a form of this, cynicism held a negative attitude toward civilization. Its fruits were deemed worthless, including private property, government, marriage, slavery, religion, luxury, and pleasures. In contrast cynics advocated a return to a simpler life, even an ascetic type. In the 4th century B.C. a school of cynics was founded by Antisthenes, a friend of Socrates. Like Socrates he saw virtue in knowledge. Diogenes, a pupil of Antisthenes, practiced a very frugal life, living in a large tub rejecting finer food and dress. Cynics believed the world to be evil and one must withdraw from it and not trust what commonly is thought to make for happiness. Salvation is within one's own virtue, and renunciation of material things must be practiced. In general cynics were anti-social; social ethics suffered at their hands. They were the "hippies" of their day.

It is erroneous to think that ethics is strictly academic. It springs from and focuses on the issues of daily human existence. One of the keynote issues is what almost everyone experiences sooner or later. It is knowing what it is to be torn between alternatives admist circumstances, on the one hand, and accepted standards or ideals, on the other. One of the most obvious cases is the civilian in time of war. Another is the choice of behavior under types of peer pressure. The philosopher as an ethicist, however, tries to systematize what the average person confronts and chooses. In so doing he is more apt to reflect on: What is basic to the good life for any and all men in the present age? What is the good for which men should strive? What is the basic principle involved? Is it happiness, duty, wisdom, social sentiment, love, religious conviction, or just what? Historically, there have been many projected theories. The existentialist philosopher is a type of thinker who qualifies the basic claims by saying that the philosophical answers are irrelevant unless they address "my" particular condition as an individual in concrete, everyday situations. In that event ethics must be more than an academic pursuit.

Whatever approach is undertaken to the study of ethics we are bound to be confronted by two types of theoretical problems fundamental to most, if not any, ethical theories. First is the problem of freedom versus determinism. One of the most long-standing of ethical issues it appears in every generation of moral thought and is still pertinent in today's philosophical inquiries. How do we reconcile moral freedom with necessitative or deterministic forces at work in our world? Can the two principles be reconciled? If not, why not, and what can be done about it? These are some of most perennial of all underlying issues in ethical studies.

A second fundamental theoretical problem is that of the dialectics of the universal versus the particular. This is akin to the ideal versus the actual, or the absolute versus the relative. Sometimes it assumes the form of the general versus the concrete, the unconditional versus the conditional, or the permanent or eternal versus the temporary or temporal. It is safe to say that nothing is more crucial to the study of ethics than these classes and subclasses of dialectical problems.

Sometimes universals or absolute ideals fail to address concrete situations. Even in the Bible we meet with this problem and Jesus, for instance, respected the law of sabbath observance yet, in overcoming legalism could say, "The sabbath is made for man, not man for the sabbath." This articulates the problem of the absolute law versus the relative situation. Likewise in the Old Testament father Abraham was challenged faithwise by God to sacrifice his son Isaac. Before the altar in the wilderness, Abraham had to choose between the will of God and the life of his son. Søren Kierkegaard was much influenced by this recorded incident and viewed it as "the teleological suspension of the ethical." The implication is that not always do universals or ideals do justice to concrete situations and not always can concrete situations do justice to universals or ideals.

But the question still prevails: Are we not responsible for universals? Different thinkers give different answers. As an idealist the pacifist, for instance, answers with a resounding 'yes.' The realist likely with a qualified 'no' and the existentialist likely with a 'yes' and 'no' as in the case of Joseph Fletcher's situation ethics, which respects both the relative situation and the ideals of love and righteousness.

Having acknowledged that there are different kinds of ethics, we must ask why they must be classified? For one thing grouping them by their similarities makes them easier to understand. It helps us see the features which make the theories distinctive. One of the most obvious classifications is the historical, when they are identified as either classical, scholastic or modern. A less obvious, but important, classification is by the types or basic emphases. For instance, though Butler and Kant were generations apart, they both belong to what is termed formalism with respective appeals to the moral reason of man. Another type is teleological ethics, which looks to the results of moral acts rather than the motive. Jeremy Bentham and John Stuart Mill as utilitarians were of this type as were William James and John Dewey as pragmatists. Each of these types of ethical theory becomes involved in a thinker's interrelating fundamental principles with practical applications, some probably catering to one pole of emphasis over the other. Dialectically, this often entails intellectual adjustments which pose tensions, leaving one torn between the alternatives of an either/or dichotomy, a both/and synthesis or a both/and paradox. Different interpreters may settle for different alternatives.

Ethics is not only significant for the individual but for our society and culture in general. It is indigenous to the very course of history and a nation's destiny. The noted Harvard sociologist Peterim Sorokin in his book <u>The Crisis of Our Age</u> indicates that our society has reached the bottom of a cycle representing a sensate culture due to a shift away from higher ideologies, values and morals. A visiting sociologist from Europe said, "What are you Americans doing-- entertaining yourselves to death?" "No, it is not that," said an American in reply, "It's our passion for escape." Escape!" said the shocked European, "what silliness is this? You have the most bountiful and most satisfying way of life in the world, yet you want to escape!" Similarly, a young man from Sweden was asked why the suicide rate was so high in his country. He replied, "Life is too easy for us."

Such exchanges deserve ethical consideration. Where are we headed in Western civilization today? It may be time to wake up culturally as ancient Rome did not. In 1787 Gibbon completed his notable work, <u>The Decline and Fall of the Roman Empire</u>. Here is the way Gibbon accounted for the fall of the Empire: 1. "The rapid increase of divorce; the undermining of the dignity and sanctity of the home, which is the basis of human society." 2. "Higher and higher taxes and the spending of public monies for free bread and circuses for the populace." 3. "The mad craze for pleasure; sports becoming every year more exciting and more brutal." 4. "The building of gigantic armaments when the real enemy was within, in the decadence of the people." 5. "The decay of religion -- faith fading into mere form, losing touch with life and becoming impotent to warn and guide the people."

The parallel between Rome and America today is most apparent. The Romans often said with a less sophisticated form of Epicureanism, "Eat, drink and be merry, for tomorrow we die." On the morrow Rome fell. Is it not possible that modern Americans have been attracted by so much pleasure and ease because so much has been available to us? America became great through the sweat of labor and industry conjoined with commitment to great principles. Have we not overshot the mark of pleasure-seeking and convenience in later decades? Have we not developed a generation of people caught in the bogs of pleasure and comfort? An editor put it like this: "We see the need all around us -- the jaded emptiness of people who get too much and give too little -- the nightclub neurotic, the painful playboy, the worried wastrel." Many people today actually need work and creative activity as a therapy for restoring mental and emotional health. If we do not earn what pleasure or happiness we gain, we shall be unhappy.

Each age reflects the spirit and degree of commitment of its people. The cynicism of the 1960's found expression among the Hippies and in primitive forms like rock music. Lack of self-discipline led to promiscuity and the decline of ethical values. Freedom has been reduced to moral license, while the human spirit still yearns for the tranquility of virtuous living. It has been shrewdly stated, "At this moment we are engaged in a great world contest for the minds of men -- the respect and confidence of the non-committed, who are grouped in the strategic areas of the world."

What people commit themselves to ethically will determine who they are and the very course of their world. It would be both ironic and pathetic if our highly advantaged and embellished nation should lose what it has stood for in her greater moments. The study of ethics is germane to retaining the intellectual, moral and spiritual principles that made those greater moments possible. It is also germane to the improvement of the moral climate of the present age, for what men believe determines the quality of their culture and the direction of their civilization. Ethical principles are the leaven in the loaf of a culture even as culture is the values by which a civilization lives or dies.

CHAPTER I

ETHICS AND CLASSICAL THOUGHT

1. The Ethics of Plato
2. The Ethics of Aristotle
3. The Ethics of Epicurus
4. The Ethics of Epictetus

The Sketch of Plato

Plato (427-347 B.C.) was born during the Peloponnesian War, a series of conflicts which almost destroyed the city-states of Greece from within. A time of political turmoil, it was marked, too, by moral deterioration. Plato sensed the need for high ideals by which his society could be salvaged. Also, he saw the need for philosopher-kings to replace the governments of the people. In general, Plato made an aristocratic appeal having royal blood on both his father's and mother's sides. Wealth gave Plato the best education available in his youth. When he was twenty he gained contact with Socrates, the noted teacher with the dialectical method and from whom Plato gained much in erudition and wisdom. The trial and death of Socrates made Plato even less confident in the democracy of Athens. He thereupon travelled for twelve years in Egypt and Italy. When he was forty he returned to Athens and established his famous Academy where he taught effectively until he was eighty. His writings are in the form of dialogues with Socrates his chief spokesman. His dialogue the Gorgias is especially important for ethics while others deal with special virtues like temperance and piety. The theory of knowledge is treated in the Theatetus and love in Phaedrus and Symposium. His masterpiece is the Republic which relates his overall philosophy to the theory of the state. Ethically, Plato sees "the good life" based on Socrates' assertion that "virtue is knowledge." Reason makes for happiness as it controls the passions and desires of life. The virtuous person is balanced between mind, body and emotions while emotions and sense perceptions are inferior to reason. The virtuous person looks to the ideal virtues of wisdom, temperance, courage, and justice.

The Ethics of Plato

Back in the fourth century B.C. the major Greek philosophers, especially Plato, stressed reason as the key to "the good life." Plato's teacher, Socrates, did much to set the precedent for this approach. As brought forth by Plato in various dialogues, Socrates believed that to know the good as the ideal of Being is to achieve it. "To know is to do," he said. This amounted to an optimistic confidence in reason with marked effects on the Platonic view of ethics.

According to Socrates a person could not act contrary to his knowledge or true beliefs, which is to say that if he loved wisdom, including truth, he could not act falsely so as to bring disgrace upon himself. To him "knowledge is virtue." In his apologia, when imprisoned, Socrates refused to suggest an alternate sentence to that of death, even though he could have saved his life.[1] To do so would have been construed by his hearers as an admission of guilt and would have abetted a lie. It also would have branded him as loving life more than wisdom, including justice and truth, and would have disqualified him as a philosopher ("lover of wisdom"). For the same reason Socrates refused to escape, when his cell was left unlocked and unguarded.

Fundamental to Plato's philosophy, inspired by Socrates, is his theory of Ideas or Forms. His ethics is based upon these Idea(1)s as principles known by reason which precede experience since logically prior to it and belonging to the realm of absolute Being quite as the perfect circle or square supercedes circular or square objects. The Ideas are unchanging, non-spatial and eternal Forms in contrast to the changing world of sense perceptions.[2] As such these Forms are more real than sensate phenomena. For instance, the ideal man is more real than Socrates or the ideal horse more real than Dobbin or Black Beauty. Similarly, the ideal of absolute Justice is more real than an act of justice, which is its "copy." Thus true knowledge is absolute, universal and objective. The highest type thereof is the Idea of the Good identified with absolute, eternal Being.[3] Offsetting the relativism of Heraclitus, it is the final goal of all things in the temporal and changing realm of Becoming. Plato's overall schematism is one of an immanental dualism in which Being, while apart from non-being is reflected in it through Becoming, the latter amounting to everyday, temporal life.

For Plato the good life was identified with a rational respect for the absolute Good identified with ultimate Being. Like Socrates, he put a premium on knowledge, since in a profound sense to know is not only to do but to be. In this light the chief vice was ignorance, the corollary being that evil is due to a lack of knowledge, especially wisdom.[4] Knowledge produced a harmonious person, for reason governs the passions and desires so that a well-balanced person is the result. Knowledge makes for virtue. When people are ignorant they are imbalanced since their passions and desires control them. When they are wise they are well-integrated.[5] Wisdom was regarded by Plato to be knowledge plus virtue or sound moral judgment. So to know the good based on wisdom was also to do it. Merely to feign the good upon seeing it is evil.[6]

Just as the Good is identified with ultimate Being, so evil to Plato is identified with its opposite or non-being. Ignorance is on the side of evil as non-being, the opposite of Good Being.[7] Reason is on the side of the latter and innately knows the cardinal virtues identified with Being, viz. Wisdom, Justice, Courage, and Temperance.[8] Thus Plato is an idealist, who sees ultimate reality comprised of absolute or universal ideals and reason as the key to the knowledge thereof. Thus to Plato discovering the good life is a rational task somewhat similar to determining the principles of mathematics.[9] Fundamental to this pursuit is one's awareness of the absolute, which divinely embraces Being, the Good, the virtues and other ideals. The Good is higher or more absolute even than Justice, while Justice as a virtue belongs to the Good. The knowledge of the Good is the ultimate knowledge upon which virtue is based, yet the Good cannot be defined or grasped by the human mind. Like the sun by which we see things, the Good is the source of intelligibility and truth, especially the ethical.[10] It provides the ideals of perfection and perfectibility, as the rational goals of life.

To Plato it was not the case that one had to have specialized knowledge to be ethical or to lead the good life, but to have knowledge itself as based on reason was to lead the good life, since "to know is to do." The shrewder thinkers follow their innate sensitivities while the less shrewd "copy" their exemplary leaders, yet all persons have a rational capacity for knowing the good virtues and can "reflect" or "copy" them in the daily life of Becoming.[11] Becoming is the temporal realm between Being and non-being, an immanental combination of both, while from within it man is moving from the lower to the higher. Only in immortality[12] will there be a total identification with pure Being and the Good.

More concretely, how do men lead the good life, according to Plato? First, by developing their mental powers through disciplines like mathematics and philosophy. Second, by developing virtuous habits based on reason. Both factors imply a looking to wisdom with its basic virtues, reason being in control of one's lesser desires, emotions and appetites. The virtues corresponding to the latter are temperance and courage while one should always look to justice and wisdom as well. These virtues are realized through reflective thought and in ideal, good proportion make for the highest excellence of the soul known as areté or a kind of rational righteousness. In Plato's Meno the conclusion is that "virtue is neither natural nor acquired, but an instinct given by God to the virtuous." It is not taught but recognizing innately what we know already, hence a form of recollection from the soul's pre-existence.[13]

It is through the virtues that man fulfills his rational nature. Ethically, it makes for what Plato and Aristotle, his student, regard as self-realization. Though this is a type of humanistic achievement, in a sense it must be understood that Plato conceded no such fulfillment apart from the soul's looking beyond itself to the objective realm of absolute Being, which is ideal Good sometimes regarded as God.[14] In the dialogue called the "Apology," Socrates stated the following:

> A man who is good for anything ought not to calculate the chance of living or dying; he ought only to consider whether in doing anything he is doing right or wrong. . . . For neither in war nor yet at law ought I or any man to use every means of escaping death. . .The difficulty, my friends, is not to avoid death, but to avoid unrighteousness. . . Wherefore, O judges, be of good cheer about death, and know of a certainty that no evil can happen to a good man in life or after death.[15]

Plato realized that some people are better capacitated than others to understand the good life and guide the majority. These are "the philosopher kings" referred to in "The Republic" in which Plato advocates that it is the hand-picked philosophers who should be the rulers of an ideal society. Rulers should be educated to know the good life. One function of these select leaders was that of ethical censorship.[16] Young people especially should be guided and not exposed to anything and everything if they are to understand and practice the good life. The young are more readily deceived by injustices, so they should be subjects of their elders and the state.[17] They should be trained in philosophy in their twenties.

Besides the philosopher kings, Plato recognized two other classes of people. There were the middle class merchants and military men. Also, the peasants and artisans. Yet all men were deemed rational reaching their best through reason as they reflect or copy "the ideal man" or "good man."

If the basic element in Plato's ethics is the rational knowledge of Good, the next in importance is the principle of the Absolute. Goodness resembles a mathematical truth, for it is equated with or indigenous to absolute or pure Being known as nous or mind.[18] Since there is but one Good or goodness, there is ideally but one good life. In no way dependent upon men's desires or inclinations, it is the standard that judges and guides men. Men do not judge it; it judges them. Involved in the knowledge of the Good as an absolute principle is reason's innate knowledge of the four great virtues: Wisdom, Justice, Courage, and Temperance. This implies the objectivity of moral principles in contrast to any theory which says morals are relative or a matter of opinion or preference. The absolute Ideas, as Plato spoke of them, are ultimate ideals including truth, beauty and goodness, which are constitutional to the universe and belong to the objective realm of pure Being or Nous. Thus principles such as these: Men should not steal or kill. . .are binding without qualifications. Since Plato stressed the rational objectivity of the virtues and ideals he has been considered an objective idealist.

Similar to self-realization and the areté or rational rightness of the soul, a person's happiness known as Eudemonia (good spirit) is attained by the rational contemplation of the great virtues with habits based thereupon.[19] Aristotle agreed with this but, being more empirical than Plato, also stressed the exercise of the virtues. In either case it is the rational person who is truly happy, for he is virtuous. This implies that he is balanced rationally, biologically and emotionally and as such is wise, temperate, courageous and just, for he reflects the great virtues. In Book V of The Laws Plato refers to false ways of honoring one's soul: 1. By praise, 2. By excuse, 3. By self-indulgence, 4. By want of endurance, 5. By excessive love of life, 6. By preferring beauty to virtue, 7. By making dishonest gains. In general the penalty of yielding to evil is to grow into its likeness.[20] To act rationally, on the other hand, is to make for one's true welfare or what Socrates called the health of the soul and moderns call integrity. The chief vice in life is ignorance, since it is the opposite of reason or wisdom. As Socrates said, "To know is to do." Only out of ignorance do men do evil.

Man to Plato is a tri-partite being with the capacities of reason, feelings and appetites or impulses. Respectively, the loci of these capacities are the head, the breast and the abdomen. Reason must control the other capacities. The natural function of the soul is similarly tri-partite. First of all it has desires and aversions; next it has active impulses and feelings; finally there is the power of reason by which one is deliberate. Reason controls the other motives, checking or releasing them as occasions warrant it. The four virtues correspond to these with temperance matching the appetites, courage matching the impulses, and wisdom matching reason.[21] Justice is the more all-embracing virtue akin to righteousness or the areté of the soul.[22] The later-known capacity of volition or the will of man was not given a place by Plato. Reason was to him the height of manhood and the core of human nature.

Parallel to the nature of man in society is a tri-partite social structure with the philosopher-kings as the heads of state and the soldiers, police and merchants the middle class with artisans and farmers at the bottom of the social scale. Though all men have reason and can reflect the virtues; the lower classes need the guidance of the philosopher-kings, who are the guardians of the state that society might be ethical to the maximum.[23]

Criticisms are now in order. First, is it always true that men will do the good that they know? For instance, do not some men steal who know it to be wrong? Plato's only answer is that one acts immorally only out of ignorance of the good or the right way of life. Only ignorance is on the side of evil. Plato does not allow for a perversion of the will, since he has no place for the will. Reason to him is never perverse. But are there not people whose reason does not seem to give them ample incentive to do the good? Like Socrates, Plato cannot accept such a claim. Thus they have a very optimistic view of human nature because of an optimistic view of its basis in reason.

A second criticism: Is it correct to say that there is but one good life implying one course of action for pursuit of the good life? If so, one must be very ascetic towards life in this world. This Plato conceded to some extent, since this world of becoming and multiplicity is tainted with non-being with its evil and ignorance. To a great extent the body is the center of competition with the good life, since it is what needs the control of reason. The logic of this is ascetic self-control and depreciation of the lesser levels of life including the emotions. This ascetic tendency is reflected noticeably in Plato's dialogues <u>Phaedo</u> and <u>Theatetus</u>. The soul must strive to fulfill and be in harmony with absolute Being, which is its source as well as good.[24] But the realistic question must be asked: Is the body the locus of evil? In the New Testament St. Paul rather refers to the problem of the "flesh" (sarx), which is not the body (soma) but the egocentricity of human nature (Romans 7). Historically, orthodox Christians often have shown the effects of the Platonic view and associated original sin with the body.

Thirdly, is not Plato's idealism too absolutistic? Are not men at times torn between difficult alternatives when knowing a universal good does not seem to settle ethical matters entirely? Consider the hungry child whose father is unemployed. Is the father totally removed from the good life because he steals to feed his child? Plato's absolutistic position can only condemn the man. Others might say the man was right; still others that he was both right and wrong. Plato's position is such that he does not allow for the realism and/or relativism of some ethical situations. Are there not times when persons must settle for the lesser of two evils? Plato's idealism does not allow for evil as a lesser good; it is completely alien to the good, contrary, for instance, to Augustine's position.

Fourthly, Plato has no room for an ethics based upon experience. In this respect he is at loggerheads with Aristotle and several modern ethicists from Locke and Hume to James and Dewey. Basically, this is because Plato has no serious role for the senses to play, only reason as a "spectator."[25] Also Plato has no place for free will. It is a concept almost foreign to the Greeks until the Stoics introduce it a few centuries later.

Despite the weakness in Plato's objective idealism he saw the vital importance of ethics. He said, "For no light matter is at stake: nothing less than the rule of life." (or) "the manner in which human life is to be lived."[26] In addition many would applaud Plato for counteracting the relativism of the Sophists and philosophers like Protagoras. In <u>The Theatetus</u> Plato refutes such as self-contradictory. If truth is held to be a matter of opinion the idealist with his absolutism would regard the claim to be false. If Protagoras says what is true for him is true for him and the same applies to others, then Socrates can controvert by stating that in his opinion truth is objective or absolute. Protagoras would then have to concede that Socrates' opinion is correct. Hence, a consistent relativism is impossible.

Notes

1. Plato, Apology, trans. by B. Jowett from The Dialogues of Plato, 17 p. 3ff, 28, p. 15.
2. Timaeus, 30-31, p. 507; Parmenides, 133-134, p. 479f; Cratylus, 439, p. 175f; Symposium 176, 217-218, 204, p. 224, 210, p. 230. Phaedo, 66, p. 59, 78, p. 75, 80, p. 81, 100, p. 99. The Republic, II, 380, trans. B. Jowett.
3. The Republic, II, 380, trans. B. Jowett.
4. Symposium, 202, p. 222; The Republic, I, 350, V, 478.
5. Crito, 48, p. 39; Phaedo, 94, p. 92f; The Republic IV, 444-445; Cf. Meno, 99, p. 168f.
6. The Republic, II, III, 397.
7. The Republic, V, 477-479.
8. The Republic, IV, 427-428; Phaedo 68-69, p. 61ff; Gorgias 494, p. 193f.
9. Phaedo, 64-77, p. 57f; The Republic, I, 334.
10. Meno, 98-99, p. 167f; The Republic, VI, 504-505, 508-509, VII, 517-519.
11. The Republic, VI, 500; Phaedo 101, p. 100; Timaeus 508, p. 571f. Note all things "reflect" or "participate in" the Ideas, which are eternal. The philosopher "copies" the Idea(1)s.
12. The Republic, X, 611; Phaedos 250, p 446; Phaedo 72, 78, 83-84, 100, 101, 105. It is noteworthy that the innate ideas are gifts from God (Meno 80-84, 99) and knowledge as such is in the form of "recollections" from the soul's pre-existence (Phaedo, loc cit).
13. Phaedo 70, p. 62. Virtue is not taught. Meno 80-82, 100; The Laws, theme, 652-654, p. 523ff. (One should not press the logic of the quotation from the Meno.)
14. God, for Plato, is equated with Absolute Being as Good. The gods are more of a product of the poets. The Apology 29, 30, p. 16x. Timaeus, 27-29, p. 507f; The Laws, Bk. X.
15. The Apology, 28f, p. 15f.
16. The Republic III, 411-412; V, 473; VI, 499, 503; IX, 591=592; Cf. Gorgias 490, p. 188; Symposium 209, p. 229. The Good is the model for the philosopher - kings and implies perfectibility.
17. The Republic, III, 389, 396; VI, 492-494; Cf. Gorgias 484-485, p. 183f. (contrast Callicles).
18. Timaeus, 37-38, p. 511f. Note, the absolute and ideals are eternal universals.
19. Gorgias, 507, p. 199f; Republic, I, 353; VII, 540. Happiness of the soul is linked, too, with justice as the more comprehensive virtue.
20. Ibid. and The Laws, Book V, 726ff.
21. The Republic, IV, 434, 440, 442-444; IX, 581. Reason controls the other faculties and appetites; Republic, III, 389-390; IV, 430; IX, 572.

22. The Republic, I, 353; V, 472. Justice is related to both "the excellence of the soul" and "the virtue of the state." Cf. The Republic, II, 368; IV, 431.
23. The Republic, IV, 434-436; IX, 581.
24. The body is inferior to the mind, since it smacks of matter and non-being. Cf. Phaedo 65, 80-81, 92; Theatetus 184-185, 473; The Republic, IV, 403.
25. Plato uses this term in The Republic, VI, 486.
26. The Republic, I, 352 also translated ". . .the manner in which human life is to be lived."

The Sketch of Aristotle

Aristotle (384-322 B.C.) was a philosopher, scientist and teacher, one of the foremost thinkers in Western history. Born in northern Greece at Stagira, he entered Plato's Academy at the age of eighteen. He studied and wrote while there until Plato died about twenty years later. After traveling Aristotle became the teacher of Alexander, son of King Philip of Macedonia who became Alexander "the Great." Later Aristotle founded his own academy at Athens, known as the Lyceum. With his fertile and creative mind he compounded almost all of the knowledge of his time and wrote extensively in a variety of fields, philosophic and scientific, from poetical theory, metaphysics and ethics to physics and biology. Many of Alexander's men and patrons collected data of all sorts and contributed them to Aristotle to work with especially in zoology and medicine. The first great scientist of the West, Aristotle's basic classification of animalia have been used until today. He studied closely the charters and constitutions of many states and wrote on political theory. He made basic contributions to logic, and his famous <u>Nichmachean Ethics</u> was the first discourse of its type.

The Ethics of Aristotle

It is quite apparent that Plato's ethics was closely related to his metaphysics, notably his idealistic ontology or theory of Being. Though Aristotle was also a great metaphysician and a more intricate system-builder with an immanental dualism of degrees in Becoming, his ethics is based less on his metaphysics than on his respect for the moral relativities of experience in temporal Becoming.

For Aristotle ethics is more empirical and amenable to the scientific, inductive approach to things. Instead of looking primarily to the theory of absolute Being as the Good, he looks to the ideas of men in the everyday walks of life. Here it is observed that some people lead "good lives" while others lead "bad lives." In this respect Aristotle is more sensitive than Plato to particular situations. However, he saw one thing in common to all persons who lived good lives; it was happiness. Bad lives are unhappy; they lack virtue. Inductively, Aristotle asserted the principle that only the good life knows happiness. This much is in accord with Plato's doctrine of Eudemonia or that happiness is based upon the contemplation of the virtues, whereas Aristotle stressed more empirically the exercise of the virtues together with similar habits; two-thirds of life, he said, was habit. Disagreeing with Socrates, Aristotle does not think that knowing the good necessarily warrants doing it. Deliberations and virtuous habits are needed in daily life.

But a problem arises when the common man is asked what is meant by happiness. Either he is left speechless, contradictory or vague. Thus Aristotle sets out to supply the answer in his chief work, <u>Nichomachean Ethics</u>, named after his son. This work is actually one of the first essays in analytical philosophy, since it analyzes basic everyday moral terms like "the good." In this respect Aristotle anticipates the metaethics of G. E. Moore of Cambridge, who, too, analyzed basic ethical terms. The Good to Aristotle was viewed in a more teleological* and empirical sense than it was by Plato. Plato's concept of the Good was transcendent of experience, its archetypes being much less attainable than Aristotle's experiential "goods." To Aristotle the Good is "that at which all things aim" and "that for whose sake everything else is done." This is akin to the entelechy principle in Aristotle's metaphysics, which sees all things in Becoming being ultimately fulfilled in Being. Ethically, "in cases where the end lies beyond the action the product is naturally superior to the activity."[1] This applies to any art or applied science.

---

*All things move toward the <u>telos</u> or end in a Being that is Good.

The end as telos is the good sought like health relative to medicine or a building plan relative to its materials. The overall view of the Good, then is teleological with a "scale of Being" in Becoming allowing for a hierarchy of goods by degrees. Aristotle held to this view of the Good relative to man as a social and political animal who fulfills himself through social and political values.[2] Yet the supreme good in life is the rational activity of contemplation of the virtues that look to the Good. The Good while an end in itself is quite practical and within the reach of human nature through the specific hierarchical goods of experience.

It is in this light that Aristotle's recognized definition of happiness is to be understood. It is "an activity of the soul in accord with perfect virtue."[3] The language may be a bit obscure but in stressing happiness as activity Aristotle seems to counteract the idea that happiness is a static end or goal. Happiness is not a final goal or attainment so much as it is what accompanies the virtue-directed soul seeking the Good. As a state of existence it is a qualitative activity that is an end in itself, not a means. "Contemplation," says Aristotle, "is the most delightful and the best" of experiences. It is "the activity of philosophic wisdom," he says, and "the pleasantest of virtuous activities."[4] As such happiness is indigenous to virtue while pleasure is admittedly an ingredient of happiness. Dynamic and not static, happiness is both the essence and fruit of "the activity of reason." Aristotle states, "Happiness by its very nature is therefore itself in the last analysis a form of contemplation."[5]

Aristotle also was aware of what is called the "hedonistic paradox," which implies that happiness is not attainable by direct pursuit the way the hedonists assume it is. It is not identified with pleasure per se; it is not hedoné or sensate pleasure but eudemonia, the beautiful state of mind that makes for good spirit. Thus happiness results from rational activity.[6] However, the masses are enslaved to their passions. The higher life is the contemplative life of philosophy, religion and cultural interests; it is also fulfilled politically.[7] This is because the rational activity is the most divine-like activity. Yet Aristotle believes strongly in the fusion of theoria and praxis, the theoretical with the practical. Both personal and political life are best when based thereupon.

Aristotle saw two forms of reasoning leading to truth. Theoretikos was based on rational speculation and contemplation. Praktikos was practical thought relating theoretical thought to the empirical problems of life. Aristotle's ethics, then, is linked with the praktikos. This, again, makes him different from Plato, whose thinking was more theoretical and one-sided. Yet Aristotle is a classical ethicist in his own way who seeks to answer the underlying questions: What is the good life? and How ought men to behave? The basic answers are that the good life is one of happiness, and men ought to behave so as to achieve happiness. But how? The answer is similar to that of Plato, viz. by wisdom as knowledge plus virtue.[8] Yet we must note how Plato's answer was more objective upon looking directly to the absolute universals, Ideas or Forms. Aristotle was more subjective in the sense that the closer-to-home empirical ideas were basic while giving rise to the objective concepts inductively. Acts of justice, for instance, are perceptive and give rise to justice as a conceptual ideal. Thus Aristotle, while a realist, was enough of an idealist to contemplate the objective virtues that human experience anticipates in the good end(s). Conjoined with happiness the human expressions of virtue must be allowed to bloom like health plants.[9] While pleasure is a part of life's experience, it is not a sufficient guarantee of the good life. Excessive pleasure is intemperate.

The overall result comparatively is that, whereas Plato in principle described but one good life, Aristotle, being more individualistic and pluralistic, saw many paths to the good life. He also allowed more for the degrees of virtue and happiness. Happiness is a product of actualized potentiality but experienced in degrees according to the following ascending order: pleasure, honor, meditation and contemplation. Much like Plato, Aristotle believed in self-realization believing that the lower animal nature of man must be controlled by the higher nature of reason. Anyone can live, but the task is to live well, which is in accord with the rational areté of the soul. Besides caring for the body and cultivating one's emotional life a person must unfold his intellectual life through science, religion and cultural pursuits.[10]

Quite as for Plato, all things aim for the Good identified with Being, thinks Aristotle. This aim and movement of Becoming is entelechy, all things moving by degrees toward the good telos, which is immanentally implicit within them. In this respect Good is the fulfillment of nature, whereas evil is its perversion leaning toward the lower level of Becoming influenced by non-being. Nothing contrary to entelechy or the teleology of nature is good. Yet man is capable of distorting his nature; animals are not. Man's truest function is to activate his soul rationally, and when he does he will live in accordance with virtue. Concurring with Plato, Aristotle sees how man's uniqueness lies in his intellect. Yet, unlike Plato, he welcomed a certain amount of pleasure associated with happiness and the virtuous life.[11] A philosopher needs recreation, for instance, but such pleasure is not his ambition.

In keeping with his degrees of virtue, Aristotle has a more specific formula for happiness. It is his "doctrine of the mean," often referred to as the Golden Mean.[12] Basically, this is the virtue of temperance in which the theoretical is interrelated with the practical. It means that extremes must be avoided. Nothing should be entered into which represents either too much or too little, be it eating or drinking or anything else. Here a matter of relativism enters in or virtue by degrees. Different people may have to live differently to be ethically sound or correct. One person may need eight hours of sleep per day, another may be happy with six. Reason alone cannot decide such things. It takes reason combined with experimentation, or the unity of theoretikos and praktikos. Inductively, trial and error may be essential.[13] Thus Aristotle is a realist who combines idealism and empiricism.

How, then, shall a person behave morally? The answer is: temperately in accord with the Golden Mean. When eating neither stuff yourself nor go away hungry. Temperance as a virtue spells moderation and is the key to other virtues like courage, liberality and modesty. Courage is the mean between fear and rashness; liberality is the mean between prodigality and frugality; pride the mean between vanity and humility. Thus happiness is an activity of the soul in accord with the temperate mean between extremes.[14] It is acting moderately. Nevertheless, there is no hard and fast standard of the mean which applies to every person. This bespeaks a certain amount of relativism and moral judgment. It depreciates the use of finalized codes and legalisms. A man who cannot swim is not to be judged the same as one who can, when another is drowning.

The Golden Mean adds to the variety of approaches or avenues to the good life. This is much in contrast to Plato for whom there is but one good life, fundamentally, though a rational identification with the Good. Aristotle sees many good lives as possible-- probably as many as there are people. For this reason Aristotle has been regarded as an ethicist closer to common sense realism. Moreso than Plato, he is sensitive to differences in life situations, temperaments, talents and dispositions. In keeping with his immanental* realism Aristotle interrelates the ideal with the practical more tightly than Plato's doctrine of reflection with its copies of the ideals.[15]

Aristotle criticized Plato on these counts: 1. Plato's view of the Good is too simple, remote and static and not related sufficiently to the pluralities of experience. 2. The eternal absolute Good does not explain the particular goods in the form of deliberations, choices and acts. 3. It has too little bearing on concrete moral situations and applied virtue. 4. It is too transcendent of human experience

*The ideal or Form of Being is within particulars much like the blueprint indigenous to the house.

and attainment. In contrast, Aristotle sees the Good attainable through specific goods, which belong to a hierarchy or scale of good acts.[16] These acts are combinations of the rational and the practical by degrees.

One of the more practical empirical virtues accentuated by Aristotle was that of friendship. Friendship is essential to happiness. There are three kinds of friendship, says Aristotle. 1. for utility, 2. for one's own good, a type of pleasure, 3. for the sake of good, as an end in itself. Friendship exists for the sake of the mutuality of interests between persons. Friendship, while reciprocal in nature, is in tune with all virtues that look to the Good. It is important in friendship to choose to love rather than to be loved. The demands of justice increase with the intensity of friendships, which contribute to the community. Even government involves friendship influencing the ruler-subject relationships. Justice, says Aristotle, is "proportioned to merit" as in friendship. Where justice is lacking friendship is lacking as in the case of tyranny. Where citizens are equal they have more in common and friendship is more prevalent. The same is true where there is more inter-change of services. Yet friendship is more than "neighborliness" or "good will," for it is more intimate.[17]

Even so, Aristotle sees friendship to be based on "self-love." A happy person needs friends to help keep him happy. Whereas "true love" is toward but one person, friendship may be with many as a kind of "partnership" in civic and social groups. But the intimacy basic to friendship is for the sake of the Good yet is mixed with self-concern. This is quite in contrast to the Christian view of friendship which is not only good will but sacrificial love (Agápe) that is out-going toward others whether or not it is of any personal gain or is even mutual.

Aristotle's view of philia is a mutual liking and mutual well-wishing. It is, therefore, fundamental to his ethics, for it is based on more than rectitude; it is a favorable attitude. But Aristotle raises some practical questions here. For instance, can unequals be friends? He argues that in partnerships friendship demands absolute equality of status, advantage and moral goodness. There are exceptions, however, in the case of husbands and wives, Aristotle being more favorable toward the goodness of men. Basic is what he refers to as friendships of character, where persons come to trust each other and love one another because of their good qualities.[18] A life of shared activities is superior to a life of purely private activities, for a solitary form of life becomes apathetic and inactive without stimulation and support from others. Friendship, then, is essential to knowing the goodness of one's life.

As a philosopher Aristotle linked his ethical concerns with his political theories. Justice is the central virtue which unites the two concerns. Justice, he said, is "the complete virtue" because it relates one's actions to his neighbors and promotes equality of rights and opportunities.[19] To Aristotle true forms of government seek the common interest of men in accordance with the "strict principles of justice." Perverted forms are those which regard only the interest of the rulers.

First, there is royalty or kingship in which one person rules. Its perversion is tyranny. Second, there is aristocracy in which a few rule. Its perversion is oligarchy. Third, there is constitutional government administered by citizens. Its perversion, says Aristotle, is democracy. Tyranny seeks the monarch's interests only; oligarchy, the wealthy; democracy, the needy. None says Aristotle, are to the common good.

Aristotle emphasizes that though it is possible for the poor to be the few in power within an oligarchy and the opposite in a democracy these situations are "accidental," and the "real difference between democracy and oligarchy is poverty and wealth."

Laws must be adapted to constitutions, thus true forms of government must have just laws, and perverted forms will have unjust laws. In political science the end is good, the highest good being justice or the common interest of men. Governments are perversions when they rest upon either of two principles, 1. those equal in one thing ought not to have an equal share in all, of 2. those unequal in one thing ought to have an unequal share in all.

Aristotle sees difficulty in government when all elements of society coexist in governing bodies. It is better than either the rich, poor, or virtuous is dominant. If government is based on wealth it is logical that the wealthiest man ought to be the ruler. In an aristocracy a similar difficulty occurs about the most virtuous man. (In a constitution if the people are to rule it is logical that the most influential man should govern.) This is the way Aristotle points out that none of the principles on which men rule is right. Aristotle strikes at democracy (as he defined it[20]) as establishing ostracism of the wealthy and prominent citizens.

The true legislator and statesman should be a specialist in political science. He should know 1. what is theoretically "best in the abstract," 2. what is best relative to circumstances, 3. how a state is formed originally, and constituted under certain conditions, when formed, how best preserved, 4. what form of government is best suited to states in general, what is possible and readily attainable, 5. what are the remedies for any prevalent defects in the present form of existing constitutions.

There are various kinds of constitutions. They are classified as democracy and oligarchy. Aristocracy is an oligarchy, and the constitutional government is a democracy. Democracy is not simply the rule of a sovereign majority, for in every government including oligarchy the majority rules. Nor is oligarchy the sovereign rule of a few; Aristotle surprisingly asserts.[21] Aristotle says, "democracy is the form of government in which the free are ruler," and oligarchy in which the rich rule. He says, ". . .it is only an accident that the free are the many and the rich are the few." Government is not a democracy in which the freemen, being few, rule over the many who are not free, nor is it democracy when the rich have the government because they exceed in number. "But the form of government is a democracy when the free, who are also poor and the majority, govern, and an oligarchy when the rich and the noble govern, they being at the same time few in number."

Of forms of democracy there is, first, that based on equality. Neither the rich nor the poor have advantages. Second, there is a democracy in which the magistrates must meet a small property qualification. Third, there is the kind in which all the qualified citizens share in the government, but know that the law is supreme. Fourth, a democracy in which all citizens without qualifications share in the government under supreme law. Fifth, a kind in which the multitude supercedes the law by decrees; in this demagogues prosper and this makes the government rally without constitution.

As for the kinds of oligarchies, there is one in which property qualifications are essential for office-holding, thus eliminating the poor who may be in majority. Another is oligarchy based on high qualifications thus resulting in vacancies being filled by co-optation. Another form exists in which the son succeeds the father. A fourth, also hereditary, the magistrates are supreme and not law. (This becomes a dynasty or rule of families.) Oligarchical states may sometimes administer undemocratic constitutions and their educational systems in a democratic manner. The opposite may also be the case in democracies. Some democracies exclude classes, demand property qualifications and have birth standards. Others[22] allow free men to share in government only as they have leisure.

A few criticisms of Aristotle may be in order. First, ought men always to follow the middle course or the Mean in their ethical activities? Does one take a middle course when telling the truth, for instance, or being honest or keeping a promise? Surely such compromise or temperate ballast does not apply well in the home or courtroom let alone the laboratory. Conditions may override the absoluteness implied at times as perhaps in the case of remaining consistent with one's one-time sincere promise, say, to marry one's bethrothed. Yet we can hardly deny that a person who keeps a promise is moral and anyone who breaks it is immoral. Either one keeps it or does not. Here the Platonic perspective of absolute virtue comes into view, offsetting Aristotle's more relative position. In this light Aristotle detracted somewhat from the absolute Good by settling for temperance as individually interpreted alone with degrees of goodness.

Another criticism: Aristotle's ethics proposes the principle of moderation as conditional to happiness and the soul's areté. But are there not times when only an immoderate behavior is right or proper? A person who is strongly passionate or temperamental, for instance, may need to curtail even a moderate behavior on the grounds that the temperate mean for them may still be extreme. On the other hand, one who is dispositionally romantic may find moderation unsuitable. It was at this point that the eighteenth century Romanticism of Rousseau was a reactionary movement against Aristotelian thought. Then, too, on the witness stand a person must be more than temperate when dealing with the truth.

In view of his hierarchy of values, Aristotle states, "The aim of education is to make the student like and dislike what he ought."[23] This smacks a bit of thought control and Plato's censorship, also Plato's claim that youth need to be guided into aesthetic sensitivity. Not all wrong, does Aristotle's view promote academic freedom? Determining just what students 'ought' to be concerned about is a big problem, especially today in view of the current relativism of morals and cultural values. This writer sees little hope for our civilization short of the recovery of respect for the Absolute on a new basis, one which will be of existential relevance to persons as whole persons with a faith-subsumed reason-in-existence similar to Kierkegaard's perspective. Why? Because even the best 'goods' that either Aristotle or Plato arrive at are products of a finite reason that cannot do justice to the infinite.

An underlying weakness in Aristotle's theory is his inordinate love of reason. The speculative intellect in the pursuit of truth is deemed the highest good for man. Moral virtue is therefore a secondary good, as A. C. Garnett reminds us. It is a means to intellectual excellence. Politically, Aristotle justifies a social system that maintains a leisured class of the more intellectual people supported by slaves and artisans. This is a type of aristocratic snobbery. The underlying weakness is a love of the intellect as an end in itself rather than as an instrument serviceable to human needs and the development of other capacities together with itself.

Notes

1. Aristotle, Nicomachean Ethics, Book I, Chapter 1:1-5; 5-10; Chapter 7:20, pp. 941-946, 950 from The Basic Works of Aristotle, ed. Richard McKeon.
2. Ibid, Book I, 2:10; I, 4.
3. Ibid, Book I, Chapter 7:15, Cf. 13:5.
4. Ibid, Book X, Chapter 7, 1177, 24-27.
5. Ibid, Book X, Chapter 8, 1178f, 31; Cf. Chapter 6, 1176, 25-30.
6. Ibid, Book I, Chapter 4, 15-20; 5:20. Cf. Book X.
7. Ibid.
8. op cit, footnotes 3, 4, 5, 6.
9. Nicomachean Ethics, Book X, Chapters 4-6.
10. Ibid, Book III, Chapter 12, 1110:15. Cf. Book VI, Chapter 1139.
11. Ibid, Book I, Chapter 8, 1099a, 8-25.
12. Ibid, Book II, Chapter 2, 1104a, 25-35; Chapter 3, 1104b, 10-13; Chapter 4:18, 1105:5.
13. Ibid, Book II, Chapter 6, 1107; 9:25.
14. Ibid, Book III.
15. Ibid, Book II, Chapter 7; Cf. Chapter 8:15f. Cf. Chapter 10:25.
16. Ibid, Book VIII.
17. Ibid, Book IX.
18. Ibid, Book IX, 3. Cf. essay by John M. Cooper, "Aristotle on Friendship,: from Essays on Aristotle's Ethics, Ed. by A. O. Rarty, Univ. of California Press, 1980.
19. Ibid, Book V, Chapter 1:25-30.
20. Aristotle, Politics, Book III, Chapters 6-13.
21. Ibid, Book IV, Chapter 1-4.
22. Ibid, Chapters 5-13.
23. Aristotle, Nicomachean Ethics, 1104, B. Cf. Plato, The Republic, 402, A.

The Sketch of Epicurus

Epicurus (341-270 B.C.), a noted Greek philosopher, founded a philosophy named after him called Epicureanism. Born on the island of Samos in the Aegean Sea he had Athenian citizenship and opened a school in Athens after studying under Plato and Democritus. The school known as the Garden accepted women and slaves among its students. But due to his stress on pleasure as basic to all of life including morals he led people to suspect that the school was promoting sexual immoralities such as practiced by many of the hedonists of that time. Commonly, the Epicureans were accused of an "eat, drink and be merry" version of life. Actually, however, life in the school was well disciplined. Students were taught that pleasure and happiness were natural and people should turn from their fear of the gods and divine punishment and live for pleasure. But actually Epicurus stressed pleasures of the mind over pleasures of the body, the latter meant to be serviceable to the former. Long-range pleasures were deemed the best. Though Epicurus wrote extensively, only three letters and some fragments remain.

The Ethics of Epicurus

Epicurus was a hedonist of a more sophisticated type by which is meant that he was more than a sensualist. To him mental pleasures such as the study of philosophy itself was of greater pleasure than sensate things. Also he believed in suspending the more immediate superficial pleasures for the sake of long-range pleasures, which are apt to be more qualitative. The basic source of the ethics of Epicurus is his Letter to Menoeceus, together with his Doctrines and Sayings.

Influenced by Democritus' atomic theory Epicurus held to a materialism in which thought and will were based on the atomic motion of the world. This was a form of determinism that really negated free will, yet the so-called uncaused, spontaneous atomic "swerve"* was such that it opened up the exception of uncaused motion making free will a possibility. Ethically, then, despite this atomistic physics, Epicurus had a positive place for man's freedom of will.

Happiness according to Epicurus is sought as an end in itself and not as a means. It is the highest good. The soul is comprised of atoms in flux, death being the dissolution thereof and end of consciousness. Though atoms remain at death, the soul does not. Thus there can be neither reward nor punishment after death, so why fear the gods? The present temporal life is the seat of happiness, the highest goal. Feelings are basic to this happiness just as sense perceptions are basic to knowledge. Happiness is freedom from pain, especially the pain of unfulfilled desires. The wise person has fewer desires.[1] This is somewhat similar to Stoic ethics except that the latter is less self-centered.

In his letter to Menoeceus, Epicurus encouraged young men to study philosophy and old men, too, for "the well-being of the soul." This alone suggests that Epicurus was more than a sensualist or what the term "epicure" has come to mean. Though he believes in the gods as paragons of virtue, they are otherwise irrelevant to men. He maintains that most people's views of gods are false. Death being the end of all consciousness, sound philosophy, he asserts, should relieve men of the fear of death. A happy life is more significant than a long life. The wise man in no way finds life an evil; he neither renounces it nor fears its end. "The act of living well and the art of dying well are one," said Epicurus.[2]

---

*Atoms deviate in their course irregularly.

Happiness, which is of basic concern to Epicurus, has pleasure as the underlying motive. The satisfaction of desires for health and peace of mind are ample for a happy life, for they are natural and "the final end" of the good life. Yet some pleasures bring pain, and this must be considered. Thus some pleasures must be sacrificed for better, long-range pleasures. Yet the fewer the desires the wiser the person.[3]

Not a sensualist, as asserted above, Epicurus overtly specified that physical pleasures do not yield the highest happiness. Rather, it is the simple life that is free from anxiety with normal needs satisfied. Prudence and practical wisdom are fundamental to this. Epicurus believes that the virtues accompany the pleasant life and vice versa. Reverence with no fear of death and the achievement of the pleasant life are marks of the good life. Implied in all this is a life of moral freedom. Thus Epicurus states, "It would be better to accept the myth about the gods than to be a slave to the determinism of the physicists. . ."[4]

Epicurus is convinced that to live the pleasant life one must know the nature of the various desires. The health of the body and the soul's "freedom from disturbance" are essential to the good life. To avoid pain and fear are basic thereto. "For we recognize pleasure as the first good innate in us, and from pleasure we begin every act of choice and avoidance," says Epicurus, "and to pleasure we return again, using the feeling as the standard by which we judge every good."[5] Yet the prudent person realizes that he, not fate, is in control of that which makes for happiness. Wise decision is more basic than either fortune or the supernatural invasion of the gods.[6]

Epicurus is mainly individualistic, yet he has minimal social concern. Justice is a social virtue which makes for mutual protection from injury. It is strictly a human virtue. It is a mutual compact not to injure or be injured. A law's usefulness is judged accordingly.[7]

In general Epicurus believed in <u>ataraxia</u>, the highest ethical ideal, that of serene happiness. Since the gods were to him personifications thereof he could not espouse atheism, despite his underlying materialism; to achieve personal ataraxia was to imitate the gods or to become godlike.[8] The underlying motivation of the pursuit of the good life was thus partly religious, a matter often overlooked by the critics of Epicureanism from St. Paul to contemporary ethicists. Ataraxia was a freedom from passion, fear and pain. Epicurus believed that the fear of death was unnecessary; rationally it need not be dreaded, for all good and evil is sensation, which ceases with death and stops the craving for immortality, for no longer do men exist.

Though Epicurus has been accused many times over for being a sensualist, it is apparent from the above observations that such is not the case; nevertheless, his ethics is subject to questioning. The hedonistic pleasure -- pain principle is quite ambivalent and can be used to support either conventional or unconventional morals. It judges an act not by itself nor by rules of reason but by the feelings of pleasure and pain resulting from the act. Feelings are the basis for ethics. Thus hedonistic ethics is relative and not absolute, since the value of an act is not the character of the act itself but in its consequences, which are also relative one person to another.[9]

Also, the term "pleasure" is ambiguous. The first thing many critics think of is what is sensuous, when actually the Epicureans were often quite ascetic. Pleasure to Epicurus was lack of pain either physical or mental i.e. it was physical comfort or peace of mind. The good life included self-discipline of the appetites and desires, yet, negatively, it included withdrawal form the life of the community in favor of a few friends. The ideal of serenity was much like Buddhistic peace except for the lack of a mystical nirvana. Yet there were degenerate Epicureans who were out in the world seeking the sensuous pleasures. They were the better known but pseudo-Epicureans who were more apt to arouse the critics.[10]

One of the strongest criticisms of hedonism is that it is not a social ethic. It was too self-centered to be a turning outward toward others. Though it promoted friendliness among a few it lacked a comprehensive concern for society in general. Though it anticipated 18th century Utilitarianism in its concern for consequences, the latter movement was centrally a social movement based on "the greatest good for the greatest number." At its best Epicureanism was a withdrawal. Whereas the one is altruistic happiness, the other is egocentric happiness. Even justice is a social contract without being an absolute principle such as a Platonic Ideal. The effects upon the self are basic, not the effects on society. Justice is valued for bringing serenity to 'me.' The result is that social injustices are not taken seriously. Yet the Epicureans had minimal social concern in their fight against the superstitions associated with the Olympian religions of their day.[11] A parallel problem exists today when our churches stress personal salvation while neglecting the socio-economic evils around them like poverty and racial prejudice. Can men know true happiness if they ignore the unhappiness of others?

The ethics of Epicurus met with some tension in the face of his atomistic physics and metaphysics. This was touched upon on the first page of this overall discussion. Epicurus was very sensitive to man's need for freedom, lest he be but an automator of nature and would have no feeling for being free mentally. All his actions would be inevitable and predictable, which would leave him less than a human or morally responsible being. The swerve theory allows an act of will to be causally free since uncaused by outside forces. Yet in view of Epicurus' atomism this leaves man as a moral being a freak of nature, since the moral decisions, logically speaking, are little more than chance events upsetting the causal economy of physical events.[12]

Plato in his dialogue <u>Protagoras</u> was anti-hedonistic pointing out the necessity of reason in measuring the pros and cons of competing pleasures and pains. This implies that pleasure cannot be regarded as the highest good. Reason is superior.[13] Though popular at times hedonism is to be questioned, for often there are bad pleasures that lead men to a kind of self-enslavement. Often momentary pleasures have long-range displeasures or subsequent pain or travail. Thus it can be questioned again whether pleasure is basic to the ethical life.

Notes

1. Cf. Introduction by Russel M. Geer, Epicurus' Letters, Principal Doctrines and Vatican Sayings, pp. xxxii-xxxiv.
2. Epicurus, Letter to Menoeceus, 122-126.
3. Ibid, 127-130.
4. Ibid, 131-134.
5. Ibid, 128, 129a and Principal Doctrines, xxvi, xxx also The Vatican Sayings, lxxxi, xxi.
6. Letter to Menoeceus, 133-135.
7. Principal Doctrines, xxxii-xxviii.
8. George K. Strodach, The Philosophy of Epicurus, p. 51.
9. Ibid, pp. 71ff, 77f.
10. Ibid, pp. 78-81.
11. Ibid, p. 82ff.
12. Ibid, p. 85ff.
13. Plato, Protagoras, 354-357.

The Sketch of Epictetus

Epictetus is reputed to be one of the more prominent members of the school known as Stoics. As a Roman teacher he adapted the teachings of Zeno (336-264 B.C.), who founded the Stoa or Porch, the last of the noted schools of Athens. Yet little is known of the time and place of Epictetus' birth though it was about 50 A.D. As a child he was sold into slavery by his parents and joined the household of a Roman soldier. When his master died he gained freedom. Typical of the less renowned Roman philosophers, Epictetus leaned heavily upon Greek thought. The school of Stoicism belonged to both Greek and Roman cultures and its impact was felt from 200 B.C. to at least 400 A.D. Accepted by all social classes it became of marked influence upon early Christians. Some scholars even have thought that St. Paul attended a Stoic school in his home town of Tarsus near the northeastern coast of the Mediterranean. Roman armies found the movement popular for contending with military difficulties. Cicero, Seneca and Emperor Marcus Aurelius espoused the doctrine as intellectual leaders of Rome at a time of much moral debauchery. When he gained his freedom Epictetus' reputation as a philosopher grew. In 89 A.D. when Emperor Domitian forced philosophers to leave Rome, Epictetus went to Nicopolis where he taught until his death around 130 A.D. His student Arrian recorded his lectures on ethics, notably the <u>Discourses</u> and the <u>Enchiridion</u>.

The Ethics of Epictetus

Stoicism has been regarded as the most influential ethical doctrine in the Western world prior to Christianity. Its heyday was between the third century B.C. and the third century A.D. After the fall of the Alexandrian Empire it dominated late Greek and Roman thought until Christianity superceded it. Philosophically, it underwent changes that eventuated in a form of neo-Platonic idealism. Most of the changes were metaphysical while Stoical ethics remained quite constant.

The founder of Stoicism was Zeno of Cypress. In the Third Century B.C. he lectured from a stoa (porch) which gave his followers their nickname. Quite like the Cynics, he and his fellow Stoics were depressed over the collapse of the city states and empire, seeing no hope for reconstruction. So, in the main, their philosophy consisted of advice to individuals concerning a personal salvation in a crumbling world. Their basic tenet was: be indifferent to external influences and practice renunciation through mental self-discipline. Another influential Stoic was Epictetus, who rose from slavery to the rank of a Roman official and teacher. He wrote the <u>Enchiridion</u> and <u>The Discourses</u>, sets of moral discourses and diatribes and stressed "withdrawal from externals" in favor of modest living. Marcus Aurelius was a third Stoic leader. He became the Roman emperor who was also a philosopher (121-180 A.D.). Seeking to be just and charitable, he had too much centralized authority in his administration and persecuted Christians probably because of accepting the second-hand calumnious reports of his understudies. His <u>Meditation</u> is not a system of thought but, strong on feelings, stressed self-control and self-overcoming. Mental peace, he said, comes through purging oneself of his passions.[1] Military commander that he was, Marcus Aurelius, nevertheless, despised pomp and favored a quiet, modest home life.

Stoicism in general stressed self-discipline and good or evil as something self-made by man. If a person could be indifferent to pain and bad treatment by others, they will not overpower him. Epictetus, the chief exponent, stressed that virtue resided in the will, which alone is good or bad.[2] Here we see a fundamental difference from Plato and Aristotle, who stressed reason. A man's good will, said Epictetus, is basic to his character and behavior, a principle which anticipates Kant and Kierkegaard. In fact, the Stoics were the first philosophers to see free will or volition as basic to life and philosophy. How does one gain a good will? Epictetus saw it in being freely indifferent to external happenings. This way character is not destroyed by circumstances. When indifferent to the latter a person is free and independent. Though the world may be in chaos one can have inner peace.[3]

Despite the free will basic to Stoical ethics its philosophy in general has strong metaphysical connotations through the doctrine of Moiroi or fate. This is a type of predestination or preconceived cosmic plan fixed by God, the cosmic Reason. It implies that nothing is accidental; nothing happens fortuitously. Virtue lies in a will that is in harmony with nature's rational laws and happenings. The virtuous person accepts what happens as a divine arrangement that he cannot change. It is immoral to resist it. So the way to avoid frustration is to despair of altering divinely ordinanced events. Epictetus states succinctly, "Demand not that events should happen as you wish; but wish them to happen as they do happen, and your life will be serene."[4] Here we observe in Stoicism a basic paradox: freedom lies in determinism. One is not free in "fighting city hall" or the cosmic system. Thus Stoicism fosters basically a passive outlook with a resolve to be free from desires or passions.

Yet the Stoics were not altogether cynical. Total renunciation of the world was not called for. One need not renounce material things or material success provided one is not bound or trapped by them.[5] In this respect the Stoics were more temperate about apatheia (renunciation) than the Cynics. They have no feelings about unsatisfied desires. Even if one is very successful and somehow loses all his gains he must remain as apathetic or indifferent as possible. The net result of this was to place responsibility on oneself for becoming a good or bad person. One should not blame social or natural factors.[6] One's frame of mind and character are what counts. Happiness requires conscientious self-discipline. If one limits his desires to what is in harmony with God, the cosmic process, then even death will appear of little consequence. What causes distress is not the divine order of events but faulty judgments and attitudes. The wise and happy soul accepts with equanimity whatever inevitably happens. For instance, "it is not poverty that causes sorrow, but covetous desires. . ." Hedonism is false, and wise persons will place virtue above externals like wealth, pleasure or honor.[7]

The Stoic view of virtue was quite productive, and Stoicism in general disseminated human culture. It had a deep interest in scientific theory. Whereas to the Cynics things of the world were of no value, the Stoics saw both positive and negative factors at work. This was viewed in the context of an ethical dualism within a metaphysical monism. Man is rational and free yet functioning within a cosmic determinism of fate. This set a precedent for the forthcoming philosophical tension to appear repeatedly in Western thought: freedom versus determinism.

Against Epictetus and hedonism, the Stoics fought for the dignity of the soul of man.[8] They visualized an ideal Wise Man based on the independence of the soul as the unity of the self. The wise person loved virtue for its own sake. For the first time in Western thought the soul of man is regarded as a free and independent phenomenon to reckon with. As pneuma or spirit a man is akin to the World Soul, the "warm breath" which pervades all things as a force of creative reason and regenerative powers. The World Soul is dualistically seen to be in contrast to the World Body composed of earth and water. Substance consists, then, of these two realities, rational force and matter. The basic Pneuma of the World Soul is the life of the university giving it a rational teleological unity within its plurality. Man belongs to the divine system. In man it is pneuma which gives unity to the self and body, even as it is an emenation from the cosmic Pneuma. This makes man a microcosm of the macrocosm in a Neo-Platonic setting. The divine pneuma accounts for man's soul and reason. At death it is released from the body and rejoins the cosmic Pneuma or World Soul.[9]

A part of the ethical dualism of Stoicism was the antagonism felt between reason and the senses. Though reason was paramount, it was seen to be fed data by the senses. The senses had no knowledge in themselves. Sensations were changed into knowledge only as tributary to reason. They then became serviceable to acts of the will. But in contrast to man's reason and free will, he has an irrational make-up as well. Reason can fail when under pressures of excitement or the disturbances of emotion. So the Stoic tried to keep emotions in abeyance.[10] From this epistemological perspective the ethical principle of renunciation or indifference (apatheia) was feasible. Man governs the world only by controlling himself. The virtue of the wise man was realized as reason and willful resolution worked together. Proud of his self control in the rational sense of <u>hybris</u>, the Stoic did not view pleasure as necessarily good, nor pain as necessarily evil.

The highest good and end of life to the Stoic was his rationality, a form of self-realization. His true happiness was based on his rational harmony and independence as when his entire being was centered in contemplation of the World Soul as reason so as to have no sense of dependence upon anything else. But, akin to Socrates, contemplation must become conduct as well. In this respect the Good is absolute and such relative matters as wealth, honor and position are matters of indifference. Even a life may be taken indifferently, when it does not serve reason.

What is the inner disposition which makes for the highest good? It is apatheia, which is not so much "apathy" as "imperturbability," the latter term being akin to the Epicurean word <u>ataroxy</u>. Positively, this attitude is virtuous. Negatively, it is the absence of control by the feelings; quite to the contrary of what is hailed by modern Romanticism. The Stoics' happiness and serenity lay in their submission to rational law.[11] Thus apatheia to them is not insensibility but firmness. It is (1) an intellectual resignation to cosmic fate, (2) an inner harmony, and (3) self-control. It is such that makes for self-realization.

Whereas the Epicurean was an individualist at loose ends, the Stoic saw the ideal man's reason akin to an eternal reason, an absolute principle giving human reason its absoluteness. Unlike Aristotle, ethics was not based on the politico-moral life of Greek culture, for that had faded. The absolute was an immanent cosmic principle and power linked with a pantheistic conception of Nature. This was adapted to the Logos doctrine of Heraclitus, a rational principle of duration through change. It was reinforced by Aristotle's entelechy of nature; however, the Stoics disavowed the form and matter dualism of Aristotle in favor of a monism of nature equated with matter equated with reason equated with fate equated with providence equated with God.[12] Man, again, was the microcosm of this macrocosm, so that nature and personality supplemented each other. Thus the Stoic view of man saw him reinforced by the cosmos.

What of Stoicism and society? Basically, there are two classes of men, the wise and the foolish, with no middle ground. Only a few are wise, the masses foolish. The attitude of the Stoics in this respect implied that they were among the elite. This condescending outlook made them dangerous politically. Not confident in democracies, their leaders were apt to become advisors to tyrants like Julius Caesar.[13] On the other hand, Some like Musonius Rufus made a puritan protest against Nero and were of influence on Rome in the second century A.D. Unlike the Epicureans who saw society inherent in human nature, the Stoics saw it as a divine institution of the World Soul enveloping everyone. A life of reason is in harmony with the cosmic reason; therefore, it leads to social life, not only of Romans but all men including slaves. In fact, the Stoics were the first to teach the brotherhood of man. Concern for justice and respect for one's fellow men were Stoical anticipations of religious freedom.[14] There are two opposing social tendencies in Stoicism: (1) Social justice, sociability, brotherly love and cosmopolitanism. (2) Unconcern about the world due to the stress on inner freedom with reason's renunciation. In general Stoicism was not a strong reform movement due to the latter and its doctrine of fate. Yet there were exceptions as in the case of Zeno and Marcus Aurelius, who even anticipated a world state.

The Stoical linking of the human and cosmic reasons elevated human conduct into a universal law of duty. Against external law it accentuated the inner moral law. (One wonders whether St. Paul, who likely attended a Stoic school in his youth, was influenced to hold a similar view in eventually denouncing religious legalisms in favor of the inner spirit of truth.) The inner law made for personal responsibility. Stressing the difference between what is and what ought to be, Stoics eventually appealed to conscience. They originated the idea that life is a struggle against society and oneself.[15] A great soul overcomes the world largely by indifference to it, yet accepts the world without doing much to change it. In these ways, it can be said, Stoicism prepared the way for Christianity, the strongest factor being the place for free will despite the unsolved intellectual tension with fate.

Some criticisms of Stoicism are in order. We have anticipated the most basic ethical criticism: the logical difficulty of accepting the notion of both freedom and fate. As suggested above, this is an intellectual tension that Stoicism never resolved and it may be questioned whether any other school of thought has resolved it; however, most existentialisms view the self as having to live with both elements. The advantage of existentialism over Stoicism in this regard is that it is not committed to a hard and fast cosmic system of reason the way Stoicism is. Fate is also inconsistent with the view that one's free resolve can alter his character through indifference or renunciation to things he formerly prized. The implied free will is hardly commensurate with the harsh doctrine of fate. This problem of free will versus determinism is not only one of the most persistent in historical philosophy and theology, but it is basic to almost all ethical theories and is germane to much in modern psychology and the social sciences. It is dubious, for instance, that criminal law can be consistent with deterministic social sciences.

Stoical indifference is itself another problem. If one loses his life savings the problem is apparent. If one's friend dies is indifference a virtue? Is an otherwise immoral act right just because it is done indifferently? The Stoical answer would seem to be affirmative if the act were based on reason, capital punishment being a case in point and mercy killing, too.

Stoical ethics may be plausible in exceptional cases today. If one knows he will be tortured by an enemy seeking military secrets, for instance, stoical resolve may be helpful. Sometimes to be indifferent toward pain may be better than concentrating on it. But Stoic ethics looking to indifference is perhaps more the exception than the rule. It is dubious that it can or should be universalized. Then, too, it seems seriously inconsistent of the Stoic to respect all men while regarding most men to be fools. A self-sufficient reason is stressed while almost ignoring the role of the irrational aspects of life.

Stoicism is a kind of formalist theory, since it looks to human reason for the ethical answers. But in so doing it does not make ethical obligation to depend on the theory of value. An act may be known to be right without considering mixed motives and/or consequences. Reason is deemed self-sufficient to attain the good. It is thought to be one with metaphysics as the law of nature.

Stoicism arose when the Greek world collapsed. It helped men withstand the rigors of life at that time. But when men came to see that circumstances needed to be changed they confronted the weakness of Stoicism. It provided no positive program for building a better world. Fate and renunciation combined to make for a nearly laissez faire attitude and outlook. Christianity became the more dynamic successor after Stoicism's 500 years of dominance. Even so the strong emphasis upon rational self-control did much both to prepare for and affect Christian ethics. Also, Stoicism's stress on Fate in a sense helped prepare men for Augustine's doctrine of predestination.

Notes

1. Marcus Aurelius Antoninus, Meditations, First Book, esp. parts V-XII, XV-XVII.
2. Epictetus, The Discourses, Book IV, p. 261, "Of Freedom."
3. Ibid, Book I, p. 3,7. Cf. Epictetus, The Enchiridion, I, p. 331f.
4. Ibid, Book I, p. 17, 40, 41, 44, 46. Cf. Epictetus, The Enchiridion, 8, p. 334. Cf. 10, 334, 17, 337, 52, 352.
5. Ibid, Book II, p. 95, 98; Book III, p. 127, 180, 193.
5. Epictetus, The Enchiridion, I, p. 331ff. Cf. 11, 12, p. 335.
7. Ibid, 23, p. 338. Cf. 5, p. 333, Cf. 13, p. 335; 23, p. 338, 34, p. 346, 48, p. 350.
8. The Discourses, Book I, 60, Book II, pp. 103, 146; Book III, 188.
9. Ibid, Book I, 26, 66, 68, 101, 103.
10. Ibid, Book I, 21, 40, 46, 55, 68.
11. The Enchiridion, 1, p. 331f; 2, 332, 3, 323.
12. The Discourses, Book I, Chapter 6, p. 17. Chap. 4, p. 12. Cf. Marcus Aurelius, Meditations, Book XII.
13. Ibid, Book I, Chapter 19, p. 52. Cf. Chapter 10, 30.
14. Ibid, Book I, Chapter 3, p. 11; Cf. Book IV, Ch. 2, p. 283; Cf. Book III, p. 210.
15. Ibid, Book II, p. 138; Book III, p. 208, p. 253.

CHAPTER II

ETHICS AND SCHOLASTIC THOUGHT
5. The Ethics of Augustine
6. The Ethics of Thomas Aquinas

The Sketch of Augustine

Saint Augustine (354-430 A.D.) was born in North Africa, the son of a pagan father and a very devout Christian mother. In his earlier years as a student he accepted Manicheanism, a belief in a rigid dualism of good and evil and a negative view of human nature. When, after a sensuous life, he was converted to Christianity under Bishop Ambrose in 386 he rejected that system of thought. Resigning his professorship in the field of rhetoric he joined a monastery, and later he was ordained a priest in Algeria and still later a bishop. His spiritual venture as a Christian was expressed with pre-existential insight in his so-called Confessions around the year 400. In this great work City of God and his noted work On The Trinity Augustine adapted a neo-Platonic frame of reference while rejecting its pantheism. The City of God (426) was the first Christian philosophy of history and became a model for the Church and Western civilization. Together these works became influential also as interpretations of ethics. The Enchiridion was an exposition of faith, hope and love.

The Ethics of St. Augustine

Saint Augustine employed a neo-Platonic frame of reference in which to couch his Christian ethics and theology. He based his ethics on the Platonic premise that God is good, ultimate Being and the Judaeo-Christian doctrine that God is the creator of all things and that they must be fundamentally good, because God is good. God creates only what is good and cannot create evil.[1]

Evil to Augustine is a basic problem to be reckoned with especially in the face of divine sovereignty and benevolence. Evil to him is not a positive reality but a negative one, which is to say that evil is what lacks the good. This is viewed as the privative theory of evil while interpreted in such a way as to make evil akin to the Platonic concept of non-being. In general this means that, practically speaking, evil is a lesser good, which implies that though its reality is goodness its lack of pure goodness, since not as pure as the creator, makes it less real than something good per se.[2] This combination of ideas is such that evil things belong to Becoming, the mixture of Being and non-being and, as such, evil things have reality but smack of non-being even moreso, since pure non-being is sheer evil. Evil things in Becoming are mixtures of Being and non-being, the former making them real, the latter making them evil.

Since specific evils are real, God can use them to bring about good or higher goods. When evil in man's life is controlled or ordered by something good it can even enhance the good; St. Paul's "thorn in the flesh," linked with spiritual self-discipline, can be viewed as a case in point. Suffering often helps keep persons humble and more amenable to divine guidance. Also, persons often appreciate the good much more when contrasted with evils in their lives; for example, health in view of illness.[3]

The question arises why God should permit men to choose evil. Also, why should God even will the possibility of evil? To Augustine the permission of evil really reflects the goodness of God, since He thereby gives men the freedom of choice between good and evil. Augustine states ". . .if man did not have free will, both punishment and reward would be unjust." Man's selection of good is to God's glory, though, whatever men choose, God's will is ultimately fulfilled. As stated above, God can use evil by bringing good out of it. Furthermore, though much is done contrary to His will, God's good will will prevail.[4]

Evil is the corruption, distortion or deterioration of what is good. This implies that the good is deprived of some of its reality. It is a good gone bad. So long as being is deprived of goodness or is being corrupted it still has some good of what it is being deprived.[5] A criminal is not totally but partially corrupt like a good apple gone bad. He is a good being that is being consumed or corrupted, since every being is a form of the good, and goodness is being. Evil, then, being privative may be interpreted to be parasitical. It feeds off of the good like the leech that lives off the blood of other creatures or the lampreys in Lake Michigan, which feed on the trout. Since evil depends on the good in Augustine's view, he has a theory of evil as privative, i.e. evil is the privation of good.[6]

Vices are contrary to both God and man and are evil, because they corrupt the goodness of man and creation. Both nature and man are basically good to Augustine, having been created so by God and belonging to the inherent order of a good creation. But they become vitiated when perverted or distorted. Though man is good by nature through a good creation by God, his sin is against God and debilitates both nature and human nature. Man corrupts himself through an abuse of his moral freedom, which, originally, led to the so-called "fall of man,"[7] which has biased his moral freedom ever since, as Christian orthodoxy has contended ever since Augustine's time.

Evil is privative due to the absence of the good quite the way a disease is the absence of good health. A cancer, for instance, consumes the good cells of a body and as such is a privative form of evil. In this light Augustine regards evils as "accidental," which is to say they are contrary to the good order of things. Vices are similarly privations of a natural good. A crime is the use of a good intelligence for bad ends. Thus evil does not exist without the presence of the good; it is parasitical. Though human nature is basically good, it is corruptible. Were it incorruptible, evil as vice would be impossible.[8] Evil, like non-being, has no source of its own. It is a decaying goodness or a disordering of order. Good can exist without evil, but evil cannot exist without good. God does not create evil but permits it to occur in the sense that he has given man a moral freedom, which is subject to abuse, which abuse is sin.[9]

Though Augustine held to the doctrine of divine predestination, he also defended the idea of free will in man. Every human action is attributable to an autonomous will. Though evil actions stem from an evil will, Augustine says nothing external to it causes an evil will. It is a state which lacks the good but does so by choice. The causal factor is a person's own consent to succumb to temptation or vicious desire. The assent of the will is the root of evil, morally. It falls to a lower plane not efficiently but deficiently, which means not so much by deliberation as by default. An evil will is one that is defective, one that fails to choose the good and only in that sense is perverse. A man who covets gold intemperately is sinful not because of the gold but by the perversity of loving it. The same for any other lust.[10]

Freedom minor, so-called by some, is ordinary free will-in-action. Freedom major, on the other hand, is what Augustine speaks of when man's will is in alignment with God's will. It spells true freedom, because it is a good will that receives divine wisdom and true happiness therein. A good will is basic to morality since it is in tune with the will of God. Thus, if the will is good the soul is truly free, since its acts are good. Man's chief good is the soul's good. It cannot be a mere sensuous or bodily pleasure as the hedonists allow, nor is it the mere absence of pain. The highest good of man's soul is in God, for the soul obtains virtue by following the will of God, and this is freedom major, the key to true happiness. Augustine states that the supreme good is what has supreme existence. This is God, whom we are to seek and love freely.[11] Attaining this is not achieved in becoming like God but in drawing close to him. This is a relational matter, so that goodness is received from God, not of him. God is the highest and immutable good, eternal and immortal, quite as for Plato but with Christian adaptations.

The greatest human virtue, thinks Augustine, is the love for God inspired by the love of God. Augustine holds that from the Christian perspective the four Greek virtues are four forms of love i.e. four aspects of the same basic virtue which is Caritas or love.[12] However, the Greek virtues in themselves or as unilluminated by divine Grace remain but proud attainments of a self-sufficient, rational man. Only under a faith-qualified perspective are the Greek virtues serviceable to God's cause. The distinctively Christian virtues of faith, hope and love are superior and basic to the life seeking peace with God and endeavoring to serve His Kingdom. Indigenous to loving God is one's love of his neighbor in relation to one's reasonable self-love and self-respect. Love of neighbor is good will or benevolence. It is a "cradle of our love to God," says Augustine. Love of God and love of neighbor rise together and are perfectible. Love of neighbor is essential to one's happiness even as it reflects harmony with God as one comes to God by faith.[13]

Augustine maintains that unless a person orientates his life around God, his will and love, he will become frustrated. In his Confessions he expressed it this way in a prayer: "Thou madest us for thyself, and our hearts are restless until they rest in thee." Every personality is in a state of moral struggle, because two forces oppose each other. They are two wills, one of the old man and one of the new, one carnal and the other spiritual.[14] Augustine himself experienced this tension existentially especially prior to his Christian conversion. At that stage intellectually he was a Manichean, who believed in a universe split into a rigid dualism of good and evil or of God struggling with Satan for rulership of the world.[15] Later he turned to a Christianized neo-Platonism while avoiding the pantheistic conception of the World Soul as held by the Stoics.

The ultimate form of knowledge in Augustine's schematism is a mystical intuition of the Supreme Good. This is more than rational, however, for it belongs to a faith-subsumed reason. One cannot obtain true knowledge or virtue without faith and the divine illumination that comes by Grace on the condition of faith. "I must believe in order to know," said Augustine. Belief in this sense means to trust God or have faith, and this opens up special insight. Intellectual knowledge, then, is superceded by a faith-conditioned knowledge. One cannot know God solely through one's own rational attainments. The Grace of God must enlighten the mind.[16] Such knowledge is salvation, which is a free gift bestowed upon the predestined souls. In this context it is understood that God foreknows what choices men will make, including who will freely accept his gift of Grace. More than that, God foreordains who will accept and reject him.[17]

Since God is sovereign and knows in advance who will choose him, Augustine argues that men cannot have a perfectly free will.[18] This he asserted strongly after his debates with Pelagius, who argues religiously for man's free will. This creates a problem, however, in view of Augustine's own defense of free will, mainly earlier in his career. He tries to show how it is possible to believe in both divine foreknowledge (prescience) and predestination, on the one hand, and human freedom, on the other. The closest he comes to a solution is to say that man's will is a causal power that functions as a part of the overall causal order of divine providence. The question still remains whether this solves the matter. Augustine settles for a kind of paradox in which God's knowledge of a cause and the cause itself are to be distinguished, so that God's foreknowledge of man's choices is not the same as His causing them.[19] Actually, this is the very argument James Arminius used in offsetting Calvinism, viz, foreknowledge is not foreordination.

To Augustine those people are wrong who not only pursue carnal or sensual pleasures but rely on reason as the sole basis of ethics. Reason is finite and by itself cannot cure the evils of life; it needs divine illumination, which is based on the revealed Word and Grace of God. To trust reason alone is to imply that the supreme good is in man alone or within his grasp. It is a false pride that claims that reason by itself can know God or his truth, including moral virtues and precepts.[20] Rather, it takes a Grace-illuminated mind.

In his work City of God Augustine indicates that there is meaning in history only as "the city of God," the forces of good identified with the Church, overcomes "the city of man" or "the city of Satan." The providential end of history will be realized only as an eschatological fulfillment wherein the divine forces of good overcome the satanic forces of evil. Regenerated men with Grace-illuminated minds are alone serviceable to that good end. Those who live in the City of God are serviceable to peace through love, not war.[21] Even so such a life of faith does not shield men from earthly problems. The major branches of Christendom outside of fundamentalism have embraced Augustine's eschatology.

Many ethicists as well as theologians would criticize Augustine for jeopardizing man's free will and moral responsibility both in everyday life and in man's free response to God and His Grace. Does not Augustine's doctrine of predestination overwhelm, if not overarch, man's freedom of will, in which case man is not truly free? And to what glory of God is a man "bulldozed" by predestination into the Kingdom and the good life?

Some would say that Augustine jeopardizes the humanistic possibilities of man due to his utter dependence upon divine revelation and Grace. The natural man of reason is not left self-sufficient. Augustine's reply would be in compliance to the criticism on the grounds that the natural man, so-called, is a sinner in need of the very things of God that the humanist rejects. To Augustine the natural man is not self-sufficient, because he is corrupt and in need of regeneration, the re-orientation of life in the Word of God on a faith-conditional basis. On the other hand, some Augustinians would say that the true humanism is religious in perspective by which is meant that the truly fulfilled person is the regenerated person whose possibilities are maximized, not minimized, under Grace.

Others would say that Augustine's doctrine of original sin or the fall of man leaves man so depraved that he has not only lost his innocence but has received a bent of inclination toward evil from birth. This, too jeopardizes free will. Some like Kierkegaard, however, would see free will overcoming the sinful bias under Grace; the same for those Catholics and Protestants alike who stress the sanctification of life under Grace and the Holy Spirit of God.

Notes

1. Augustine, Aurelius, City of God, Books VIII and X.
2. Augustine, The Enchiridion on Faith, Hope, and Love, Gateway Editions, Chaps. XI, XII, CII.
3. Ibid, also C1.
4. Augustine, "On The Free Will," Book II, Chapter I from Selections From Medieval Philosophers, Vol. I, p. 11f. Quotations from p. 13: Cf. Enchiridion, Chaps. XCVI, C, C-CI.
5. Enchiridion, op cit, Chapt. XI, XII, CII.
6. Ibid.
7. City of God, op cit, Vol II, Book XIV: i, xi-xv.
8. Ibid, Book XIV::iii, v, xi.
9. Enchiridion, Chaps. XCVI, C-CI.
10. City of God, Book V: 9-10 and Book XI: 7-8.
11. "On The Free Will," Book II. Chap. XVII: 45, p. 62f; Chap. XIII: 37, p. 53f and City of God, Book XXII.
12. Augustine, Faith, Hope and Charity, Chaps. 31, 32 (not The Enchiridion).
13. Enchiridion, Chaps. CXXI, VII, VIII and City of God, Book XIX: 4.
14. Augustine, Confessions, Book VIII and City of God, Book XIII, 4, 10, 11; Book XIV: 6, 11.
15. Ibid, Book III, Book VII. Cf. "On The Free Will," op cit, Chap. 2, no. 6, p. 16f. Chap. IX, no. 25, p. 40; Chap. XIII, no. 35, p. 52f.
16. City of God, Book XIX: 4, 25.
17. Enchiridion, Chaps. XCVI, XCVII, XCVIII, C-CI and City of God, Book V: 18; Book XII: xcii, xxvi.
18. City of God, Book V: 9-10.
19. Ibid.
20. Ibid, Book XIX: 4. Cf. Confessions, Book XIII: 14, p. 31.
21. Ibid, Book V: 18; Book XIV: 1-2, 23; Book XIX: 14; Book XXI: 12, 15; Book XXII: 29, 30.

The Sketch of Thomas Aquinas

St. Thomas Aquinas (1224-1274), Roman Catholic philosopher and theologian, was born in Italy and educated under Benedictine and Dominican orders at Naples and the Universities of Paris and Cologne. He received his doctorate in theology at the University of Paris and taught there until 1259 when he was thirty-five years old after which he spent a decade teaching in monasteries in and around Rome. Thereupon he returned to Paris to teach and continue his writings. One of his major areas of study was the works of Aristotle. Aquinas wrote several works in both theology and philosophy including essays on the Bible and Aristotle's philosophy. He is most noted for this work <u>Summa Contra Gentiles</u>, finished in 1264, and <u>Summa Theologica</u>, finished in 1273. The first was designed to convert the Moors, the latter being a systematic synthesis of Aristotle and Christian theology. In 1323 Aquinas was canonized as a saint after scholars saw his work was not heretical as first suspected because of his departure from Plato's frame of reference. Those who follow his philosophy closely are known as Thomists. Some in recent times who have modified his views somewhat are Neo-thomists.

The Ethics of St. Thomas Aquinas

It can be said that Thomas Aquinas wrote his Christian ethics and theology within the framework of Aristotle's ontology while greatly influence by St. Augustine's views. Basically, this implied two types of religious knowledge, the one from a natural philosophy of reason's observations and the other from a revealed, Grace-conditioned or more-than-natural source. Yet the two kinds of truth are thought to synthesize or coalesce without losing their distinctiveness. Aristotle's ethics, which is based on a natural reason, is deemed to be sound but inadequate.

In his ethics and moral theology Aquinas is teleological. Moral acts are conducive to man's happiness, the ultimate end of which is the eternal contemplation of the Perfect Good. The chief problem is the selection of prudent means to that end. In God there is eternal law that provides man with the ultimate standard of good and evil. Some of it is known by natural philosophy and some by being revealed through the scriptures, the Decalogue of Moses, for instance. These principles are covered by Aquinas in the third book of his Summa Contra Gentiles. Moral virtues and vices are discussed in his Summa Theologica including the supernatural virtues of faith, hope and love.

Aquinas adapts Aristotle's doctrine of entelechy, which sees all things moving toward the good end of Being, so human activity is likewise directed toward ends. The teleological principle implies a final end in God, and God is also the efficient cause for bringing about such an end. The happiness men pursue through reason is linked with the final end. Aquinas is much in agreement with Aristotle but sees a higher form of happiness attainable through divine Grace; it applies to both this life and the next with both reason and revealed truth contributing to it, since both look to divine law from their respective vantage points. Accordingly, philosophy deals mainly with immanental truths; theology with the transcendent.

In his famous work Summa Theologica Aquinas treats the existence and perfect Being of God and how God is known by men. Aquinas also deals with the features of God's character and personal nature. These factors are largely presupposed when Aquinas comes to his other great work Summa Contra Gentiles in which he discusses the divine creation and purpose of all things. As perfect being God bestows being on all existents not by necessity but by his free will. As the agent behind creation, God wills a good end for all things. In this respect God is the sovereign ruler of all.

Intelligent beings crated <u>imago dei</u> resemble God and are not only directed but freely direct themselves to the good end, since they are moral agents. This implies that such creatures as human beings have a free will that seeks to attain ends, some of which are means to higher ends. In addition all human ends on this basis are attainable. All natural ends of concern to a moral agent are good. They are that in which the "appetite of the agent or mover comes to rest," says Aquinas, good being the "object of every appetite" and all movement being for a good. In agreement with Aristotle it is contended by Aquinas that the highest end for man is the contemplation of truth; however, Aquinas qualified this by asserting the highest truth contemplated to be divine, for God is the highest good and end of all things.[2]

Aquinas respects Aristotle's claim that men seek happiness through reason but believes it to be too optimistic a view, because human nature finds it difficult to achieve the moral and intellectual virtues of life while trying to overcome evil tendencies. A natural reason cannot find the higher divine wisdom on its limited terms. Hence honor, wealth and bodily pleasures are not happiness. Human passions compete with rational harmony and divine wisdom. Also the empirical pursuits of the sciences are inadequate when it comes to contemplating the most noble truths and divine wisdom. Man's highest happiness lies in contemplating God, yet it is not achieved ultimately in this life. It is realized in immortality, when all desire will be fulfilled.[3]

Moral acts are voluntary or moved internally toward their end by their own inclination. They are free choices. A virtue is what links a good with an action; a vice links a bad with an action. The good has the rational quality of an end. Actions done by choice are done for an end. Aquinas definitely believes some actions of men are evil, yet every action has some goodness, since it has being. Man's evil is due to the evil objects which he loves, his goodness due to the good objects he loves. Good and being are convertible concepts with being providing both form and end of goodness; reason points us to both.[4]

Upon contemplating God a man must come to respect that God is the moral lawgiver. Being an intelligent moral agent created <u>imago dei</u> man can understand and observe the eternal law of the Supreme Reason of God. All is under providence, for the whole "universe is governed by the divine reason." As a rational being man partakes of that rational law by what Aquinas calls "the natural law." The natural reason discerns what is good and evil, insight into which is "the divine light." Thus the natural law of reason belongs to the eternal law.[5]

Man, then, participates rationally in the eternal law of God. Aquinas even suggests that man has a natural disposition to know and choose things in this light. The good is that which man seeks naturally along with the avoidance of its opposite, evil. Good is an end pursued, evil is not, thus what man naturally apprehends and pursues by reason is good. "Man has a natural inclination to know the truth about God, and to live in society," says Aquinas, " and in this respect, whatever pertains to this inclination belongs to the natural law. . ."[6] The natural law of reason, then, is grounded in the eternal law of God. In this way philosophical ethics and religious ethics become a working team.

In the light of these principles Aquinas asserts that a free or voluntary act is that of a moral agent and is done for an end contemplated by reason. Since reason controls fears and passions the latter do not minimize moral responsibility. Rational movements are intrinsically for ends, and knowledge of the end is necessary; therefore, such acts are voluntary or morally free since done "from their own inclination." It is voluntary if "the will is moved to it." What is done from fear is involuntary, but what is done from concupiscence is voluntary since based on desire.[7] In most instances ignorance is not grounds for disclaiming moral responsibility unless it causes involuntariness.[8] Good and bad moral acts are to be judged by the goodness or badness of the object or end to which the will looks under the direction of reason.[9]

This much calls to mind the role of conscience in relation to reason. Contrary to some who contend that as long as persons willfully choose things according to their rational power of conscience their acts are moral, Aquinas argues that a person's conscience may be in error at times, mistaken about a moral issue and not merely ignorant of details involved. When one accepts the imperatives of an erroneous conscience his act will be evil. On the other hand, if the will of a person does not respond to conscience the act is apt to be evil also. Yet when conscience erroneously commands something evil or forbids what is "good in itself" it is not binding, so the will that varies with such a conscience is not evil. Ignorance as seen above can make an act invol-untary at times, for it removes "the character of moral good and evil." Only as ignorance is voluntary, supported by the will as one chooses not to know what he ought, is it blatantly evil. The conscience cannot excuse the will in that case.[10]

At times Aquinas reminds his readers of Kant's ethics when he asserts that what is good about an act is what the rational will intends rather than the results or consequences brought about by the act. In other words it is one's motive that is basic to a moral act. If a person fails, however, to foresee evil consequences his will is not evil. "The consequences," says Aquinas, "do not make an act that was evil, to be good; nor one that was good, to be evil." An act of charity done for a poor man, who uses the alms for evil ends, is not evil. Likewise, if one bears a wrong done to him, the wrongdoer is not excusable. Also any consequence of an act by accident does not make the act more evil or good.[11] It is motive based on reason that is basic to morality.

Good and evil pertain to the will, and the goodness of a person's will is derived from its object. Where an act of the will is fixed on a good no circumstance can make that act evil. "The will's object is proposed to it by the reason." "Therefore the goodness of the will depends on its being subject to reason."[12] Yet the reason and conscience can err and this does not excuse the will which abides by them. As for the means employed by the will it is to be judged by the intention of a certain end. If the will is to be good it must will the good end for its own sake. Goodness or malice in the will depend on the good or evil in the intention. A good will intends a good end. "Now the last end of the human will is the highest good, namely, God," says Aquinas.[13] The truly good will is "ordained to the highest good," the absolute Good identified with "the divine will as its proper object."[14] Thus the highest form of moral conduct is that which is in harmony with God and his will. This is given a special moral quality in the light of the Christian virtues of faith, hope and love, which supersede but yet blend with the Greek virtues of reason.

Thomas Aquinas is criticized by some philosophers and theologians for his claim that natural rational ethics and the Christian virtues of faith, hope and love may be synthesized. Thinkers who are not as confident in reason may not accept this, nor do thinkers who think the Christians virtues totally supersede the natural. The latter type of thinkers are apt to maintain theologically that the Christian virtues are transcendent of the natural or rational, which are immanental or innate.

A parallel matter is how Aquinas asserts that God as Being creates all existents by free will. How can this be known save by revelation or a faith-conditioned unveiling? Likewise how God wills a good end for all things even as God is the highest good and end of all. Similarly, how the natural law is akin to and grounded in the eternal law. Is not the ethics of Aquinas then dependent more on theology than philosophy though very much attached to Aristotle's metaphysics?

More practically speaking, Aquinas maintained that in accord with divine providence our material goods are meant to meet needs; therefore, property based on human law must not hinder meeting the needs of others. Abundance of worldly goods must be shared with the hungry, the naked and the penniless that freedom may be theirs.

Notes

1. Thomas Aquinas, <u>Summa Contra Gentiles</u>, Book III, Chaps. I, p. 3f and Chap. II, p. 5, also Chap. III, p. 7.
2. <u>Ibid</u>, Chap. III and Book III, Chap. XXXVII, pp. 59f; also re imago dei see <u>The Summa Theologica</u>. Question 93, Articles 2, 3, and 4. Cf. Question 75, Articles 1, 2.
3. <u>Summa Contra Gentiles</u>, Book III, Chap. XLVIII, p. 84ff. Chap. LXII, p. 108ff, Chap. LXIII, p. 111ff, also Chap. XXXVII, p. 59f. Cf. Cf. Chaps. XXVII, XXVIII, XXX, p. 51ff.
4. Aquinas, <u>Summa Theologica</u>, Question 18, Second Article thru Eleventh Article, pp. 319-333.
5. <u>Summa Theologica</u>, Question XCI, Article 1, 2, p. 748ff.
6. <u>Ibid</u>, Question XCI, Article 2, p. 774f.
7. <u>Ibid</u>, Part II, First Part, Question 6, Articles V, VI, VII, p. 226f, 234ff.
8. <u>Ibid</u>, Article VIII, p. 237f.
9. <u>Ibid</u>, Question 19, Articles I, II, III, p. 335ff.
10. <u>Ibid</u>, Question 19, Articles V, VI, p. 339ff.
11. <u>Ibid</u>, Question 20, Article V, p. 356f.
12. <u>Ibid</u>, Question 19, Articles 1-10, pp. 335-349, quotation from p. 337.
13. <u>Ibid</u>, Question 19, Article 9, p. 3-6.
14. <u>Ibid</u>.

CHAPTER III

ETHICS AND SOCIAL THEORY

7. The Ethics of Thomas Hobbes
8. The Ethics of the Earl of Shaftesbury
9. The Ethics of David Hume

The Sketch of Thomas Hobbes

Thomas Hobbes (1588-1679) attended Oxford University and became a tutor to a wealthy family that favored him with books, people and travels. His sympathies with the crown when England was at civil war caused him to flee to France where he was made familiar with the philosophy of René Descartes and others. The sciences and mathematics impressed him greatly. Hobbes turned away from the Scholastic philosophies of medieval thinkers, based on Plato and Aristotle, and tried to apply materialistic concepts to philosophy and the mental life. His most notable writing was Leviathan, authored in 1651, which interrelated man and society with nature and a materialistic psychology, the first of its kind. Human nature, he maintained, was to be understood in its original state prior to the development of societies or states. Human existence in that original state was competitive, animalistic and warlike. In order to control it people had to develop governments to sustain peaceful relationships. In order for such to succeed the people had to surrender their wills to the state in the form of a social contract that yields total sovereignty to the state with a form of pre-utilitarian understanding.

The Ethics of Thomas Hobbes

Thomas Hobbes chose to stress the materialistic side of René Descartes' rigid dualism. In his major work, The Leviathan, he not only set forth a pro-mechanistic to pre-behavioral psychology and epistemology but enunciated a hedonistic type of ethics.

Upon asserting that man seeks happiness Hobbes overtly sees man as egoistical. Human beings are entirely selfish, he says. Thus prudential concerns are egocentric in that even prudence or good judgment in private affairs is solely out of self-interest. Man is an intelligent being in that he seeks his own well-being. Though Hobbes does not relate this to religious view in any positive sense he does so negatively by simply saying this self-concern belongs to the way we are made.

Man to Hobbes is a social animal who in the face of his competitive and warlike tendencies enters into "social contract" with others mainly to avoid war and similar social tensions. War is "not in actual fighting, but in the known disposition thereto. . ."[1] The natural state of man is competition, diffidence and war. Paradoxically, self-preservation is natural also; in fact it is "the primary end of nature in man," says Hobbes. Social contract, then, is purely an expediency, a mutually prudential undertaking for the sake of personal security. It is entered into not out of the desire to promote social welfare benevolently but purely out of selfish interests. People yield property rights to a third party, as it were, the government, to prevent social tensions. The right to protect one's own life is retained as a natural disposition while the government is given ultimate authority to control human affairs by law, which is the logical outgrowth of the social contract. Without the state there is no moral law.

Basically, then, Hobbes' ethics is hedonistic and egocentric with no motive of true benevolence beneath the social contract. Benevolence is based only on the desire for power, says Hobbes in his work entitled Of Human Nature.[2] Desires ever progress without end. Power is the means of obtaining good desires especially for a "commonwealth," honor being a sign of such power. Only as there is coercive power in society can there be justice.[3] Thus the undergirding nature or motive of Hobbes' ethics is self-interest. This is linked with the absolute sovereignty of the government as a necessary condition of a peaceful society.

Hobbes was influenced by his seventeenth-century contemporaries, who catered to naturalism, Copernicus, Galileo and Harvey being among them. Thus he became the first philosopher to systematize such views and relate them to the study of man and society. Basic to his views is a mechanistic materialism, which had become prominent in the Newtonian physics of his day. In The Leviathan he extends it into psychology and ethics. Mentality is reduced to physiology or a variety of animalistic motions. Speech precedes reason, says Hobbes.[4]

Good and evil are merely the object of people's desires or aversions. All values are transient, relative and temporal. Self-gratification is the basic concern of man and his happiness, even in relation to the "commonwealth" based on social contract whereby a civil society is made possible through law. Hobbes makes civil authority and law the basis for morality, not vice versa. Justice, for example, has no place in the state of nature; it only belongs to man in society.[5]

In Leviathan Thomas Hobbes presents a psychological theory based on the so-called "motions" of the body and mind. Besides the vital motions of animals basic to their physical nature there is voluntary motion basic to deliberate acts or motions like "going or speaking." The latter, unlike the former, fall under the category of endeavor or desire. What men desire they love; what they have an aversion for they hate. Good and evil similarly are given a mechanistic interpretation. What a man desires is good, and that which he hates is evil, desires and hates being forms of motion. Furthermore, the general inclination of men is a restless desire for power.[6]

Prior to developing a society or state, Hobbes contends, people make judgments of good and evil relative to their desires and aversions while their uppermost concern is security or self-preservation. Success in this endeavor is deemed happiness. Friends, wealth and intelligence help promote it. Desired objects which promote such felicity are regarded as "powers." Men seek more and more of such powers the longer they live, but when people desire the same objects of power tensions arise. Confederations develop and overt conflicts break forth.[7]

Where civil society is not yet developed people are apt to be in contention. As mentioned above, Hobbes brusquely asserts that the natural human condition or state of nature is war. There are three principal causes of this in human nature: competition, diffidence and glory or pride. The first leads men to "invade for gain," the second "for safety," the third, "for reputation." Without government or "a common power to keep them all in awe" men are at war, which is not only battle but the "known disposition thereto," for they lack security.[8]

Thus in reaction to the natural state of war, Hobbes states, men develop societies by "social contract" while strictly out of prudential self-interest and fear, not benevolence. One's own interest is a natural concern for one's own happiness. The natural law of life is self-protection, and men have a natural right to promote it. Organized society is designed for gain or glory based on "love of ourselves," says Hobbes. These interests are served by "mutual help" based not on goodwill but fear. The basic right is that every man should "protect his life and members" and have the means to do so. Social contract assures them of this.[9]

For Hobbes the natural, pre-social state of man is one of self-interest, social relations being artificially developed. Society is only a more clever way of furthering one's individual interests and happiness. The natural man, he maintains, has no moral sensitivities or obligation. Concepts of right and wrong, justice and injustice develop only with the rise of a civil society. Every man is basically at war with every other. "Where there is no common power," Hobbes says, "there is no law; where no law, no injustice. Force and fraud, are in war the two cardinal virtues." There is "no *mine* and *thine* distinct," only to each his own. What inclines men toward peaceful relations is fear of death and desire for commodious living. Reason instrumentally works out agreements which are called "the Laws of Nature."[10] Reason thereby works for the end of warfare of nature, first as the individual sees his need of security and, second, as it discovers the laws of nature that affect peaceful relations. The laws of nature are rules learned by reason where by men are forbidden to do whatever destroys life or prevents its preservation. They promote peace by voluntary acts which seek security for the individual through mutual efforts.[11]

Hobbes, as asserted at the outset, stresses the egoistic nature of men. Even the covenants or social contracts they draw up are in self-interest, but without them war would prevail. Justice exists only where a covenant of mutual trust exists. To break the covenant is unjust. For justice to prevail there is need of a coercive power to compel compliance. This can be brought about only through a commonwealth with "the constitution of a civil power" to compel compliance and promote propriety.[12]

Despite his materialism Hobbes concludes that the laws of nature boil down to the Golden Rule, or really, the Silver Rule: "Do not that to another, which thou wouldest not have done to thyself."[13] Reason in this light promotes peace and the means to attain it. Government is needed as a civil power to determine right and wrong, i.e. a single sovereign power either topped by a monarch or an assembly to prevent disputes between lesser authorities. Such a power becomes even the moral conscience of the people; it should even dominate church matters. Civil law decides what is good and evil and the judge is the legislator representing the commonwealth.

Individuals do not judge good and evil actions. Rather, "the law is the public conscience."[14]

The logical outcome of Hobbes' ethical theory is the political doctrine of the state's absolute sovereignty. Individuals give up certain powers and self-interests so that this may be possible; yet it is done out of self-interest, for it is designed to end the natural state of war between people. All that is done by the sovereign power is warranted as just by law and is meant to prevent the hurting of people. Yet Hobbes actually states that the sovereign power must be accountable to God, the "author" of law.[15]

Critically speaking it is questionable that men are either as hedonistic or egoistic as Hobbes' materialism and psychology contend. His ethics, therefore, fails to embrace any form of benevolent motivation, since his portrait of man is such that he is only selfish. Even mutual human interests in the social contract do not allow for any outgoing concern for others or for the welfare of mankind. Rather, they rest on fear. Self-gratification is the sole concern of men, who are left by Hobbes on an animalistic level.

Hobbes has no place for an intuition of morality, in fact no basis for morality linked with human nature; it is solely of the sovereign state. Hobbes makes civil authority the basis of morality instead of morality the basis of civil authority. Philosophically, this makes law the basis of morality, not morality the basis of law. The problem then arises: What does law look to in order to be substantial? Hobbes says next to nothing philosophically that law can appeal to that warrants its morality. The closest he comes to such is to say government must look to God as the author of law. The logic of this is for Hobbes to keep law and religion in opposite pockets. His philosophical framework fails to coordinate, let alone synthesize, the civil and religious referents. The fundamental problem is that Hobbes' materialism is short-sighted and he has no philosophical superstructure that can interrelate his ethics and the God to whom civil law must eventually look for authenticity.

Then, too, it can be questioned whether war is the closest to the natural state of man, lest the perennial yearnings for peaceful relations be of no consequence. While Hobbes does much to offset the superficial optimism of romanticists and many humanists by stressing that man is egocentric, proud and competitive, he neglects the more positive aspect of human nature. Even his own confidence that reason works for peace through social contract is not justifiably accounted for. Hobbes is much too pessimistic when he states that the natural man has no moral sensitivities. The logic of this is that morals and laws can exist only where there is civic power. It may be that just the opposite is the case. While Hobbes conceded that the Golden Rule expresses the laws of nature he fails to account for the motifs of love and good will whereby such a principle is made possible. Love can do what law cannot. This is fails to see.

In theory, Hobbes is a teleological ethicist who looks to self-centered results. He has no place for an innate or rational principle of moral intuition of "ought" or duty, nor a definite respect for the will of God. Though he respects the reality of God, Hobbes sees the will of God only in keeping with man's social contract principle. His ethics is a matter of prudence linked with psychological egoism.

Notes

1. Thomas Hobbes, Leviathan, Chapter XIII, p. 64.
2. Thomas Hobbes, Of Human Nature, Chapter IX, p. 299 in British Moralists, ed. by S. Bigge.
3. Hobbes, Leviathan, Chapter X, XV. Note last paragraph.
4. Ibid, Chapter V, p. 21.
5. Ibid, Chapter XIV, last two paragraphs.
6. Ibid, Chapter VI, p. 23ff. Cf. Chapter XII re. power.
7. Ibid, p. 63ff.
8. Ibid, Chapter XII, latter on p. 64.
9. Ibid, Chapter X, XIII, XIV, p. 66ff.
10. Ibid, Chapter XIII, p. 66, Chapter XV. Cf. Chapter XVIII, p. 90.
11. Ibid, Chapter XIV, XV.
12. Ibid, Chapter XIV, XV, p. 74f.
13. Ibid, Chapter XIV, p. 67.
14. Ibid, Chapter XXIX, p. 172ff.
15. Ibid, Chapters XXX, XXIII, p. 203. Cf. Chapter XXIX, p. 173.

The Sketch of the Earl of Shaftesbury

Anthony Ashley Cooper (1621-1683), Earl of Shaftesbury, was an English statesman and philosopher. In 1679 he managed to secure the passage of the Habeas Corpus Act, one of the bulwarks of British democracy. The ruling demands that police have sufficient basis before the court for holding a prisoner. Both England and America have adopted it as a guarantee of freedom. Cooper was born at Wimborne in Dorsetshire and studied at Oxford University. In 1640 he entered Parliament becoming prominent under Oliver Cromwell during a civil war. After the death of Cromwell he helped restore the monarchy, his efforts being appreciated notably by King Charles II who pardoned him for certain previous actions. The king made him Baron Ashley, Earl of Shaftesbury, and Lord Chancellor. He worked to establish the Whig party and supported the Test Acts against the Catholics. In 1679 he became president of the Privy Council and passed the Habeas Corpus Act, but he was arrested in conjunction with a plot against the king, whereupon he escaped to the Netherlands where he died. In philosophy he modified the egocentric hedonism of Thomas Hobbes in favor of a more benevolent position of enlightened self-interest. He was influenced by his near contemporary John Locke.

The Ethics of the Earl of Shaftesbury

The third Earl of Shaftesbury was a liberal Anglican deist who disliked the egoistical type of thought basic to the ethics of Thomas Hobbes. His was an empirical approach to ethics influenced by John Locke, who contended all knowledge is a product of experience. Shaftesbury rejected both a moral intuitionism and all views based on special revelation while favoring an empirical ethics of social implications.

The Earl of Shaftesbury catered to a prudential view of ethics of a benevolent type. Though men seek their own welfare naturally they are social creatures, who at times act out of benevolence with marked concern for the welfare of others. To Shaftesbury personal prudence and social benevolence seldom conflict. So he greatly modifies Hobbes' view by toning down its psychological egoism. His conception of virtue is much closer to the Christian view. The motive of good will is paramount rather than the observance of law for the sake of one's security as in Hobbes' ethics. Public welfare and one's own are thought to blend.

To Shaftesbury men seek more than hedonistic interests and pleasures. Anticipating John S. Mill, he says men seek higher goods as well. Even preceding one's security good will may be experienced to the extent of making sacrifices for others. Basically, then, virtue is grounded in a rational understanding conducive to the well being of both oneself and others. Good will can be a dominant motive rather than a mere expediency. Thus virtue can be viewed as "enlightened self interest" when personal and social welfare are seen to blend. Pure hedonism is selfishness, and it is erroneous, because man is more than a self-centered individual; he is a social being. Whatever is a man's good must be seen in view of the social whole. It promotes the good of society, which contributes, too, to one's own enjoyment.

The Earl of Shaftesbury is regarded as the founder of the "moral sense school" of ethics. He is basically concerned about what makes for merit or character. Moral worth is not based on fear or self-interest alone but on what he calls "affection" basic to benevolence.[1] This pertains to the inner motive or "moral beauty" that directs a person to "the public good."[2] This "moral sense" is a sense of right and wrong with which all men are endowed by nature yet subject to development in different degrees.[3] It is what makes for public interest and is rooted in human nature. Yet it can be weakened through social conditioning or custom.

Unlike John Locke, Shaftesbury viewed justice and honesty as innate or instinctive, i.e. potentialities of the human spirit which develop in the social context. Locke regarded such as unnatural and without basis. Though Shaftesbury does not refer to intuition his moral sense theory is based on intuitive functions. He refers to good "taste" and to the "heart," which significantly are later adapted by David Hume. Reason makes for the discipline of the moral judgments, i.e. helps prevent emotional failure. In this respect the Earl of Shaftesbury synthesizes the intuitive and logical judgments. He does not accept Hobbes' claim that there is no right and wrong in nature prior to the organized commonwealth.[4] He sees the need and reality of moral sensitivity before men can have a commonwealth, so it belongs to nature with moral values preceding social contract. Conscience is related to this with religious implications, it being a reflective sensitivity to affections, positively, and a sensitivity to what is odious, negatively.[5] Happiness is for Shaftesbury based on conscience and the natural, social affections, which promote the general good.[6]

Critically, Shaftesbury makes a good case for virtue being basic to happiness, but are there no exceptions relative to prudence? Hobbes is shown to be deficient in his egoistical view, for man is seen to have social interest, not just selfish ones. Social cooperation is a more basic impulse than Hobbes allows. Even so, Shaftesbury's argument for social impulse is weak in the sense that self-interest is still present in the form of catering to one's own group.[7] It can be contended that the Earl of Shaftesbury does not fully overcome Hobbes' psychological egoism, for his enlightened self-interest theory still has an underlying egocentric appeal. Even so his "natural affections" which include love, gratitude, pity, friendship, love of truth, and all sorts of mental pleasures are intensified when shared with others. Shaftesbury thus greatly improves upon Hobbes' theory, for he sees that man's disposition is strongly social in outlook, even apart from his self concerns. This allows for a synthesis of benevolence and personal prudence.

Notes

1. Anthony Cooper, Earl of Shaftesbury, <u>An Inquiry Concerning Virtue or Merit</u>, from <u>British Moralists</u>, edited by L. A. Selby-Bigge, pp. 11f, 14-18, 23, 26-62.
2. <u>Ibid</u>, pp. 6-8, 13, 27f, 49, 66f.
3. <u>Ibid</u>, p. 24. Cf. pp. 21-23.
4. <u>Ibid</u>, pp. 17, 21, 23, 32, 60. Cf. Stanley Grean, <u>Shaftesbury's Philosophy of Religion and Ethics</u>, pp. 199-216.
5. Shaftesbury, <u>An Inquiry Concerning Virtue or Merit</u>, note the religious implication of the moral sensitivity, pp. 49f, 67, 211.
6. <u>Ibid</u>, pp. 38f, 49f, 66.

The Sketch of David Hume

David Hume (1711-1776) is next to John Locke in the eighteenth century beginnings of modern empiricism. As such he made a strong attack against rationalistic metaphysics in his 1739 work, <u>A Treatise of Human Nature</u>. Revised in 1748 it appeared as <u>Philosophical Essays Concerning Human Understanding</u>. In 1751 Hume published <u>An Enquiry Concerning the Principles of Morals</u>, which he considered his best work. Posthumously his work, <u>Dialogues Concerning Natural Religion</u> was published in which he questions the proofs of God. Hume was noted, too, for his classical <u>History of England</u>. Born of aristocratic parents he attended Edinburgh University in Scotland. He failed to gain chairs of philosophy in Edinburgh and Glasgow Universities and for five years served as librarian to the faculty of law at Edinburgh. A modest man, Hume felt that the empirical method of physical sciences could apply to philosophy, since to him nothing is in the mind save through the senses. Moral issues are treated also as matters of fact and are only contingently true and not necessarily true, yet moral matters are rooted in human nature's feelings dealt with empirically in terms of behavior. Feelings of approval and disapproval are basic to this as matters of social sentiment. It appears, then, that ethics is reduced to a matter of taste, yet Hume assumes all men have basically similar preferences and he tries to deal with them as objective phenomena, not merely subjective. Differences of opinion stem, then, not from human nature but misunderstandings. Also, men act justly solely out of social utility.

The Ethics of David Hume

The Scottish philosopher David Hume expressed a different refutation of Hobbes' ethics with its psychological egoism. As a thoroughgoing empiricist Hume stressed that men know ethical values through social experience.

Hume denied a unified, enduring self in favor of a stream of perceptions and saw all knowledge based on sense experience. Yet Hume qualified his sensate epistemology with an appeal to "social sentiment" or feelings as the locus of ethics. He credited this to neither reason nor intuition. For him ethics is conditioned entirely by social experience as centered in a "moral sentiment" that is a product of social forces. Though admitting egocentric and hedonistic elements, Hume sees them modified by a benevolence as interpreted by society. Socially, men have favorable feelings toward acts of benevolence and it is by this that society gives us our moral norms.

The basis of the social sentiment is "an immediate feeling and finer internal sense" much like the perception or "taste" of beauty, says Hume.[1] While he does not appeal strongly to reason or innate ideas to justify morals Hume is favorable to the idea that reasoning can point one to an appreciation of moral sentiment, much like the use of reason in art and the appreciation of beauty.[2] But the final source of morality does not lie with reason, for it is not the basis of inspired action but is only what procures the "cool" assent of the understanding. Essential to virtue is "the warm feelings" that "regulate our lives and actions."[3] Thus sentiment is the source of morality. Virtue, then, is what receives social approbation and vice is what receives disapprobation. Even so, reason helps men make moral decisions in this light, especially in the face of doubtful circumstances.[4] The underlying appeal is still made to what Hume calls "the heart."[5] "Nothing," says Hume, "remains but to feel, on our part, some sentiment of blame on approbation, whence we pronounce the action criminal or virtuous."[6]

Hume recognizes that men have long endorsed the virtue of justice and that it is universally accepted, but benevolence is even more approved. Justice is based on utility and equity, whereas benevolence is based on friendship and generosity.[7] The latter are more basic, since they reflect an inner concern for others over usefulness. "The notion of morals," says Hume, "implies some sentiment common to all mankind, which recommends the same object to general approbation . . ."[8] Yet it is "without any dependence on the intellectual faculties."[9] Morals, then, are of the heart with its warm sentiments.

Hume allows for no objective ideals or standards. Rather, moral life is intrinsic to human nature as socially dispositioned and conditioned. Is a universal ethic possible in this event? Hume answers the question affirmatively on the grounds that men share a common human nature on which the empirically developed social sentiment is based. The net result is that absolute public norms and innate moral ideals are rejected in favor of morals based on social sentiment. On this basis right acts are whatever evokes a feeling of approval on the part of others. The universal factor is that men make similar value judgments that are basic to social sentiment. The benevolent factor to Hume is that selfish interests are offset by a disinterested concern for the public. Here he shows a marked optimism about human nature.

In general Hume sees right conduct determined by social approbation. This group consensus is a kind of "social subjectivism" that anticipates the ethics of John Dewey. Personal opinion has its place but is not the locus of moral judgment. Rather moral judgment is based on the sentiments of the society to which the individual belongs.

Critically, an empirical relativism enters the picture with differences from one society to another, sometimes even contradictory mores and codes. This is a challenge to the universality claimed by Hume. Also, ethics is reducible to statistics or a vote. For example, slavery is moral providing the social sentiment favors it. In addition, moral judgments amount to emotional attitudes. Something is moral or amoral, logically, until people express disdain for it; child labor and the Nazi holocaust being cases in point. Then, too, on Hume's terms any moral reformer could not possibly be right, because his precepts run counter to the current social sentiment. Logically, people could only condemn the reformer. This is symmetrical to our claim that on Hume's terms a society could not improve, because its only frame of reference is the present social sentiment. On such a basis a moral reformer could never be considered moral during the initial stages of his movement for his views are not yet socially endorsed. Such a situation is absurd. Today civil disobedience could only be condemned on Hume's terms. How can a minority group protest an unjust law save in the name of a higher principle not condoned by the social sentiment. Higher principles do not arise from a static social sentiment.

Is Hume's ethics fair to minority opinions? Hardly. Whence the social norms basic to social approval? Does not Hume lack such a reference point? Do all men view social approval alike? If so, why do different cultures, empirically observed, have different sentiments and morals? If the moral reformer is logically wrong how can social ethics improve? These are questions Hume does not sufficiently answer.

Though Hume finds useful conduct to be virtuous he has no basis for saying such conduct is an obligation or "ought" to be done. He sees nothing in human nature that gives rise to moral obligation. He rests his case merely on prudential customs based on self-interest. The only moral obligation is what is based on social pressures and sentiment. Yet, though he failed, Hume set an important precedent by taking an empirical approach to ethics.

It can be questioned, then, whether Hume's empirical claim for social utility is a sufficient basis for moral obligation. Though justice is socially useful must it not be an integral part of a moral theory before it is applied socially? Is it not respectable prior to its utility and, if so, it must have a more-than-empirical basis either rational or divine, in which case Kant's view is more feasible.

Notes

1. David Hume, <u>An Enquiry Concerning the Principles of Morals</u>, p. 4f.
2. <u>Ibid</u>, pp. 4-6, 127-129.
3. <u>Ibid</u>, pp. 5-6.
4. <u>Ibid</u>, pp. 107, 129-132.
5. <u>Ibid</u>, pp. 108, 129, 131.
6. <u>Ibid</u>, p. 109.
7. <u>Ibid</u>, pp. 9-10, 14-21, 110ff.
8. <u>Ibid</u>, p. 93.
9. <u>Ibid</u>, p. 111.

CHAPTER IV

ETHICS AND RATIONALISM
    10. The Ethics of Benedict de Spinoza
    11. The Ethics of Joseph Butler
    12. The Ethics of Immanuel Kant

The Sketch of Benedict De Spinoza

Spinoza (1632-1677), was born in Amsterdam of Jewish parents, who were refugees from the Spanish Inquisition. He had a thorough knowledge of the Old Testament and the Talmud as well as Hebrew mystical works and those of Jewish theologians as well as Christian philosophers and the scientists of that day. Spinoza rebelled against Jewish orthodoxy, yet threats to his life drove him into an outward conformity thereto resulting in his excommunication in 1656. He changed his first name to Baruch and continued with his nonconformity while not becoming a Christian. Some have regarded him as an atheist, but this does not stand the test of inquiry. Eventually, Spinoza settled in The Hague as a lens grinder and avocational but creative philosopher. He corresponded with Christian Huygens, the physicist and Gottfried Leibniz, the philosopher. He wrote a commentary on Descartes and made a strong plea for freedom of thought in his <u>Tractatus Theologico - Politicus</u> (1670). Protests followed. His main work was entitled <u>Ethics</u>. In 1673 he was offered a professorship at Heidelberg but he turned it down.

The Ethics of Benedict de Spinoza

Spinoza of Amsterdam was a pantheist of unorthodox, non-conformist leanings who was described by Novalis as the "God-intoxicated man." He endeavored to write a religious philosophy that blended with the spirit of the seventeenth century rationalism of his time. For him all things which transpire do so within the laws of the infinite nature and necessity of God. God is synonymous with Nature or Reality, the rational unity of the universe accounting for all things. God is fully immanent and neither transcendent, free, providential nor loving. God is the rational unity of the whole of things.

Human minds can know God or Nature, thinks Spinoza, because they belong to the rational, divine order of the cosmos. Yet the minds of men are limited, because of their self-centered perspective, causing illusory judgments of good and evil as objective. The very distinction of good and evil is erroneous, since the universe or God is perfect. Bondage to ills based on emotions must be overcome if men are to be happy, and this is the basic problem of ethics. Rational minds accept the unchangeable order of events under eternity seeing all events fixed in the order of Nature. This makes for happiness through the perfection of the intellect in union with Nature's God. Seeing all under eternity becomes an "intellectual love of God," which is the true state of freedom in the life of reason.[1]

In his <u>Treatise on the Correction of the Understanding</u>, Spinoza begins by referring to his experience, asserting that his mind is affected by fears, and if happiness is to be attained honor, riches and pleasure must needs be debarred from his mind. Such things prevent the mind from "thinking of anything else." As "perishable" they make for a mental "disease." The cure is the superior happiness based on meditation and "the union which the mind has with the whole of nature." The latter is based on the true rational pleasure in what is eternal and infinite.[2] Looking to these one aspires to a perfection for self and others. The mind will itself be perfected "when it has regard for and reflects on the knowledge of a most perfect being."[3]

In his <u>Ethics</u> Spinoza exposes misconceptions which encumber men's search for true happiness. One of the basic errors is to assume that things in nature move toward an end as does man. Akin to this is the idea that God purposefully directs all things to a "definite good" and that the phenomena of nature are either good or bad. Spinoza, in contrast, states ". . . that nature has no fixed aim in view, and that all the final causes are merely fabrications of men."[4] And, ". . . all things in nature proceed eternally from a certain necessity and with the utmost perfection."[5] In other words any event belongs to a perfectly completed, deterministic whole. Spinoza argues that if things have a final end, it follows that they transcend other things, which claim "destroys the perfection of God: for if God seeks an end, he necessarily desires something which he lacks."[6] This competes with perfection. Also, to trace end results causally back to the will of God, says Spinoza, is "the asylum of ignorance." Another error of men is to assume all things were made for the sake of men and those things are best which are beneficial to mankind.[7]

Free will to Spinoza is a pernicious doctrine that men falsely espouse out of ignorance of the true causes of their actions. It is erroneous, he thinks, to assume that what we do could be other than it is. Volition is simply an aspect of reason and must act on fixed laws of nature governing all thought.[8] Men think they are free since conscious of their actions and unconscious of what determined them, even unto infinity. What is viewed as decision relative to thought is a "conditioned state" when viewed in the context of "extension" and the laws of motion and rest. Spinoza says men are dreaming who believe they have free decisions.[9]

Spinoza rejects free will also because it makes for elements of uncertainty in life. It also raises false hopes. On the contrary, true freedom is action taken in accord with the laws of reason and nature. "All things follow from the eternal decree of God by the same necessity, as it follows from the essence of a triangle . . ." This also implies that each person should be "content with his own" and helpful to others not out of pity but by the guidance of reason. This is best, too, for the commonwealth so that people not become slaves but to do freely what is best.[10] In general Spinoza seems to have the same problem as the Stoics, a kind of fatalism yet respect for active freedom, a tension which goes unresolved.

Spinoza also remains strongly deterministic in his psychology. Even emotions, he says, should be studied as natural phenomena subject to the same laws of reason as all else in nature. Some thinkers, he maintains, are in error for believing "that man disturbs rather than follows the course of nature, and that he has absolute power in his actions and is not determined in them by anything else than himself."[11] Spinoza wishes to treat emotions in a "geometrical manner" whereby emotions like hate and envy "follow from the same necessity and ability of nature as other individual things."[12] Thus Spinoza's psychology is as deterministic in its way, rationally, as modern behaviorism is in its way, physically.

Spinoza stresses human striving for perfection and self-preservation as a natural, rational disposition. They are the basis of all behavior as well as of virtue, since the nature of man is rational.

In part IV of his <u>Ethics</u> Spinoza accentuates this in a series of propositions. He asserts that the more one seeks to preserve his being the more virtuous he is. "The effort for self-preservation is the first and only foundation of virtue," he says. To obey virtue is likewise to preserve one's being in accord with reason seeking what serves the self usefully. This is what Spinoza means by "understanding." He adds, "We know nothing to be certainly good or evil save what is conducive to understanding or what prevents us from understanding."[13] "The greatest good of the mind is the knowledge of God, and the greatest virtue of the mind is to know God."[14]

Conformity to reason is the basis for self-preservation and perfectibility. It also appraises the emotions, desires, pleasures and pains. Yet moral evaluations are inferior to reason's moral attainment. Judgments of good and evil are determined by emotions, for men view the good as what is conducive to pleasure or what is believed to foster perfectibility. Evils are things of pain which compete with perfectibility. Something good is deemed by Spinoza to be what is desired, not vice versa. Emotions judge what is good or bad, useful or useless.[15]

Men sometimes fall prey to their emotions, and when they do they are not masters of themselves but lie at "the mercy of fortune." Freedom is present only when the laws of reason are respected. The mind's ability to understand emotions affects the extent of one's freedom. The power of reason must appreciate the strength of the emotions if bondage to emotions is to be surpassed by rational freedom. "An emotion," says Spinoza, "therefore becomes more under our control, and the mind is less passive in respect to it, in proportion as it is more known to us."[16] When reason governs us we sense that the universe is determined and that what <u>is</u> must be as it is. Spinoza thinks that on this basis we are better equipped to control our emotions.[17] Also on this basis of reason the mind views things not merely as finite and temporal but as eternal, even as a person understands himself to be a part of God or Nature both mentally and physically. This makes for the greatest good, "the intellectual love of God." By it the mind also realizes it is "conceived through God."[18] Because of this Spinoza states with finality:

> "Whereas the wise man . . . is scarcely at all disturbed in spirit, but, being conscious of himself, and of God, and of things, by a certain eternal necessity, never ceases to be, but always possesses true acquiescence of his spirit."[19]

Critically, while Spinoza gives us a model of manhood correlated with nature's God he can be attacked for essentially the same weaknesses reflected in Stoicism. His deterministic rational metaphysics leads to universal necessity, a kind of fate, and overwhelms the moral freedom of man as accepted in the usual sense. His only freedom is one within his obeisance to reason as that which belongs to Nature as God. To a degree this parallels St. Augustine's determinism and what he calls "freedom major" in contrast to "freedom minor," the natural moral freedom of man. Similarly, the criticisms brought to bear against pantheism apply to Spinoza's ethics. He does not distinguish between natural physical law and natural moral law. His monism fully betrays a doctrine of evil that is more than emotional. It renounces anything and everything which might be viewed as dualistic. Consequently, evil as a serious static of competition with a rational harmony of man and Nature is soft-pedaled if not ignored. While God is respected rationally there is no room for any form of religious liberation or redemption, in fact no need of it, for man is basically at one with God and simply needs to be made aware of it through reason. At best religiously, Spinoza's views make for an abstract deism that absorbs man. His only serious problem is the control of emotion and illusory judgments both of which point to a minimal metaphysical problem of evil, because they are within the jurisdiction of man's rationality or lack thereof.

As a thinker Spinoza was commendably against dogmatism despite anathemas and threats to his life. He stood by his principles consistently while addressing his works to the more philosophically mature of his day. Yet his greatest work, Ethics, is more of a metaphysical treatise on pantheism with immortality attained by reason's overcoming of emotions and passions together with rational union with Nature as God. Religiously speaking, this is a type of Stoic monism combined with humanistic self-sufficiency without respect for divine transcendence as superior to immanence. God is nature and in no way a personality, lest anthropomorphism* take over. Man's intellectual love of God is akin to the Ultimate and is deemed eternal. Religion is man's life in God and God's life in man, their unity based on reason.

---

*Ascribing human features to the divine.

Notes

1. George Santayana, "Introduction," <u>Ethics and De Intellectus Emendatione</u> by Baruch (Benedict) Spinoza, pp. vii-xii and the book proper, I and II. Also, Spinoza <u>Ethics</u>, Part I and Appendix (and) <u>Great Traditions In Ethics</u>, ed. by Albert, Denise and Peterfreund, pp. 145-148.
2. Benedict (Baruch) Spinoza, <u>On The Correction of the Understanding</u>, I, II, pp. 227-231.
3. <u>Ibid</u>, VII (30), p. 239. Cf. (49), p. 241.
4. Benedict Spinoza, <u>Ethics</u>, Part I, Appendix, p. 30ff, esp. p. 32.
5. <u>Ibid</u>, p. 32.
6. <u>Ibid</u>, p. 33.
7. <u>Ibid</u>, p. 34f.
8. <u>Ibid</u>, Part III, Prop. II, p. 86ff. See: Note. Cf. Part II, Prop. 7, 12, XLVIII, XLIX p. 75f.
9. <u>Ibid</u>, Part III, pp. 88-90. Cf. Part II, Prop. XLVII, p. 74f.
10. <u>Ibid</u>, Part II, Prop. XLIX, Note p. 81.
11. <u>Ibid</u>, Part III, Introd. p. 83.
12. <u>Ibid</u>, p. 84.
13. <u>Ibid</u>, Part IV, Props. XX-XXVI and Prop. XXVII.
14. <u>Ibid</u>, Prop. XXVIII.
15. <u>Ibid</u>, Part III, Prop. XXXIX, Note.
16. <u>Ibid</u>, Part IV; Part V, Prop. III, Corallary, p. 203.
17. <u>Ibid</u>, Part V.
18. <u>Ibid</u>, Part V, Prop. XXV-XXIII, pp. 214-218. Cf. Footnote 2 above.
19. <u>Ibid</u>, Part V, Prop. XLI, Note p. 224.

The Sketch of Joseph Butler

Bishop Joseph Butler (1692-1752) was an erudite Christian philosopher who combined faith and reason. He was born three years after the Toleration Act was passed allowing all sects to worship freely, and his father was a Presbyterian Dissenter and shopkeeper, who saw his son's talents and helped him receive training for the ministry. While at Tewkesbury Academy he turned away from the doctrine of the Dissenters to the theology of the Anglicans. In 1714 he entered Oriel College, Oxford. In 1719 he became preacher to the Rolls Chapel in London, where he began his ecclesiastical career. In 1726 he published his <u>Fifteen Sermons</u> containing his ethical theory. In 1736 he was recalled to London to serve as court chaplain under Queen Caroline and he published <u>The Analogy of Religion</u>. In this book Butler defends theism against deism and free thinking. Butler became Dean of St. Paul in 1740, and at the time of his death he was Bishop of Durham. For Butler the basis of morality is conscience, considered a rational faculty somewhat like Kant's later view. Moral reason supercedes feelings, contrary to Hume's claim. Butler in this sense is more of a philosopher than a theologian, for he does not make his appeal to revealed truth, though he believes in such. Christian truth is found by any man within himself. Reason, then, confirms rather than conflicts with Christianity. Thus Butler rejected the then popular Hobbesian notion that moral obligation is limited to an egocentric human nature. He rejects psychological hedonism, asserting that men desire objects of concern to them, not merely the pleasures that may accompany them. Passions can be controlled by a conscience related to both self-love and benevolence. Anticipating Kant's ethics, Butler sees conscience prompting us to do our duties, for it yields a moral knowledge of what is right.

The Ethics of Bishop Joseph Butler

Bishop Joseph Butler of 18th century England expressed an ethics based on conscience as the ground of morality. In pre-Kantian manner he conceived of conscience as a rational capacity which discerns the moral nature of deeds. Conscience is not a matter of feelings but of moral reason. Instead of appealing to theological principles of revelation, however, Butler confirms Christian principles through what he sees in the nature of man.

In taking his position as he does Butler resists the irreligion of his time, which saw people as egoistic and morality as something valid only if within their self-centered capabilities. He also is against the strong hedonistic and psychological egoism of Hobbes. He refutes the notion that pleasure is the motive of all conduct; it is rather an accompaniment or consequence and not the desired object. Passions and impulses are behind many actions but they can be controlled by true self-love, conscience and benevolence. Anticipating Kant's theory, Butler sees conscience giving us a sense of duty and making us moral agents who know what is right. This concurs with St. Paul's words about "the law written in their hearts, their conscience also bearing witness." (Romans 2:15).

Upon expounding his ethics Bishop Butler examines human nature, and he asserts that vice is contrary to human nature and virtue is in harmony with it. By "nature" is not meant acting as we please or by passions but by self-love and benevolence, which to Butler are not opposing practices.[1] He says benevolence is to society what self-love is to the individual. Self-love is self-interest. Benevolence is an affection for the good of others and is what "we were designed for," he says. While benevolence seeks the public good, self-love seeks the private good. Yet the two work together, so to foster the one is to promote the other even as God "intended we should be instruments" of both kinds of good, says Butler.[2]

Thus Butler refutes the popular idea that self-love and benevolence are alien to each other. He says, ". . . that any affection (that) tends to the happiness of another, does not hinder its tending to one's own happiness too."[3] Butler also refutes the notion that self-love is reducible to the mere gratification of one's impulses. Self-love is concerned about an internal lifetime of happiness not merely momentary gratification. Self-love does not seek external things for their own sake as ends but only as means to happiness. Even the love of our neighbor is a form of self-love in this respect; it is gratifying to the self.[4] Self-love is natural, however, and in human nature is superior to passion. Thus "reasonable self-love must govern."

Happiness and its desire proceed from self-love while linked with the satisfaction of affections and passions. No pursuit is justifiable or of any consequence except as it is conducive to our happiness, says Butler. It is all any person has a right to. This being the case all we owe to other men is to make them happy. It is our duty.[5] Injustice and pain are contrary to nature regardless of "the balance of happiness" produced by them for some people at times. Men are often as unjust to themselves as to others.[6]

The highest governing principle in man is conscience, which both influences and evaluates behavior by approval and disapproval.[7] It does not supply a set of rules but judges each case individually. Even if conscience fails to control conduct at times its authority is undiminished, Butler believes. This is the case even should benevolence and self-love fail to dominate desires and passions. Conscience belongs to "the constitution of our nature" and is "our proper governor" designed to regulate all passions and motives of action. Regardless of how men rebel against it conscience is an inner sense of duty and a sacred "natural right."[8] Conscience is its own authority and need not look to another source, contrary for instance, to Hume's theory of social sentiment. As an authority it is a "guide assigned us by the Author of our nature," says Butler.[9] In this respect virtue consists in following human nature; however, Butler at times suggests a dual human nature with passion necessarily under the control of conscience lest vices appear that are contrary to conscience. "Every bias, instinct, propension within is (also) a natural part of our nature, but not the whole . . ."[10] That man is virtuous in whom the superior judgment of conscience masters the appetites and passions. He is also religious, for morality and religion, virtue and piety are held to coincide.[11]

Conscience to Butler has an immediate disposition regardless of the individual's tendency toward happiness.[12] It does not look to social approbation or disapprobation or to what is worthy of reward or punishment.[13] Men were meant to care for their fellows quite as for their own health. Thus benevolence is a natural inclination,[13] for we were meant for each other or "made for society."[14] Conscience when resisted is acting against man's nature, says Butler.[15] Man in this respect is a "law unto himself" with the "rule of right within"[16] when he follows his "heart" or what is also called the "moral sense" or "divine reason." This is a standard of virtue universally acknowledged, thinks Butler.[17] Every affection looks to its object as an end, so virtue is desired as an ultimate end.[18]

To Butler the only moral attribute of God is benevolence. God desires the happiness of the world. Piety is based on benevolence and the authority of conscience. By benevolence is meant "all that is good and worthy."[19] Benevolence is not opposed to self-love. Vice often reflects too little self-love -- a keen psychological observation by Butler. Virtue, then, coincides with self-love. To love our neighbor as ourselves includes all virtue. Even prudence is approved by the conscience as a virtue.[20] Thus Butler sees virtue as a natural propensity and possibility based on the human conscience with its sense of duty toward one's fellows. His ethics is a remarkable anticipation of Kant's theory with duty a sensitivity within reason intuitively related to the "heart" and its "natural right." Yet fulfilled duty can be coincidental of enlightened self-interest as well. Overall, Butler has a type of self-realization theory on which his ethics rests. His ethics is basically deontological, stressing an inner moral sense, while embracing, too, a teleological perspective of benevolence.

Religiously, Bishop Butler has a broader or more liberal view of human nature than, say, the Protestant Reformers, because his place for self-love is a positive rather than a negative disposition. He so much as looks with favor on Jesus' words, "Love thy neighbor as thyself," and not only regards them as referring to an intensity of love but a legitimate rather than an inordinate type of love. Thus Butler can interrelate self-love with benevolence so that they are not in conflict.

Also, Butler in his ethics so much as links Christian ethics with a natural disposition. Those of a more liberal religious persuasion will think this to be sound. Those of a more conservative disposition will think it too optimistic. One way to defend the conservative position is to observe that Butler resists a looking to revelation and has little or nothing to say about divine Grace, the relationship and power whereby men are enabled to love when inclined to hate. In this light Butler appears to have an overly optimistic view of man, a criticism that some would also make of Kant whose views Butler strongly anticipates.

As for Butler's strong case for an authoritative conscience, again he may be optimistic. A more realistic position would do more to recognize the mixed motives of men and morally dualistic tensions that often appear in man's inclinations and nature. Though Butler acknowledges that man sometimes yields to his passions so as to act contrary to his conscience he says little, if anything, about the cause of such moral violations of conscience. Functionally, conscience is deemed humanistically self-sufficient, for it need not look beyond itself, either to society or to revelation.

Empirical critics like Hume, the Utilitarians and John Dewey would counter-argue that man must look to society for moral approbations and disapprobations. Dewey would charge Butler with a form of subjective moral idealism, which fails to lean realistically upon social mores, the experimental source of moral principles. Yet, to defend Butler, it can be contended that society would have no moral principles, even experimentally, except as men have a basic moral sensitivity that functions in the midst of all social trial and error and to which the latter must look. Butler views men as moral beings by nature. Dewey looks to society, almost forgetting that society is comprised of such moral beings as more than products of social experience.

Notes

1. Joseph Butler, <u>Sermons</u>, Sermon II and I.
2. <u>Ibid</u>, Sermon I.
3. <u>Sermon</u> XI.
4. <u>Ibid</u>,
5. <u>Ibid</u>, Sermon XI (228, 235f, 239, 281); Sermon XII 241, 244; Butler, <u>Dissertation II</u>, 249f.
6. <u>Ibid</u>, Sermon I, the end.
7. <u>Ibid</u>, Sermon II.
8. <u>Ibid</u>, Sermon I and Sermon III (223).
9. <u>Ibid</u>, Sermon II.
10. <u>Ibid</u>, Sermon III.
11. <u>Ibid</u>, Sermon XII, (243) the end.
12. <u>Ibid</u>, Sermon XII, note.
13. <u>Ibid</u>, Joseph Butler, <u>Dissertation II</u>, "Of the Nature of Virtue," (246).
14. Butler, Sermon I.
15. <u>Ibid</u>, Sermon II (217).
16. <u>Ibid</u>, Sermon II (220), Sermon III (221, 222-223).
17. Butler, <u>Dissertation II</u>, <u>op cit</u> (244).
18. Butler, <u>Sermons</u>, Preface (202), Serman II (218), Sermon XI, XII, (228).
19. <u>Ibid</u>, (202) and (220), Sermon XII, (243). Cf. Butler, <u>Dissertation II</u>, (249).
20. <u>Ibid</u>, Sermons, Preface (200f). Cf. Sermon III (225), Sermon XII, (240f); <u>Dissertation II</u> (249).

The Sketch of Immanuel Kant

Immanuel Kant (1724-1804) was one of the most influential thinkers of the past two centuries. He lived a very modest, disciplined life in Konigsburg of East Prussia. He came from a devout, middle class family and was sent to a pietistic college followed by studies at the University of Konigsberg where he turned from theology to science and philosophy. For about nine years he was a tutor and later became a professor at the university, where he was very popular. As a writer Kant was a profound and critical scholar and developed a new kind of philosophy both in epistemology and in ethics. He wrote on astronomy before his famous <u>Critique of Pure Reason</u> (1781), which combined scientific thinking with empirical skepticism. His basic ethics was capsulated in his 1785 work <u>The Metaphysics of Morals</u> and <u>The Critique of Practical Reason</u> of 1788. He is also noted for his work, <u>Religion Within the Bounds of Reason</u>. Though he is comprehensive about science he is skeptical epistemologically about experience while confident about a moral reason independent of experience. For Kant the conscience reveals moral precepts that are universal and binding while practical experience yields but relative knowledge.

The Ethics of Immanuel Kant

Kant's ethics is known as Formalism, since it is based upon reason. It is a form of moral idealism, which places the seat of ethical authority in human nature itself in contrast to Plato, who saw the seat of moral authority in the objective ideals identified with absolute Being. Whereas Plato's ethics was an objective idealism, Kant's is subjective. Also, Kant's ethics is viewed as a deontological ethics, which is to say it observes "the moral law within" as an a priori principle or category of reason preceding experience, while reason does not arrive at Being. As such Kant's ethics is not empirical and does not look to axiological, utilitarian or pragmatic results, for it is inward, not outward. He stated, "Two things fill the mind with ever new and increasing admiration and awe . . . the starry heavens above me and the moral law within me."[1] Centering in man himself Kant's ethical theory is freed from the determinism of the Stoics.

Ordinary knowledge for Kant consists of judgments or appearances based on the combination of sense perceptions and a priori mental categories like substance, space, time and causality. The latter are the preconditions of knowledge. This mixture makes for a relativistic form of knowledge yielding appearances only.[2] However, moral knowledge is based on a priori principle of reason that is pure, i.e. not empirical or mixed with sense perception and yielding, therefore, a clear or absolute form of knowledge, not just an appearance or opinion.[3]

The basic a priori form of moral knowledge on which Kant rests his case in ethics is the Categorical Imperative. This is a mental category which is a moral imperative in the form of an innate sense of duty. As such it yields an inner sense of "ought," which is fundamental to all ethics. Being a priori, it precedes or supercedes experience and is an authoritative sensitivity from within reason itself. It may be viewed as a moral quality or dimension of reason, a category of reason that is moral in nature. Duty is the core of this inner rational imperative rather than any desire, object or impulse. What is right is distinct from what is desired; it is what answers to the dutiful "ought."[4] Rightness entails the duty to perform it. Telling the truth is a case in point. Lying is self-evidently a wrong act, since not based on the inner sense of oughtness or duty.

For Kant consequences are not the locus of the moral worth of an act, even if foreseen. Rather, moral acts are unconditional and absolute in nature, because the Categorical Imperative is not related to the world out there but is in the moral agent per se. As such it is the Categorical Imperative that gives moral character to the agent's will. "Nothing . . . can possibly be conceived which could be

103

called good without qualification except a good will," said Kant.[5] Yet good acts sometimes serve evil ends, for the ends are not always good in themselves. The value of the acts and their ends is derived from the good will. Thus to Kant it is the motive of an act that is basic to morality, not the consequences of the act.[6]

No act to Kant is good save as it is prompted by good will. But what accounts for a good will? we must ask. It is the will's response to one's sense of duty or "I ought." It is that which makes for the right and is what makes for rational control of one's impulses and desires. A good will, then, is based on a rational, moral will rather than on impulse or appetites. The moral reason does not guide the will toward the satisfaction of human impulses and desires but rather guides the will into being a rational will, hence a good will. This is because the moral reason answers to the Categorical Imperative intrinsic to reason itself. Thus only a rational will is good.[7]

For Kant a valid principle of morality is independent of sense experience or even the empirical data of morality. Moral consciousness, or conscience, discloses to every person that moral precepts are necessarily universal. Morality, then, lies in the rational nature of man, since it is the same in everyone, whereas desires and impulses differ among persons and are fickle and change.[8] A moral principle implies that all men should act upon it. Thus the Categorical Imperative is the unconditional directive for conduct and is dutifully binding, because rational beings must follow reason. This moral law is viable whether accepted or rejected.[9] Good will is based upon respect for this, since it is a rational being's effort to do what he ought to do, not what he feels like doing.

An act based on good will is judged by its intrinsic quality, its motive, and not whatever good results it may achieve. Even if it fails to attain certain ends sought, it would be good in itself and the act would be of higher significance than an act that achieves its ends by immoral means.[10] Kant differs markedly from the hedonists and even Aristotle here, for happiness to him is not the highest achievement. A moral reason is designed to make for a good will regardless of happiness or unhappiness. Moral acts are done out of duty, which is what makes for good will. Actions done out of self-interest, even if the results accord with those done from duty, are of no moral worth.[11] If, for instance, a business man contributes to the Downtown Improvement Fund to draw business his way and not out of a sense of duty, his action is immoral; duty and good will are missing. Kant is not saying that it is unpleasant to do one's duty. But to act in accordance with duty but not from duty is wrong; the act lacks inner worth. Sometimes praise-worthy behavior lacks altruistic or dutiful motivation and is morally inferior-to-immoral.[12]

Kant distinguishes the Categorical Imperative from a "hypothetical imperative." The former gives moral worth to an act or maxim, whereas the latter lays down conditional means for attaining an end or consequence. The one implies, for instance, we should tell the truth as a matter of principle; the other implies that we should do it, say, to avoid punishment or to build up one's business reputation.[13] The former can be universalized as a rule of conduct, the latter cannot. To will something rationally is to will consistently. The "law of contradiction" in this respect demands that an act cannot be right for one person and wrong for another. This observation leads to the first of three Laws of Conduct or binding moral criteria that Kant articulates roughly as follows:

1. The Law of Universality:

This, the first law of conduct, asserts that you should act always so you could will your action would become a universal law. This implies that whatever you do should be allowable to others any time or place. Can everyone do it? is the underlying issue. If not, it is wrong. An act cannot be right for me and wrong for my neighbor. There is no exception to the law of universality. One must always tell the truth or keep a promise.[14] Here Kant is anti-existential in that neither relativistic judgments nor exceptions are allowed for. The physician who lies to a terminal patient to help buoy up his spirits is positively immoral. And in no case should suicide be condoned, for if the act were universalized it would wipe out the human race.

2. The Law of Humanity:

This, the second law of conduct or criteria of morality, asserts that we should always treat persons as ends and not as means to our ends. Right is always person-affirming and respectful of others. Influenced by Christianity, Kant had reverence for divine law and the worth of individual persons.[15] Philosophically, Kant was arguing in favor of the Golden Rule. This second moral law or law of conduct, unlike the first, has received little, if any, criticism. As rational beings people must be respected as such i.e. as ends in themselves. While we may use physical things for our ends we must not do the same to persons. Hence, slavery, prostitution and various forms of economic exploitation are immoral, for they degrade persons and violate their selfhood. Here the Categorical Imperative intrinsically serves the welfare of others and does not serve what is derogatory.

3. The Law of Autonomy:

This, the third moral law or criteria of moral conduct, implies that the good will is autonomous or self-ruling. As such it is inwardly free and self-motivating and not looking to results, even if foreknown. A right act is thus good without qualification in keeping with a good will. The moral laws or principles which a man of good will obeys are not external impositions but self-induced impositions, i.e. duties or laws which he imposes upon himself freely and inwardly. The sense of duty based on reason is obeyed from within oneself as expressions of his higher self. In dealing with others we respect their autonomy as such as well as our own. Autonomy makes for dignity.[16]

The Categorical Imperative and all that relates to it is a universal respect for selfhood. Not only is every self of intrinsic worth but other person's ends are one's own.[17] One's own happiness is good not as an objective, goal or aim in life but as an accompanying reward of good will and virtue.[18] In this respect Kant has much in common with Plato and Aristotle's view of Eudemonia as accompanying the virtues, yet happiness to Kant does not necessarily follow or accompany virtue. One may be virtuous and have to pay a price for his virtue. If happiness were a necessary accompaniment of virtue man would not need a moral reason. Morality would come easier and on a hedonistic basis or out of "instinct." Furthermore, to Kant happiness is not always good, since often it is not based on "good without qualification" or a good will. Some evil people are happy. Good will to Kant is not merely good intention but the summoning of all the means in one's power to do one's duty.[19] It acts. In this respect Kant has much in common with Socrates' dictum: "To know is to do." The test of moral character lies in doing the "ought" whether inclined to or not.

In appraising Kantian ethics it can be said that Immanuel Kant articulated a rational ethics with a subjective basis while seeking to save the objective nature of morality through its necessitative quality. While the spirit of Platonic idealism is related to the latter, Kant's ethics improves upon it by his concern for human motive. Together the necessitative quality and the subjective motive contribute to the moral worth of an act. On the other hand, while the hedonist was right in appealing to motive he was wrong in identifying it with pleasure. Many would say that Kant corrects the utilitarian error of looking to the effects or results of actions by stressing the moral motive behind the action. Kant realizes that one can fail effectually while having high motives; for example, a surgeon and his mistakes.[20] Furthermore, Kant realizes that some motives are wrong stemming from lesser desires, caprice or inclination. Often moral acts done out of a sense of duty may be against one's inclinations such as paying taxes or observing the speed laws. To a degree Kant's ethics not only expressed philosophically the Golden Rule but Jesus' teaching that "as a man thinketh in his heart, so is he." On the other hand, the spirit of Kant's ethics differs from Jesus' statement: "By their fruits ye shall know them."

One of the basic contributions of Kant's ethics is a philosophical grounding for "common law." Common law is what is appealed to in the public's mind or conscience when historical documents like the Magna Charta and the Bill of Rights of the United States Constitution are drawn up. Kant provides philosophically the undergirding principle of common law, viz the inner sense of duty as anchored in the moral reason implicit in human nature. By this a "people could have imposed such a law on itself,"[21] said Kant.

Other positive appraisals of Kant's ethics include the following: He provided a philosophical basis for human conscience and thereby helped keep individuals responsible and conscientious. In so doing Kant protected the uniqueness of man as a moral being and enhanced the dignity of man. In addition Kant's ethics provided background for his moral argument for God. Morality bespeaks a moral dimension to the universe, the principles of which are implicit in God as the law-giver of the laws and the one before whom we are ashamed when morally remiss.[22] Also, man's moral sensitivity is no less than a yearning for the divine Absolute beyond all relative judgments. It is the subjective corollary of the objectively moral nature of the universe or God.

Turning to negative appraisals of Kantian ethics there are three leading criticisms: 1. Kant surreptitiously introduces consideration for the consequences of acts even though he tries not to. When treating his law of universality he appeals to results to support the claim, e.g. reference to suicide. In sympathy with this one might ask: Why be concerned with universality of an act save for the consequences appertaining thereto? Kant overtly argues that if one lies he is apt to be paid back in his own coin. 2. Kant is not too strong when it comes to a conflict of duties. Suppose you promise to keep a secret and another friend asks about the matter. How can you keep your promise and tell the truth at the same time? The Kantian ethic would seem to demand respect for both prongs of the moral dilemma, which is a paradox which cannot be rationally synthesized. Such behavior cannot be universalized, for to tell the truth is to break a promise, and to keep the promise is to obviate the truth. 3. Kant's moral idealism is too Absolutistic. More moderate views see morality in terms of less stringent generalizations like the categorical proposition that there can be no exceptions to telling the truth. There are instances when a lie or "white lie" is the better course of action. The physician who lies to a terminal patient may be a case in point, or, if a man with a smoking gun asks for your whereabouts, may I not say, "I saw him leave the building five minutes ago." Telling the truth, keeping promises and paying bills are duties, to be sure, but at times there may be over-riding factors present. The captured soldier who gives away military secrets on the grounds of the Categorical Imperative might well be put in question.

In addition, is Kant altogether correct about ignoring in principle the consequences of moral acts? Does he not minimize the influence of situations? Are all impulses bad or removed from good will? Are there not times when we need to act on feelings as much as reason? As for the absolute good, do not different persons at times differ over what is good? Does not Kant remove his moral reason from his practical reason? Do we have a sense of duty without value judgments of end results preceding the good will? How shall we deal with irrational persons like bullies or criminals? Is there no place for exceptions here? Is good will ever misled? Questions of this sort are pro-existential in perspective.

Furthermore, being non-empirical about ethics does not Kant overlook the socio-psychological conditioning of the human conscience? Jean-Paul Sartre sees this as the sole source of conscience, thus rejecting Kant's idealism, yet, unlike Kant, Sartre minimizes or ignores the inner moral capacity of man that can be developed.

Is it possible that Kant's ethics is based on a very optimistic view of human nature? The answer, contrary to popular interpretations, is a yes and no. What has been set forth above really represents an optimistic view of man, but this is one-sided. Kant actually saw an ethical dualism in human nature. Besides the moral reason with its dutiful and good will, Kant conceded to <u>ein verderbter Hang</u> in the nature of man, "a corrupt propensity" based on a perverted will that violates moral law. It is an acquired "concupiscence."[23] This combination of dualistic elements provides a more realistic picture of man as a moral agent. It is commonly overlooked that Kant, being a Christian and often called "the Protestant philosopher," eventually appeals to divine grace for the resolution of this tension in man.[24]

Notes

1. I. Kant, <u>The Critique of Practical Reason</u>, Pt. II, Conclusion, first statement, V, 162, p. 258.
2. Kant, <u>Critique of Pure Reason</u>, basic thesis. Cf. <u>Foundations of the Metaphysics of Morals</u>, Second Section, pp 105-107; 72-74.
3. Kant, <u>Foundations of the Metaphysics of Morals</u>, Preface, pp 52f. Cf. pp 58, 63. Cf. Second Section, pp 60f, 68ff, 71, Third Section, p. 107.
4. Kant, <u>Foundations of the Metaphysics of Morals</u>, First Section, pp 61-64. 56. Second Section pp 72-75, 83.
5. Kant, <u>Foundations of the Metaphysics of Morals</u>, First Section (First statement), p. 55.
6. I. Kant, <u>Foundations of the Metaphysics of Morals</u>, Preface, IV, 390, p. 53, Second Section, IV, 428, p. 428, Third Section, IV, 458, p. 112. Cf. <u>Critique of Practical Reason</u>, Pt. I, V, 72, Chapter III, p. 180f. Part II, (V, 151), p. 249ff.
7. Cf. Kant, <u>The Foundations of the Metaphysics of Morals</u>, First Section, pp 61, 94f.
8. Kant, <u>Critique of Practical Reason</u>, V 162, p. 259.
9. <u>Foundations of the Metaphysics of Morals</u>, Second Section, p. 87.
10. Cf. footnote 5.
11. <u>Ibid</u>.
12. Kant, <u>Foundations of the Metaphysics of Morals</u>, First Section, p. 58f.
13. Kant, <u>Foundations of the Metaphysics of Morals</u>, Second Section, pp. 63, 72-75, 78, 80ff.
14. Kant, <u>Foundations of the Metaphysics of Morals</u>, First Section, p. 63f. Second Section, p. 80f, 85, 87, 89.
15. I. Kant, <u>Critique of Practical Reason</u>, V. 162, p. 259. Kant, <u>Foundations of the Metaphysics of Morals</u>, Second Section, p. 93.
16. Kant, <u>Foundations of the Metaphysics of Morals</u>, Second Section, pp. 90, 93, 97ff; Third Section 101f, 107, 111, 115.
17. <u>Ibid</u>, p. 86f.
18. Kant, <u>Foundations of the Metaphysics of Morals</u>, First Section, p. 55f.
19. <u>Ibid</u>, pp. 56-58, Second Section, p. 75ff, 92.
20. Cf. footnotes nos. 5 and 9.
21. See I. Kant, <u>Critique of Practical Reason</u>, VI, "Perpetual Peace: A Philosophical Sketch," Section I "Containing the Preliminary Articles for Perpetual Peace Among States," Section I, esp. sub-sections 3, 5, 6. Section II, p. 312, 316, 320. Cf. Appendices I and II. Cf. "What Is Enlightenment," p. 289f.
22. Cf. I. Kant, <u>Critique of Practical Reason</u>, "Natural Theology and Morals," Section 2, p. 282ff. Cf. "Orientation in Thinking," VIII, 142, p. 301f.

23. Immanuel Kant, *Religion Within the Limits of Reason Alone*, pp. 15ff, 21, 23f, 28. Re Grace and Holiness see pp. 103, 179, 180-189. Cf. Kant, *Foundations of the Metaphysics of Morals*, Second Section, p. 60f.
24. Cf. The author's essay on Kant in *Religious Issues in Contemporary Philosophy*, U.P.A., 1988, p. 13ff.

CHAPTER V

ETHICS AND UTILITARIANISM
    13.   The Ethics of Jeremy Bentham
    14.   The Ethics of John Stuart Mill

The Sketch of Jeremy Bentham

Jeremy Benthem (1748-1832) was the founder of the philosophy known as Utilitarianism. Born in London, he graduated from Queens College, Oxford in 1763. Mindful of what serves society he believed that men should base their ideas, actions and social institutions on their utility value or usefulness. This was the ability to produce happiness. His thesis was adapted from Francis Hutcheson's promotion of the greatest good for the greatest number, and his aim was to bring about the maximum happiness in society. He believed that it was based on maximum pleasure over pain, and pleasure was measurable on this basis. Bentham sought to make a country's laws and institutions to foster the general welfare of men over the individual's pleasure. This philosophy led to several reform movements including that of British courts. He wrote his noted <u>Introduction to the Principles of Morals and Legislation</u> in 1789 and <u>Fragment on Government</u> in 1776.

The Ethics of Jeremy Bentham

Jeremy Bentham was a secular utilitarian, who, unlike John Locke, did not have a religious justification for the egocentric factor in man. In fact, he did not see any particular danger or seriousness in psychological egoism. Unlike Francis Hutcheson, Bentham saw a possible blend of egoism and ethical hedonism.

Bentham is a teleological ethicist who looks to the social results of moral acts rather than to the motive. This implies that intentions are basic, not motives, since intentions look to social results. If consequences are satisfactory in that they are productive of happiness for self and others the acts are moral. This is to see the utility value of the acts. Right acts are useful. But in pursuing our own happiness Bentham believes we should seek the general happiness of society as well.[1] On what grounds? On the grounds that this bifocal concern amounts to "enlightened self-interest" much like Shaftesbury's claim, though Bentham does not use the term. Bentham supports this position by asserting that it is natural, legal, social as well as religious.

Basic to Bentham's ethics is his adaptation of Hutcheson's emphasis upon "the greatest good for the greatest number." His hedonistic adaptation becomes "the greatest happiness" of the greatest number.[2] A right deed, then, is one that has the utility value of happiness for the majority of persons directly or indirectly involved, i.e. the amount of usefulness or serviceability to the interests of the greatest number of people effected by the act. It is every person's right to seek happiness, as Locke also stressed, so one should cater to the majority, the implication being that the minority are not served accordingly. This is pro-democratic ethics much in accord with John Locke's position and Thomas Jefferson's adaptations thereof. It is different from Thomas Hobbes' theory, since it is socially benevolent and not selfishly expedient. Legal and social sanctions are usually supportive of this view, Bentham felt. David Hume's social sentiment theory, to a degree, anticipates Bentham's position inasmuch as both have an egocentric and social reference.

In his work __Introduction to the Principles of Morals and Legislation__ Jeremy Bentham asserted hedonistically that pleasure and pain govern life and point to what men ought to do and shall do. Nothing is good except pleasure and the means thereto. To Bentham the empirical, hedonistic "is" or fact of the matter implies a moral "ought." The ought has no meaning apart from utility.[3] This combines psychological hedonism with ethical hedonism. The two doctrines combine with psychological egoism or what is often called "the principle of self-preference." This means that in every instance a person acts favorable to the highest degree of his own happiness.

For Bentham enlightened self-interest is seeing the social dimensions of that self-concern.

Bentham has a quantitative view of happiness that relates to a "hedonist calculus." Pleasures differ merely in quantity. He stresses that men will strive for the greatest amount of pleasure and least amount of pain. This is what measures the greatest happiness. Thus he says the moral significance of an action is judged by seven criteria: 1. the intensity of the pleasure, 2. its duration, 3. its probability of reoccurrence, 4. its promptitude, 5. its fecundity or promotion of more pleasure, 6. its purity, and 7. its social extent or influence on others.[4] By these criteria one is expected to add up the pros and cons or the credits and debits of pleasures to determine whether an act is worth performing. Yet Bentham does not tell us how these different pleasures are calculated by a common measurement. They are admittedly hard to calculate.

Bentham rejected the idea of rights and obligations and believed they were used by writers interested in preserving unjust traditional social systems. They are not empirically apprehended, he claimed. An obligation is dependent upon some pain or loss of pleasure attending its neglect. A so-called right is merely a product of social opinions. Bentham has here no criterion for justice.[5] Social approbation is considered sufficient grounds for moral utility, ideal moral principles being an external standard adverse to such utility.[6] The dictates of utility are no more nor less than enlightened benevolence, says Bentham. Utility makes for right and is based on good will. Right and wrong are notions derived from utility, with the fitness of actions based on what men like.[7] Men like pleasure and it is the only good.[8] Next to benevolence in this context of utility men love reputation, says Bentham, as a useful motive.[9]

One might wonder whether religion has any bearing on Bentham's ethics. Only minimally. The will of God as a moral standard can only be claimed as "presumptive." Men must first know whether a thing is right to know whether it conforms to the will of God. This is done only by projecting human pleasure on God, since men cannot know the pleasures of God. Barring revelation through the scriptures God, then, cannot be used as a standard of right and wrong.[10]

Critically, Bentham fails to see that pleasure or happiness may not be the chief end of ambition of man and that it may be a product of benevolence in which case benevolence requires a different basis. This is parallel to how Plato, Aristotle and Kant saw happiness as an accompaniment of virtue. Then, too, Bentham does not clarify why we must seek the general happiness of men and on what basis when we are so egocentric. He does not see the danger of psychological egoism. It was in the face of this that Thomas Carlyle said that Bentham's utilitarianism is a "pig philosophy," an allusion to everyone's dashing to a sensate trough.

As for Benthem's theory of "enlightened benevolence" linked with self-interest, his doctrine of "self-preference" is still basic. How can a genuine social ethics be possible on that basis? If one must always seek his own interest and happiness, how can he have a moral obligation to serve the interests of others except as they serve his own interests? At times the interests of people clash. Bentham fails to resolve such tensions. Much like Hobbes, he takes for granted, erroneously, that there is in the nature of things a merging of egoistic interests that conduce to the good of society. Furthermore, there can be no justice appealed to beyond the contemporary social mores, in which case a moral reformer ahead of such mores would be out of order.

Then, too, Bentham overlooks the sacrifices of many men in history whose expendability or martyrdom looked away from their own interests. Often men have sacrificed contrary to their interests or desires, commonly for the sake of a principle. Does not Bentham keep human deeds so self-centered that there cannot really be any unselfishness on his terms? Furthermore, because pleasure is measurably desired does that make it objectively good? On what grounds can what men inevitably desire make it what they ought to desire? As for the hedonist calculus, how can the intensity of a pleasure be measured? It is questionable whether Bentham's quantitative view of happiness is an objective standard for determining moral values. Happiness is a mere feeling that cannot be measured with precision, and a vice is merely a miscalculation of pleasure over pain. Bentham is weak in his claim that utility is the meaning of what is right, though often such an association is thought to be the case. He fails to show how people may be persuaded to do the right regardless of consequences.

Notes

1. Jeremy Bentham, <u>An Introduction to the Principles of Morals and Legislation</u>, Chapter I, (I, II, III, IX), p. 107ff; Chapter IV (I, II, III, VIII). Re intentions, see Chap. viii, (I-XIII), p. 359ff.
2. <u>Ibid</u>, Chapter I (IV), (L), (II), p. 339ff.
3. <u>Ibid</u>, Chapter I, (I) p. 358, (X) p. 363; Chapter VIII, (XIII), p. 362, Chap. X (X), p. 369.
4. <u>Ibid</u>, Chapter IV (II-IV).
5. Philip Wheelwright, <u>A Critical Introduction to Ethics</u>, pp. 224-226.
6. Jeremy Bentham, <u>op cit</u>, Chap. II, (XI), p. 346f.
7. <u>Ibid</u>, Chap. X (XXXVI), p. 378; Chap. II (XIV), p. 348f; also Chap. I (XIII), p. 345.
8. <u>Ibid</u>, (X), p. 369.
9. <u>Ibid</u>, (XXXVIII), p. 379.
10. <u>Ibid</u>, Chapter II, (XVIII), p. 350f.

The Sketch of John Stuart Mill

John Stuart Mill (1806-1873) was an ardent Utilitarian who succeeded Jeremy Bentham in a similar vein of thought. In his early childhood his father expected much from him educationally in arithmetic and languages; by his twelfth year he was reading in philosophy and economics. At twenty-one he experienced a nervous breakdown, but after some years he resumed his career. After a short time in legal studies, in 1823 he joined the East India Company, a position he kept for three decades. When he retired he was elected to Parliament, though he did not campaign for it. In philosophy he published a System of Logic in 1843 stressing induction and empiricism. Five years later he wrote Principles of Political Economy, which applies utilitarianism to economics. His essay On Liberty in 1859 expressed his socio-political philosophy. In 1861 he wrote Utilitarianism devoted to his ethics. Also in 1861 he published Considerations on Representative Government. Mill expanded the philosophy he derived from Bentham promoting the greatest happiness of the largest number of people based on pleasure over pain. It was a philosophy meant to support social legislation based on utility through a "hedonistic calculus." Basically, Mill combined a psychological hedonism with an ethical hedonism.

The Ethics of John Stuart Mill

John Stuart Mill is in basic agreement with Jeremy Bentham but improves upon his position by stronger appeals to conscious, benevolent concern for others and qualitative pleasures while toning down somewhat Bentham's psychological egoism.

In his work entitled Utilitarianism, Mill stresses that the only thing desirable is what people desire.[1] He still caters to the greatest happiness principle; however, where Bentham had a more quantitative view of pleasure John Stuart Mill emphasizes a qualitative view. In reply to Thomas Carlyle's criticism of Bentham's ethics as "a pig philosophy" Mill asserts that men are capable of "more elevated" appetites than those of the animal or biological level. So Mill included intellectual pleasures, cultural concerns and aesthetic matters as nobler pleasures.[1] Mill said some pleasures are more desirable than others, hence more valuable. For instance, solving an intellectual problem can be more satisfying than a meal.

In Chapter II of his essay Utilitarianism Mill stresses that this movement of thought rests on utility as pleasure. Actions are right which promote happiness i.e. "pleasure, and freedom from pain, are the only things desirable as ends."[2] In reply to the claim that this doctrine is "worthy of swine" Mill says there are pleasures that vary in degree and in kind above sheer sensation and quantity.[3] Mill adds that people who have experienced both quantitative and qualitative pleasures commonly prefer the latter i.e. the pleasures based on the "higher faculties," even should they prove more costly. In this light Mill overtly states, "It is better to be a human being dissatisfied than a pig satisfied; better to be Socrates dissatisfied than a fool satisfied."[4] Also, "Men lose their high aspirations," said Mill, "as they lose their intellectual tastes . . . they addict themselves to inferior pleasures . . ."[5]

Mill gives reply to those who object to Utilitarianism including the claim that happiness is impossible to attain. He says that many people are content with a moderate share of happiness. He also states, "The utilitarian morality does recognize in human beings the power of sacrificing their own greatest good for the good of others."[6] Thus utilitarianism is not selfishness, for there is always a minority who serve the majority, though the sacrifice is not in itself a good. Right conduct is not what fosters an agent's own happiness but that of all concerned.[7] Mill believes this is pro-Christian. Though people do not always show forth social concern, Mill maintains that the utilitarian view of happiness as utility is still true. The greatest happiness principle may not describe all conduct but it does sanction and judge what is moral conduct. Ethically, it tells us what is our duty whether or not we have a Kantian motive of duty. It promotes public utility and avoids whatever is pernicious to society.[8]

In Chapter III Mill takes up what sanctions the utilitarian principle or what is the basis of its obligation. Although social and religious sanctions support the principle according to Mill, he says they do not obligate men to apply it. Men must feel inwardly the relevance of the theory in terms of a "feeling for humanity" which to Mill is "the internal sanction," even called a "mysterious law" and "conscience," a "subjective feeling."[9] Yet these moral feelings, Mill asserts, are "not innate but acquired" and are so by educational "cultivation." They add up to "a natural basis of sentiment for utilitarian morality."[10] It is the individual's feeling that he wants harmony between his aims and those of others, thus the desire for general happiness is the fulfillment of one's own desire for happiness.

John Stuart Mill, fundamentally, did not come up with a new ethical theory so much as he improved upon that set forth by Jeremy Bentham. For him Utilitarianism was philosophical support for much-needed social legislation to improve the socio-economic and political climate of his day. What Mill set forth in his essay <u>Utilitarianism</u> is foundation for what he sets forth in his essay <u>On Liberty</u>. His ethical theory is thereby applied to the cultural and governmental scenes. Basic to it is the contention that "rulers should be identified with the people; that their interest and will should be the interest and will of the nation."[11] Basic to this is liberty of conscience, thought and feeling; "freedom of opinion and sentiment on all subjects."[12]

But it can be questioned whether Mill succeeded in altering Bentham's position appreciably. He seems to argue that qualitative pleasures are little more than greater intensities of pleasure, hence still quantitative in nature. Some interpreters think this is because Mill did not wish to appear conspicuously different from Bentham. But how is a moral value determined as superior to others? It is by the intensity of pleasure, yet with respect for a human being's higher-than-animal pleasures. But what makes it better for a Socrates to be dissatisfied than a pig satisfied is not accounted for, since Mill is still speaking of a dissatisfied human being on a quantitative basis.

The logic of utilitarianism being based on a hedonistic premise combined with psychological egoism is weak, for it fails to account for those persons who undergo great sacrifices for the sake of an ideal or principle. It cannot be established empirically that everyone seeks his own greatest pleasure at all times. Utilitarianism is in error also because of the claim that the "ought" comes from the empirical "is" quite in agreement with David Hume. The only actions that ought to be done are those done inevitably, i.e. naturally out of desires. Also, to quantify pleasures is weak, because they cannot be reduced to homogenous components nor to exact measurements of intensity.

Then, too, to claim the moral "ought" springs directly from the empirical or social "is" is to imply, again, that the moral reformer is out of order, since he moves beyond the contemporary social mores. In addition, Mill's view that men have "feelings" for the social welfare of others is really a trans-empirical notion not unlike the appeal to intuition. Kant's intuitive or a priori sense of duty comes close to this while being less nebulous or more direct and rationally authoritative. The fact that Mill sees how such feelings are educationally acquired still implies an inner faculty that can be developed. This moves the problem out of the strictly empirical domain to the existential perspective of the self. Thus what Kant saw rationally and Mills saw empirically can, and perhaps must, be seen holistically as belonging to the whole, concrete self with the existentialist.

Henry Sidgwick as an empirical utilitarian saw the importance of the role of intuition from within the empirical perspective. His keynote idea was that a person intuits the utility results of an act for the happiness of others. Man intuits the "ought," which is indefinable. Not quite like Butler and Kant in this respect, Sidgwick sees a person intuiting the results and utility value of an act before it is done. In this respect he combines utilitarianism with intuition and anticipates the ethics of G.E. Moore.

Mill's utilitarianism supports what belongs to democracy due to his appeal to human nature. It makes a preference for what is utilitarian dependent upon a preference for democracy. It does not provide a contention for slavery, for example, to be wrong. Of this A.C. Garnett states,

> "It is not the sort of ethics, therefore, whereby one could prove that democracy is right and that it would be wrong to overthrow it and re-establish a system of slavery. All one can do . . . is to try to show that a system of slavery cannot be used to promote the happiness of those who have the power and will to enforce it on others. . . It would only show the one system more expedient than the other in the pursuit of personal happiness for the slave owners."[13]

Notes

1. John Stuart Mill, <u>Utilitarianism</u>, Chapter II, pp. 6-7. Cf. p. 10f.
2. <u>Ibid</u>, p. 5f.
3. <u>Ibid</u>, p. 7.
4. <u>Ibid</u>, p. 9. Cf. pp. 8, 10f.
5. <u>Ibid</u>, p. 10.
6. <u>Ibid</u>, p. 15.
7. <u>Ibid</u>, p. 16.
8. <u>Ibid</u>, p. 17f.
9. <u>Ibid</u>, Chapter III, pp. 24-27.
10. <u>Ibid</u>, p. 28f.
11. John Stuart Mill, <u>On Liberty</u>, Chapter I, p. 69.
12. <u>Ibid</u>, p. 75.
13. A.C. Garnett, <u>Ethics, A Critical Introduction</u>, p. 177.

CHAPTER VI

ETHICS AND IDEAL UTILITARIANISM
15. The Ethics of G.E. Moore
16. The Ethics of John Rawls

The Sketch of G. E. Moore

George Edward Moore (1873-1958) was a teacher of philosophy for many years at Cambridge University. In ethics he was notably influenced by his professor Henry Sidgwick. In 1940 he became a visiting professor at Smith College in the United States. He remained in this country for several more years teaching at Princeton University and Columbia University. Between 1921 and 1947 he edited the noted journal, <u>Mind</u>. In 1903 he wrote his greatest work <u>Principia Ethica</u>, in 1912 <u>Ethics</u>. In the former he set pace for philosophical analysis and meta-ethics by examining elemental terms and questions before erecting a system of thought. "How is good defined?" is a case in point. The indefinability of the good is still meaningful since linked with a kind of realism with ethical properties independent of consciousness. Moore regards ethical truths in the same manner as other realistic matters, i.e. they are either self-evident or have eternal or objective evidence.

The Ethics of G. E. Moore

Some of the reputable twentieth century discussions of ethics have shifted from pre-conceived systematic attempts to start with basic issues beneath the study of right conduct to the meanings of such basic concepts as "good," "right" and "ought." G.E. Moore is one such interpreter who saw the need of posing such meta-ethical questions before seeking to answer the practical questions of ethics dealing with conduct.

Upon posing such basic questions as: What is the meaning of 'good,' Moore contributed to analytical philosophy in the form of linguistic analysis while related to ethics. Moore sought that which is unconditionally and intrinsically good. Analytically, this posed two questions: How is good to be defined? and What things are good? The former is the more basic question, but Moore contends that 'good' is indefinable, like 'yellow' or 'sweetness,' while other ethical matters are definable through it.

In general Moore is an ethical realist who not only sees empirical foundations in ethics that are utilitarian in nature but that good points to a metaphysical property independent of human consciousness, something intrinsic and absolute. So in speaking of goodness not only is there external evidence related to sense perception but what he calls self-evident quality. Thus something good is both empirical and metaphysical, the latter, which is basic, being indefinable.[1] Thus ethics does not rest upon the study of conduct, but on the inquiry into the good that is primary in ethical inquiry.

Moore's linguistic approach to ethics led to a new form of intuitionism[2] as well as to more empirical revolts from this, especially those of Dewey and the positivists. The intuitionism centered in the awareness of goodness from beyond sense perceptions.

Moore's teacher, Henry Sidgwick, had anticipated the new intuitionism before 1900. He saw in man a moral, transempirical sensitivity not subject to empirical definition. It was man's sense of "ought." However, Sidgwick saw the "good" to be capable of definition empirically in terms of what was "reasonably desired." The latter is teleological and utilitarian in nature including the hedonistic formula that the only intrinsic good is pleasure. Thus Sidgwick appealed to a direct intuition of the "ought", while to prudence and benevolence when referring to the "good."[3] In combination, this meant that a person intuits in advance what he ought to do in the form of good or desirable results.

Successors to Sidgwick questioned his position. G.E. Moore (1873-1958), also of Cambridge, attempted an adjustment called "ideal utilitarianism" that combined intuition and ethical teleology differently.[4] In his 1903 work entitled Principia Ethica he refuted idealisms in favor of a common sense realism. To him ethics deals with the property of universals like goodness, which is more metaphysical than empirical since mentally conceivable but not perceivable to the senses. Some things have the property of goodness just as they may have the property of number.[5] Not empirical, 'good,' nevertheless, is applicable to things of experience. It is intuitively recognized. Here Moore overcomes what he calls the "naturalistic fallacy" of many empiricists,[6] viz: the tendency to identify the 'ought' with the 'is' of experience. The 'ought' is something intuited and not empirical. Like the 'good' it is indefinable but known intuitively.

The chief problem in ethics, thinks Moore, is the meaning of the term 'good' when speaking of good things. To some there is but one kind of intrinsic good, viz pleasure or the satisfaction of desires.[7] This much is empirical. While to Moore it has its place he cannot settle for it, for in itself it is the "naturalistic fallacy" that confuses the metaphysical good with empirical states like pleasure or the desirable.[8] This confuses the metaphysical 'ought' with the empirical 'is.' Instead, Moore sees the good as an undefinable, universal property necessarily attributable to all good (desirable, pleasant) things while being more than an empirical feature of such things. Like 'yellow' the 'good' is indefinable yet known intuitively though applied to empirical phenomena.

The naturalistic fallacy is erroneous, then, because it gives an analytic definition of 'good' in empirical terms, thus confusing the metaphysical with the physical/psychological. It makes 'good' to apply to things, whereas it is, says Moore, a non-natural reality similar to mathematics as properties of things and not the things themselves. For example, merely to say with Sidgwick the "good" is "what satisfies desire" still does not account for the "good." It is like saying "X" is good because it is desired without preventing the question: "Is X good?" or "Is it good to desire X?"

Hedonism is especially guilty of "the naturalistic fallacy." It is reflected in utilitarianism. If "good" means the same as "pleasure," the statement that pleasure alone is good is a mere tautology, i.e. "pleasure alone is pleasure."[9]

For both Moore and Sidgwick men cannot know whether the choice of X, or desire of it, would be morally right or wrong until they know whether X is good. Being teleologists, both thinkers believed that wrongdoing consists in failure to do the greatest good possible within the circumstances. The situation, therefore, is that we do not know whether it is right or wrong to choose X but we might say X is something anyone would desire who knew all the consequences of attaining it. Does this make X good in itself? Intrinsically good? No. A thing may be desired teleologically without being intrinsically good. But to Moore the ideal situation is to be able to combine the intrinsic good as property and the teleological good as desired. When this is the case Moore's "ideal utilitarianism" seems to be fulfilled or actualized. Moore thinks the "ought" and the "reasonably desired," as differentiated by Sidgwick, can be interwoven.[10]

For Moore "what is good in itself" is synonymous with "what ought to exist for its own sake." Honesty would be a case in point. A synonym of "good" is "ought to be" or as of "intrinsic value."[11] Thereby the metaphysical property of goodness is an ought-to-beness and is attached ideally to the thing or action under consideration. But Moore agrees with Sidgwick that a voluntary action only ought to be done if we first know that its consequences, physically and mentally, are good or "ought to be." We cannot know what we ought to do, until we first know what is good or ought to be.[12] The latter is an intuited property of things as acts, i.e. it is the intuition of "the good."

Critics of Moore say they have no such intuition of what "ought to be" -- that all they have is an awareness of "ought to do." If they are right, Moores' ethics seems to fall to the ground. But do we not intuit states of justice, for instance, as what ought to be? John Rawls later combines the two elements, the deontological and the teleological as related to justice.

Moore's "ideal utilitarianism" is an ethical theory which is teleological in terms of what men "ought to do" that is desired and desirable but not out of relation to what "ought to be." The "ought" is a unique, simple property; like "yellow" or "sweetness" it cannot be analytically defined. Goodness is an indefinable property, so to indicate what we mean by "good" we can only give examples of diverse good things and say goodness is their common property.[13] What things, then, have the property of goodness? Moore's reply is based on his intuition of goodness as a property which ought to be the case.

While teleological, Moore is against Benthem's idea of "good" based solely on pleasure and desirable consequences. Rather there is an intrinsic good to be respected, an organic unity in which the whole is greater than the sum of its parts -- a Gestalt or pattern-- also a metaphysical property. For Moore ethics, then, is as much of a metaphysical matter as it is an empirical science. It deals with conceptual objects or properties much like mathematical properties, which, to Moore, are not empirical in themselves but applicable to things. Goodness is not an entity but a non-natural property and is intuitively recognized. Undefinable, goodness cannot be analyzed empirically but, only apprehended intuitively as a principle. Empirical "goods" while teleological may reflect this metaphysical goodness and not only do good but "be" good. Hence, the hedonistic reference to the good as something experienced to be pleasurable is false. Moore, then, is anti-hedonistic, yet teleological. While honesty and fair play are good principles they are also good consequentially.

A value judgment about goodness is different from a factual appeal to pleasure. This is because there is an "ought" within the "good" act, i.e. an intrinsic value in a choice or deed because of its being good in its own right or for its own sake, not merely for the sake of something else like pleasure. Even so, the "ought to be" property or intrinsic good can blend with the "ought to do" or good results. Thus Moore, on the one hand, tries to keep the good connected with an intuitively discerned "ought," while, on the other hand, a good act that "ought to be" may also yield good results. In fact, Moore says a person's awareness of the oughtness or goodness of an act will help lead him to do it; thus the ideal and the practical can blend realistically. A voluntary act, if good, ought to be done as an end in itself, but if the foreseen consequences are good (desirable) then all the more so; however the teleological result (the ought to do) is to be judged by the metaphysical property or nature of the act (the ought to be factor.) Charitable acts might be cases in point. The ought to be factor is the undefinable intuited metaphysical property of goodness. In this way again Moore pleads for an "ideal utilitarianism"[14] -- one without either psychological egoism or hedonism. The net result is this: A good act has the intrinsic property of goodness yet also yields desirable results.[15] The intrinsic good is basic yet only part of a good act -- what might be called the character or quality of the act.

There are a few problems that arise, however. Can the quality of an act, its ought-to-beness, be separated from the ought-to-doness or the desirable? On the other hand, is it not possible that an act that is intrinsically good does not necessarily yield desirable or pleasant results teleologically? Kant is often criticized for such a dichotomy, but Moore tries to prevent such. In this respect John Rawls' current combination of the deontological and the utilitarian motifs is akin to Moore's position.

Moore seems to condone only the right combinations of: (a) a good act by property or intrinsic quality with (b) a good act teleologically by desirable results or ends. The one property makes the act a duty and makes Moore's ethics deontological;[16] the other feature makes it a teleological expediency, hence empirical, utilitarian.

The two elements are ideally coincidental; adultery would be wrong and marital fidelity right both in principle and in fact. The two features must not be separated. Moore hits this point strongly suggesting that an action is a duty, whenever it responds to a sense of 'ought' in view of the best possible consequences.[17] Here he is a bit anti-Kantian.

Another problem: How do we know the goodness or what ought-to-be in advance of the act? If we cannot know that an act ought to be done until we see its results, can we really perform it at all? Moore's reply would seem to be this: Yes, we can perform it, because we know intuitively in advance that the act is of a "good" property. But then another problem arises: Why the teleological reference at all if we know the act to be good? Why not join Kant? Moore's likely reply: We can proceed on the good property of what "ought to be" but should carry it through sensitive to what we "ought to do." G.E. Moore is opposed to a naked intuitionism (Cf. Kant), since it can claim that a virtue like justice can be practiced regardless of consequences. This he cannot condone. To him intuition of the good must be combined with the best teleological results. There can be disastrous results at times of revealing a truth; therefore, it should not be one's duty to tell the truth always. A physician, for instance, would not necessarily be wrong in lying to a terminal patient. Moore's appeal to actual consequences includes respect for both means and ends as well as motives. Contrary to Kant, motive alone, then, does not make a deed right -- nor do positive results alone make it so, contrary to early utilitarians. The immeasurable quality or metaphysical property of goodness must be interrelated with the measurable quantity of results.

For some philosophers who define truth as the definition of the real, Moore's claim that the good is indefinable would be tantamount to saying it is unreal. Moore could rebut with the claim that reality is not restricted to the definable; much basic experience being undefinable.

More serious is the question we raised earlier: How could one know whether we did perform an act of best actual consequences? We cannot know it at the time of the act. Even later, how could one know he did the right act when most acts have immeasurable and unobservable consequences? Why, for instance, should one be bound to an obligation impossible to fulfill?

Probably Moore's greatest contribution to ethics is his claim that we cannot define good or right in terms of natural desires like pleasure. Pleasure does not necessarily equal the good, for good is a metaphysical state of the ought, not merely a subjective affection.

Thus we cannot define ethical terms in the natural language of egoistic desires. Intuition is what perceives the good.

However, it may be that Moore's underlying realism is inadequate when it comes to describing man and his place in ethical concern. Moore needs epistemologically more of a critical realism that moves him toward an existentialist phenomenology so that the intuition employed is seen to be indigenous to consciousness and conscience while kept akin to a balanced existentialist anthropology, which interrelates the intuition and conscience with the empirical elements of the teleological side of Moore's ethics. One reason for this is what the empirical factors do not contribute epistemologically in a realistic manner to the role of intuition. Intuition is more phenomenological and existential than realistic.

Notes

1. G.E. Moore, Principia Ethica, pp. 6-16, 41, 79, 110f, 142-144.
2. Ibid, pp. 59, 77, 108.
3. Ibid, pp. 17, 59, 92-94, 145.
4. Ibid, pp. 183-185, 205-207, 220f.
5. Ibid, pp. 8f, 183-186; 99-102.
6. Ibid, pp. 9, 13f, 18-20, 38f, 48, 57f, 61, 64-69 et al.
7. Ibid, pp. 46, 56, 53f, 68, 104f.
8. Ibid, pp. 39, 58, 110-115, 139f.
9. Ibid, pp. 59, 63f, 81-87, 91-96, 108f.
10. G.E. Moore, Ethics, Chapters I and II, VII.
11. Ibid, pp. 31f, 68. Cf. pp. 26-32, 68-71, 96, 103ff; Relate to what is good "intrinsically."
12. G.E. Moore, Principia Ethica, pp. 17, 115, 118, 127f, 148, 173, 180, 223.
13. Ibid.
14. Ibid, pp. 96f, 105, 167. Cf. psychological hedonism, pp. 11, 130, 140, 148; 18, 68ff.
15. Ibid, pp. 65-70, 73.
16. Ibid, pp. 24f, 105, 146-148, 167, 180, 223.
17. Moore, Ethics, p. 97.
18. Ibid.

The Sketch of John Rawls

John Rawls (born 1921) is an ideal utilitarian who sees social morality as both personal and institutional, so that he combines the concerns of social theories like Hobbes and Locke's social contract view with the personal ethics of Kant. Rawls received his Ph D from Princeton University in 1950 and became a Fulbright scholar at Oxford University in 1952-53 after which he became a professor at Cornell University until 1959, also becoming there co-editor of Philosophical Review. Between 1960 and 1962 he was professor of Philosophy at M.I.T. and since then has taught at Harvard. His main work in ethics is his 1961 book, A Theory of Justice.

The Ethics of John Rawls

John Rawls in <u>A Theory of Justice</u> enunciates an ethical theory which to a great extent is a critique of social and political institutions. To him social morality is more than matters of personal morality or institutional policy; it is both. Not a Platonic idealist, Rawls is pro-empirical much like the social-contract theorists from Hobbes to Locke and Rousseau. Rousseau blamed social-institutions for human corruption. Rawls, however, is somewhat like Kant inasmuch as he has a place for the intuition of what is good.

Rawls disagrees with Hobbes, however, since he does not think social contract is based on individual self interests for security purposes as men make concessions to a sovereign power. Rawls believes that the Hobbesian man can still do illegitimate things and avoid detection. Rawls sees social obligation as something pertaining to more than one's own position in a given society. A person's commitment to social agreements is based on more than his social circumstances. It is tied in with mutual self-interests.[1]

Rawls maintains that every person has an equal right to liberty. Inequality between persons still implies equal opportunity. In this respect Rawls is pro-utilitarian in promoting "the greatest happiness for the greatest number." The difference between people need not imply inequality of opportunity or freedom. Equal opportunity must still be fostered, unless the situation is a matter of survival. The promotion of equal opportunity has been fostered in recent centuries unto the social well-being of persons despite "difference" - e.g. minority groups. Equal liberty is prior to individual differences. This is egalitarian in principle and in this light utilitarianism has not always been on the side of justice, since it has viewed social well-being and liberty as contingencies, slavery being a case in point. Utilitarianism has no basis for accounting slavery unjust. Its looking to satisfactory desires is inadequate. Though the old utilitarianism seemed to promote the happiness of the majority it overlooked the liberty of the different individuals. Rawls sees how every person has a dignity in the face of justice, which a society has no right to override or ignore by political maneuvering or social "bargaining."[2]

Justice is basic to the social contract, and equal liberty is basic to justice, thinks Rawls. He sees justice as a complex of liberty, equality and reward for services rendered to the common good. Justice is like fair play, a kind of socially endorsed "tit for tat." Fair play, however, is more of an individual matter whereas justice is a social matter, a share or balance between competing interests. Justice implies social rules which define rights and duties. It is basically a reciprocity that grants "equal liberty" to all and rewards men for services rendered to the common good of all. Equal liberty avoids partiality in that it does not favor some over others. Yet respect must be shown for some offices to which special benefits or responsibilities are attached - though such offices must be won in fair competition as based on merit.[3]

Here Rawls introduces what he calls the "veil of ignorance." It amounts to saying we cannot think of pure justice unless we detach ourselves from our conditions in this world as we know it and must think rather in terms of a kind of unfallen world. This reminds us of Plato's state of pre-existence when the soul of man was uncontaminated by conditions in the temporal realm of Becoming. Or, one might say Rawls is looking to a form of Utopia for contrast purposes. In this present world we have self-interests and advantages, which bias us and, therefore discolor justice through realistic inequalities. In order to promote justice, then, we must try to think in unbiased terms removed from our economic and political circumstances.[4] A critic, David L. Schaefer, says we cannot arrive at such a "veil of ignorance," since we are involved inextricably in our present state of affairs and cannot have a "memory lapse." It is pretentious to think otherwise, i.e. self-deceiving.[5] The present writer agrees with Schaefer. Even if one could engage in the veil of ignorance it is doubtful one would have any knowledge to work with. What Rawls seems to be seeking or yearning for is a kind of uncontaminated, unbiased intuition of what is good and what is basic to justice. Only a Platonic, unfallen world can afford us such goodness and allow such a perspective Rawls concedes.[6] But his respect for the "veil" is unrealistic and should open up a return to classical idealism, which Rawls does not condone.

Rawls has a strong place for the idea of social contract as essential to justice, but he readily sees the deficiencies of the historical theories of social contract. He is different from Hobbes in that he tones down the egocentricism implicit in Hobbes' social contract theory. Rawls stresses the mutual self-interest of people. This seems to be closer to the "enlightened self-interest" principle of the Earl of Shaftsbury in that benevolence as a matter of mutual respect is linked with self-interest. The family, says Rawls, is the basic social unit, which reflects such mutual self-interest.[7] There are other social institutions with similar outlooks, however. Unless justice is based on the mutual respect of free and equal persons it becomes contingent upon circumstances, which weakens justice for all. Reciprocity in that event is missing.[8]

Thus justice is a form of social contract. It is more than an idealistic executive mandate such as Plato made of it. Geared to mutual self-interest, it must be worked out from within the socio-economic and political conditions. It must be done with concern for equal liberty for all, despite the differences among people and their circumstances. Rawls views this theoretically as a modified utilitarianism, which includes a basic intuition of the good in terms of mutual welfare. As such Rawls' theory reflects the "ideal utilitarianism" of Henry Sidgwick, who saw how men intuit the good of favorable results in advance of their acts.[9]

Rawls believes his view of social contract has a higher view of justice than that of the previously mentioned social-contract philosophers and utilitarians. In some respects he is more Kantian in that he appeals to an intuitive view of respect for others on which justice in institutions is dependent. This respect is for "free and rational persons concerned to further their own interests . . ."[10] and in doing so do it mutually with others through government and other institutions with "fairness." Upon planning for such, persons must decide in advance what is to count as just and unjust. This seems to be an intuitive insight and reminds us of Sidgwick, who said we need to intuit the good in order to do it, a view which combines deontological insight with teleological results. In general, as previously suggested, Rawls has more benevolence in his theory of social contract than do Hobbes and Locke in that he stresses mutual self-interest, which is less egocentric. Nevertheless, despite the weaknesses of the historical view of social contract, with corrections, it is essential to justice.

A basic aspect of the intuitionist feature of Rawls' theory is that the implied "concepts of 'good' and 'right' are unanalyzable"-quite as G.E. Moore contended. They are not rational but are held to be self-evident first principles or moral claims, though related to various economic, social and political affairs.[11] Ethics to Rawls is a combination of the deontological and the teleological. In this respect he reminds us of G.E. Moore, again, who interrelates the two motifs. Here the subjective intuitive judgments and the objective empirical principles or results are seen to blend in social action and institutions. It is here, too, that justice blends with fairness or what Rawls calls a "fair game." The latter amounts to the techniques of the social sciences. The game theory or techniques are the empirical and teleological aspects of what is deontological in principle.[12] It appears that the goodness known intuitively is corroborated by experience in terms of teleological results favorable to the mutual self-interests of all people. Institutions that facilitate such are on the side of social justice. In principle it seems that Rawls' position is an elaboration of the views of G.E. Moore and Moore's teacher Henry Sidgwick.

Rawls gives priority to the principle of equal rights to liberty. This is meant to supersede the justification of social inequalities and is thought to benefit everyone. Unless justice as fairness is respected there is no justice. However, there are times when inequalities favorable to some in society can serve the interests of those not so well off. One is reminded in this light of the favorable positions of some people in government who are serving the welfare of all. The economic parallel in capitalism seems to be that the poorer minorities are often upgraded economically through the favored positions of those in economic positions of leadership or advantage.

Rawls in stressing liberty desires to preserve the liberty of all. With it, he believes, should come equal opportunity, something it would appear fostered by democracy but only sometimes promoted through capitalism. Liberty is viewed by Rawls as a right.[13] But is it an equal right? we must ask. Basically, Rawls affirms that it is in principle, but we can question whether it is a social fact. Do all men have the capacity to freely act or assume equal freedom? Is what is morally acceptable socially viable? Is it available to all persons?

Rawls makes justice to apply to basic liberties so as to tie egalitarian liberty to the goods of society. The chief goods are "rights and liberties, powers and opportunities, income and wealth" as well as "self-respect."[14] But the critical question is whether Rawls can consistently maintain the priority of rights and liberties over economic and social benefits. The relationship between them is significant for ethics, because principles and practices in society must be interrelated.

The principles of right and liberty lack the highest meanings if not tied in with social and economic benefits to all men including the minorities. Both kinds of factors are essential to a truly just society. So the priority given by Rawls to rights and liberties over economic and social benefits can be questioned philosophically. As Bertram Morris states, "A right that relates to no social action is meaningless; one that is not exercisable is empty; one that is capable of being exercised only through changes in the institutions of a society is at best potential."[15] A person may have rights and liberties in principle but if the socio-economic circumstances necessitatively hedge him in, he is not perfectly free to do what he wants to do. Is this full-blown liberty? Rawls would say in reply that a person has a right to liberty, even if he cannot exercise it. His view of liberty ostensibly "varies in worth according as the obstacles to its exercise, e.g., ignorance and poverty, are absent in varying degrees."[16] While in principle all have equal liberty in a just society, its significance or worth varies realistically from one individual to another due to the socio-economic constraints they find forced upon them. Thus the worth and meaning of liberty varies among people much in relation to circumstances. Bertram Morris makes a fine distinction in this regard. He says Rawls is in error, for it is not liberty that is equal in his scheme but the right to liberty.[17] Though liberty may be experienced in degrees, equal liberty is not. Rawls' makes liberty absolute but its worth relative. This tends to make justice an ideal but something that is somewhat vacuous for many when it comes to concrete socio-economic relationships. In this respect Rawls is remiss, for he does not keep coherent or consistent the kinship between the deontological and teleological elements espoused in his basic theory. Or, at least, the just society to which Rawls points us remains an unrealizable fulfillment of his bi-focal theory. Thus it appears that the actualization of such a just society remains untenable. Furthermore, it can be questioned whether Rawls' endeavor to offset or modify popular utilitarianism with an appeal to a more idealistic theory of justice as fairness has fully succeeded. In principle or theory it is reassuring but in point of fact questionable. His own "veil of ignorance" concept, and its criticisms, tends to underline this claim. In addition, it is questionable whether Rawls' ethical epistemology is adequate, for he combines the intuitive and empirical elements in a way that suggests a realism but in actuality implies a creative kind of thinking which is phenomenological and existential, if by "existential" we allow for a balanced epistemology that respects the empirical elements without making them authoritative.

Notes

1. John Rawls, <u>A Theory of Justice</u>, Chapter I, pp. 4, 11; Cf. 178f, 337f.
2. <u>Ibid</u>, pp. 4, 22, 25ff, 30-33, 139f.
3. <u>Ibid</u>, pp. 14, 33, 499f; 104f, 511.
4. <u>Ibid</u>, pp. 12, 19, 136-142, 172, 200, 139f.
5. David L. Schaefer, <u>Justice or Tyranny</u>, p. 29.
6. The writer is in concurrence with Schaefer.
7. Rawls, <u>op cit</u>, pp. 74, 300.
8. <u>Ibid</u>, p. 178f; 158f, 248; 14, 33.
9. Rawls gives considerable recognition to Henry Sidgwick throughout his book.
10. Rawls, <u>Theory of Justice</u>, p. 11.
11. <u>Ibid</u>, p. 35.
12. <u>Ibid</u>, p. 111ff, 525ff.
13. <u>Ibid</u>, pp. 73, 83-89; 201-205.
14. <u>Ibid</u>, p. 62.
15. Bertram Morris, "Rawls' Egalitarianism," <u>Philosophic Research and Analysis</u>, Vol. V, no. 8, Winter, 1975, p.2.
16. <u>Ibid</u>.
17. <u>Ibid</u>, p. 3.

CHAPTER VII

ETHICS AND POSITIVISM

    17. The Ethics of A. J. Ayer and Charles Stevenson

    18. The Ethics of Bertrand Russell

The Sketch of A. J. Ayer

Alfred Jules Ayer (born 1910) was Professor of Mind and Logic at the University of London after studies at Eton College and Christ Church College, Oxford. After serving as a lecturer and researcher he received his M.A. at Christ Church in 1936. Between 1944 and 1946 Ayer was a Fellow of Wadham College, Oxford and Dean, 1945-46. During World War II he served in the Welsh Guard doing intelligence work. In 1946 he was appointed Professor of Philosophy at the University of London. 1948-49 was spent as visiting professor, New York University. A.J. Ayer became one of the foremost spokesmen for logical positivism and analytic philosophy through his 1936 work Language, Truth and Logic, revised in 1946; also Logical Positivism in 1959.

The Sketch of Charles Stevenson

Charles L. Stevenson (1908-1979) was Professor of Philosophy at the University of Michigan and became noted for a modified positivism which sees human attitudes serviceable to ethics. In 1930 he received an A.B. from Yale University and in 1933 a B.A. from Cambridge and in 1935 a Ph.D. from Harvard. Between 1934 and 1939 he did graduate work and taught at Harvard. From 1939 to 1946 he became assistant professor at Yale and in 1946 he went to the University of Michigan to teach. In 1945-46 he was a Guggenheim Fellow. His most noted work was Ethics and Language published in 1944.

The Ethics of A.J. Ayer and Charles L. Stevenson

A.J. Ayer is a British philosopher of the school of Logical Positivism, as expressed in his jarring book Language, Truth and Logic, 1936. For him no proposition has meaning save as it is verifiable by either sense perception or logic, the two basic criteria of scientific thinking. Since ethical propositions usually do not lend themselves to these criteria basic to empirical verification, A.J. Ayer says moral claims are meaningless or merely emotive, a matter of feelings. This position is in apposition with David Hume's claim that morals are a matter of "social sentiment."

What Ayer is asserting is a non-cognitivist position in ethics, which amounts to saying that ethical propositions are not based upon genuine forms of knowledge. Two theses accompany this position of "non-cognitivism": (a) the sole acceptance of the "verifiability criterion" of meaning as based on either logic or sense perception.$_1$ This implies that all metaphysical claims for ethics are meaningless.^{2} (b) the rejection of any imperical definitions of ethical terms, since they are guilty of what G.E. Moore called "the naturalistic fallacy," viz making an "ought" appear to be based on an "is" or something desirable.

In Britain G.E. Moore was followed by deontologists like H.A. Pritchard and W.D. Ross in the claim that the basic ethical concept of the "ought" is indefinable and non-empirical. These thinkers rejected as inadequate all naturalistic or empirical views of "good." For them ethical thinking demanded that some experiences are intuitively seen to have a unique property called "good," "fitting" or ought-to-be." A whole generation of British philosophers followed in their train for the first three decades of this century.^{3}

However, many students of this deontological school became dissatisfied with the elusive "ought." They welcomed newer developments in linguistics and the analysis of meaning. One distinction of importance to come to the surface was that of the positivists including A.J. Ayer. To them there was a big difference between (1) descriptive or factual meanings of terms and (2) prescriptive or expressive meanings. For example, to state, "It is good (or right)" is not to describe a fact about a thing or act but merely to express one's feelings or to prescribe for one's hearers a certain reaction. There would be no need to look for an "ought-to-be" quality, for the statement is merely emotive.$_4$

A.J. Ayer and other positivists including Bertrand Russell subscribed to this distinction. To them meanings are determinable by reference to something observable, which either verifies or discredits it. Since their position appeals to the senses for what verifies or discredits a proposition, they rule out a wide range of mental and metaphysical referents as meaningless. This position disallows a supra-empirical, metaphysical or non-natural character referred to in the phrase "ought-to-be" as a property intuitively discerned through psychological states. In short, there is no operation known to the senses which either verify or discredit such a claim; therefore, it is held to be meaningless, i.e. neither true nor false, hence a proposition that is not intelligible. Thus the moral "ought" as something supra-empirical, non-naturalistic or intuited (i.e. not desired, not hedonistic) is rejected. The philosophical result was that a generation of philosophers including Moore who had accepted naturalistic ethics as fallacious were backed in a corner, for now their deontological, non-naturalistic position was refuted. All ethical moral utterances were now held to be factually hollow or meaningless. Theirs was not a cognitive use of language, not descriptive but only prescriptive or expressive -- what A.J. Ayer means by "emotive."

As recognized by C.E.M. Joad one effect of Ayer's positivistic position was this: An atomic bomb could be verified to be able to kill 50,000 people, but it could not be verified that it was right or wrong. The same could be said for slavery. Another effect was this: To say, "You acted wrongly when you stole the money" is no different than to say: "You stole the money." The fact is verifiable; the claim that it was wrong is only emotive disapproval, and to call it bad does not refer to anything verifiable, either by analytic or synthetic propositions. Hence, "non-cognitivism" is the result, the net result being that there is here no real moral issue. Nothing is done for ethics, since moral judgments are held meaningless. "Ethical judgments have no validity," says Ayer. This is ethical skepticism or nihilism.[5]

Ayers joins G.E. Moore, in rejecting naturalism, but he also rejects Moore's non-naturalism or intuitionism. He contends that there can be no observable fact to verify the ethical intuition of an ought. Normative or prescriptive claims resting on intuition (subjectivism) are meaningless, since in no way are they empirically verifiable. He says the intuited concepts are pseudo-concepts since unanalyzable. To say, "you acted wrongly in stealing that money" is, again, no more than like saying "you stole that money" while expressing disapproval. Ethical symbols only express one's feelings and arouse the feelings of others. This boils down exactly to what David Hume said back in the 18th Century, viz that morals are only social sentiments.[6]

Another consequence of Ayer's position is moral relativism. This he admits, for ethical statements to him are merely expressions of feelings. Different people may differ in their interpretation of the facts, and there is no security with respect to an objective base for ethical judgment. Slavery can be a fact, but it is not a fact that it is wrong, the latter is merely an emotive reaction. If agreement on facts does not produce agreement in feelings there is nothing to be done about it but to pass derogatory remarks about your neighbor's feelings. The result is that there cannot be a science of ethics or a true system of morals. All you can have is a psychology of moral feelings and a history and sociological study of related practices and customs.

Thus A.J. Ayer so much as says we have only a weak expressionist theory of ethics, not a strong descriptive theory. It is a non-cognitivist view. Even when an ethical "ought" or "duty" is uttered in the form of a command, it is still only an emotive expression in the hands of an authority of some kind. The only recourse for ethics is a subjective, ejaculatory or emotive one that is philosophically unsubstantiated, since its statements are not verifiable as true or false. Morals do not exist, since outside the scope of scientific criteria. Ayer overtly says, "Ethical concepts are pseudo-concepts . . ." The philosopher is in error who presumes to construct ethical judgments when all he can do is analyze and classify ethical language. This is a linguistic approach.

An absolutist like Kant is held to be wrong, since his intuitive base for moral value is said to lack an empirical test. Ayer sees neither innate nor empirical grounds for ethics. Yet it can be counter-argued that Moore's form of deontological ethics has an empirical test.

Critically, it is contended by A. Campbell Garnett that although "ought" sentences may not be commands, they have a prescriptive force. They tell us what to do or not to do; they lay down guiding principles of action, hence are more than emotive. They convey a decision and imply for the hearer that there are reasons for the decision and demand. In time A.J. Ayer and other positivists came to see this point and that Ayer's basic claim was an oversimplification. By 1949 Ayer conceded that "The moral judgment expresses the attitude in the sense that it contributes to defining it (a pattern of behavior). This opens up a prescriptive element that is more than emotive. His adjustment moves Ayer closer to the views of R.M. Hare and P.H. Nowell-Smith expounded a few years later. It also anticipates an intermediate position taken by Charles Stevenson, to be treated below.

Ayer fails to answer the question: What sort of qualities are morally good, whether as ends or as characters of action? Likewise, what rules are morally right? Are laws merely emotive? Stevenson also failed in these respects as we shall see.

Ayer's ethical skepticism may be self-contradictory, since to say there is no moral knowledge is to admit that moral skepticism, too, is unknowable. If value does not exist, what makes Ayer's position any better than any other? He cannot claim to have a superior view, because he has destroyed the very rule by which values are measured as good, better or best. For him to say a moral value is merely emotive is to say he values the emotivist's view as the best position on the subject -- which is self-contradictory, since it is tantamount to saying, "The most valuable philosophy denies the existence of value." His logic would seem to imply that his own philosophy is of no value. Why should he or anyone else argue about ethical values, if there are none to argue about?

In the final analysis if society adopted Ayer's view of emotivism it would become disrupted to the point of peril, for people would drop their best customs, folkways and integrity in favor of total relativism, which logically spells moral anarchy.

Charles Stevenson of the University of Michigan is also in the positivist vein of thought, but he modifies Ayer's approach through his "emotive-prescriptive theory." People may hold similar beliefs while having differing attitudes, one in favor of an act, the other against it. Attitudes, then, affect ethical interpretations, so that favoring an act may not only be emotive but also prescriptive. Attitudes bespeak values, because the language associated with them does more than express emotion. It conveys meaning as it seeks to evoke certain psychological reactions in the hearer and stir conduct along certain lines; therefore, there is a cognitive response involved, contrary to Ayer and Russell. This, in turn, implies that there may be good reasons for one's feelings and the attitudinal persuasion or demand for certain conduct in others.[8]

Stevenson's prescriptive element, though linked with emotion, is an advance upon Ayer's view, because it allows an ethical attitude to effectuate a rule of conduct. Other people can confirm an act by their feelings of approval or disapproval, and thereby it can be made a rule or law of universal proportions. For someone to say, "The act is right (or good)" is to express that they approve and want others to act accordingly. This implies good reasons for one's feelings. Such reasons include (a) beliefs that arouse similar feelings of approval or disapproval, (b) the reasons for those beliefs per se, and (c) the reasons for demanding the emotive agreement of others. The attitude involved allows an ethical pronouncement to become a rule of conduct, even a universal rule. It implies that other people can confirm the attitude toward the act, so that a rule or law can be set up.[9]

But Stevenson's emotive-prescriptive theory leaves us with the question: What sort of reasons are relevant reasons why everybody should adopt an attitude of moral approval toward something? Are they utilitarian reasons? Also with the question: "What sort of qualities are morally good whether as ends or characters of action, and what sort of rules are morally right?" The element of "ought-to-beness" seems lost sight of in Stevenson's naturalistic context of the "good" as what is desired or approved. Pro-empirical, he seeks an "ought" from an "is" of attitude. Isn't this still a naturalistic fallacy?

So the question remains: How can Stevenson move from an emotional response or attitude to a prescription of conduct, i.e. and "ought" when he is persuading others of a desirable act which is still a naturalistic preference? He seems to be saying: the emotive element reflects the desired, and it is what is desirable or ought to be a rule -- but is not this still at fault for upholding what G.E. Moore called "the naturalistic fallacy," viz of making the "is" into an "ought" when such is impossible? Is it possibly correct to reply that the "is" can be productive of the "ought" via attitudes? For example, if slavery is condoned or condemned, it ought to be. But, we ask, why? On what basis, especially when condoned?

Notes

1. Alfred Jules Ayer, Language, Truth and Logic, pp. 5, 9, 44, 108.
2. Ibid, pp. 33ff, 48.
3. A. Campbell Garnett, Ethics, pp. 268-77; 277-83.
4. Ayer, op cit, pp. 22-24, 38f, 60-62, 68f, 109; 44, 108.
5. Ibid, pp. 22, 105, 197f, 21f, 107f, 110-112.
6. Ibid, pp. 33, 118-120, 129, 136f, 106, 137f, 53f, 47.
7. Garnett, op cit, p. 303ff.
8. Charles L. Stevenson, Facts and Values, pp. 8f, 16f, 21-27, 29f, 64f, 78-80, 115-117, 133-135, 167-169, 204-208.
9. Ibid, pp. 1-3, 6-8, 26f, 49-54, 56-63, 65-68, 80-85, 90-100, 117-134.

Sketch of Bertrand Russell

Bertrand Russell (1872-1965) was a recognized British mathematician and philosopher, who received the Nobel Prize for literature in 1950 as an exponent of freedom of thought. He was born in Wales and graduated from Cambridge University in 1894. For a short period he worked in the British Embassy in Paris, whereupon he went to Germany. In 1903 he wrote <u>Principles of Mathematics</u>. In 1914 he lectured at Harvard and later in China, University of Chicago and the University of California. For several years he taught at Cambridge University. In 1910 Russell co-authored <u>Principia Mathematica</u> with Alfred North Whitehead, a provocative work opening up new vistas in the field. Russell wrote over 40 books on a variety of subjects from philosophy and education to marriage. In 1918 he wrote <u>Mysticism and Logic</u>, in 1930 <u>The Conquest of Happiness</u>, in 1932 <u>Education and the Social Order</u>, in 1940 <u>An Inquiry into Meaning and Truth</u>, in 1954 <u>Human Society in Ethics and Politics</u>. Lord Earl Russell was liberal and outspoken from time to time. During World War I he was imprisoned for his pacifism. For several years he was head of mathematics studies at Cambridge University. In 1940 the College of the City of New York cancelled his professorship there due to his radical views on religion and morality. That year he returned to Harvard to teach. In the late 1950s he wrote <u>The Impact of Science on Society</u> in which he not only stressed the implied thesis but expressed the need for social and moral changes in modern society.

The Ethics of Bertrand Russell

For some time I have been sensitive to the inconsistency of Bertrand Russell as a positivist philosopher who was very much interested in ethical and social issues. His inconsistency lay in the fact that his atomistic positivism disallowed any cognitive significance to his own moral concerns about public policy. His official philosophy, as it were, did not pave way for his applied philosophy. His positivistic skepticism about ethics did not logically allow him to be the world citizen and practical ethicist that he proved to be.

To put it positively, was not Bertrand Russell a broader thinker than his narrow-scoped positivism allowed him to be? If so, is it not possible that he left the door open to both trans-analytical and pragmatic-prescriptive insights into moral values? The purpose of this discourse is to see the announced problem as well as the feasibility of the latter claim.

Much like A.J. Ayer, as an analytical philosopher Russell could ascribe neither truth nor falsity to ethical assertions and values.[1] In sort, they were deemed meaningless, since not verifiable by the positivist criteria of logic or sense perception alone. Rather, ethical pronouncements were only wishes or desires lying outside the bounds of scientific knowledge, therefore lacking cognitive meaning. As Russell overtly stated, "Science has nothing to say about 'values'."[2] He similarly stated, "There are no facts of ethics."[3] By such statements he meant that science cannot evaluate human desires. Values and desires belong merely to emotive prescriptions rather than empirical descriptions. Hence ethics is not linked with knowledge.[4]

For Russell values and ethical principles lack any criteria of either truth or falsity, because the latter cannot be predicated of them objectively. Science and its methods and criteria must then remain silent about morals and values. This implies that we cannot deduce a moral "ought" from an empirical "is." Here Russell was influenced by G.E. Moore and his claim that to attempt to arrive at an "ought" from an "is" is a "naturalistic fallacy."[5] To say that the good is pleasure or satisfaction is only to say that good is good. Only an absolute good could give meaning to any other good, but that is lacking. At first Russell agreed with Moore's view that the Good, a central concept in ethics, is indefinable like yellow, for instance, and of "intrinsic value," but later he abandoned this theory under pressure from George Santayana, who argued that values have no basis apart from desires.[6] Russell then came to the point where he felt the analysis of ethical concepts could only disclose how men feel about facts or react to them in terms of their desires.[7]

157

Thus, Russell, like Ayer and Carnap, contends that values and morals are non-cognitive or beyond knowledge. While values lie outside the domain of science, as Russell contends - and as most defenders of religion concur - does this place ethics beyond all knowledge? Russell's positivism says[8] 'yes' and that all moral claims are reducible to emotive expressions. This view is not unlike David Hume's theory of "social sentiment."[9] Values have no empirical or naturalistic basis. All that any ethicist can do is either to employ emotive expressions of persuasion to get others to agree with his feelings or condemn other peoples' feelings or desires. Russell himself resorts to this in his applied social ethics. Even a concept of the ultimate Good has no objective evidence and is merely a subjective, emotive matter, thinks Russell.[10] The term "good" only expresses an emotion, not a fact, which implies that ethics cannot be a science, because while social sciences can deal with sources of desires and their means to fulfillment, they cannot evaluate them scientifically with a reason for their selection. In short, we cannot argue logically about tastes and preferences.

Bertrand Russell's inconsistency is that as a social ethicist he is caught in his own positivistic trap but does not let it bother him. His is an irreconcilable position as (a) an ethical skeptic on the one hand, and (b) a moral reformer and critic, on the other. Succinctly, as a positivist he is an ethical nihilist, while as a citizen of the world he cannot abandon the moral values he has said to be meaningless. In theory he is ethically subjective while in practice he is ethically objective.[11] By the latter we mean, for example, that Russell as a man would not be content with the analytical assertion that an atomic bomb can kill 50,000 people but that it is meaningless to call it bad or evil. For him killing 50,000 people would be an immoral atrocity. Thus, Russell's applied ethics is objective while his positivistic theory makes him subjective, since the analytical claim is that ethical matters are non-verifiable, non-cognitive and meaningless and, therefore, only emotive.

Ethical pronouncements, Russell held, were linked with emotional desires, as is "the whole idea of good and bad." Good and bad are merely what people adjudicate through their preferences. "Ethics is thus closely related to politics; it is an attempt to bring the collective desires of a group to bear upon individuals" or vice versa. "The philosopher," says Russell, "who values Truth, Goodness and Beauty seems . . . to be pointing the way to the welfare of all mankind."[12] Yet Russell has no confidence in this. When a man says, "This is good in itself," he really means he wishes everyone would desire it, which amounts to his expressing a mere emotive preference. Ethics, to Russell, contains no statements of truth or falsity but merely the expressions of emotions, preferences or desires.[13] Thus Russell's analytical theory reduces ethics to the subjectivity of values. On the other hand, he states, "Ethics is necessary because men's desires conflict."[14] Here Russell is glaringly inconsistent, if not illogical, because he is either conceding there is an objective ethics to settle men's differences or else he is asserting that desires are necessary because of desires, which is a mere tautology.

Fortunately perhaps, Bertrand Russell was one analytical philosopher who was conscientious enough to be dissatisfied with his own positivistic position which implied ethical nihilism. He even recognized the validity of some objections raised by his critics. But his peculiar stance is to accept his contradictory position and live with it.[15] The contradiction is one of being technically skeptical and subjective while practically confident and objective.

Sometimes those who believe in a more objective theory of ethics accuse Russell of advocating a skepticism of immoral consequences. But he believed their reasons to be faulty. He did not think that his positivistic nihilism meant a "decay of all sense of moral obligation," since he saw how men can still have socially constructive desires. Yet here the critic can accuse Russell of treating desires as teleological forms of universal moral obligations, which he treats as objective in his practical ethics but derogates as meaningless in his analytical thinking. The closest Russell seems to come to defending himself is in his statement, "A desire cannot, in itself, be either rational or irrational . . . it cannot be considered 'irrational' merely because no reason can be given for feeling it."[16] But this leaves the door open to the possibility of feelings being intelligible or rational. How then can they be regarded as meaningless?

In books like The Conquest of Happiness and Marriage and Morals Russell tries to treat ethics as more than emotive, whereas in his book What I Believe he makes pronouncements about many social situations and is overtly provoked at people who seem indifferent to moral issues or refuse to see the immorality of certain practices. Here we see concretely how logically incongruous are Russell's different approaches to ethics. He has a duplex philosophy, one side being analytically silent about morals, the other side practically vocal. This contradiction shows how exclusive, neutral and irrelevant to ethics positivism is apt to be by itself. It needs supplementation by other philosophies, if ethics is not to be ignored altogether.

Russell's inconsistency is more concretely reflected, for instance, in his view of cruelty. William S. Sahakian calls to our attention that Russell says that "science alone cannot prove that it is bad to enjoy the infliction of cruelty,"[17] yet in Schilpp's book on his philosophy Russell says, "Pleasure in the spectacle of cruelty horrifies me, and I am not ashamed of the fact that it does."[18] Elsewhere we find Russell saying, "I find myself incapable of believing that all that is wrong with wanton cruelty is that I don't like it."[19] Here we see a plain contradiction between Russell's positivism and his applied ethics. The one assertion implies a non-cognitive view of cruelty and the other an empirically meaningful view that is more than emotive. As for the latter, Russell often linked intelligent living with love and often expressed disdain for social evils like war and nations possessing atomic bombs. During World War I he chose to be jailed as a pacifist rather than be silent about war. He also maintained that people with power should promote cooperation with other groups and nations.[20] Was he only being emotive about these things?

The intellectual integrity of Bertrand Russell is so pronounced, however, that as anticipated, he admittedly recognizes the inconsistency of his philosophy while refusing to back away from it.[21] It is almost as though he agreed with Ralph Waldo Emerson who said, "a foolish consistency is the hobgoblin of little minds."[22] Russell frankly says of his philosophy, "If there is any inconsistency, it is one I cannot get rid of without insincerity."[23] Does not this acknowledged inconsistency demonstrate the primacy of the existentially situated philosopher and his trans-empirical involvements in what he knows? Does it not imply that he is a creative thinker before he is an analytical thinker or scientist-in-action, which is to imply pre-scientific forms of cognition before he is scientific? One aspect of this would be the ability to understand words and communicate ideas before they are subjected to linguistic analysis. Must not a proposition have some meaning or relevance even before it can be tested by positivistic criteria?

Even Russell's sincerity respecting his duplex view of ethics implies not only the meaningfulness of the ethical values he adjudicates but a value judgment on his part, a value judgment of his own sincerity, which he leaves ungrounded. Yet he does not succumb to his ethical skepticism entirely, for he also claims he has a "right" to speak up on moral issues. But is it not the case that a moral right is something not verifiable by Russell's positivistic criteria? Even so, he says no kind of logic, including his own, will dissuade him from making ethical judgments.[24] Actually, this amounts to a repudiation of his ethical skepticism and the finality of positivism's delimiting criteria. This being the case Russell even leaves the door open further to a trans-analytical perspective. This he does in two ways. First, he says, "Even more important than knowledge is the life of the emotions. A world without delight and without affection is a world destitute of value."[25] In asserting this Russell sees emotive desires associated with group consensus and utilitarian results, which implies a form of empirico-teleological verification. Second, he said at Columbia University in December, 1959, "We must return to the Christian ethic."[26] Even more emphatically he stated in his book The Impact of Science on Society, "The root of the matter, if we want a stable world is a very simple and old fashioned thing . . . The thing I mean is love, Christian love. If you feel this you have a motive for existence, a guide in action, a reason for courage, an imperative necessity for intellectual honesty."[27]

But for Russell to be able to say this is for him to respect trans-analytical ethics, especially an agape such as humanistically borrowed from religion by psychiatrist Eric Fromm,[28] which is dubious due to human egotism, or else an agape as remotivating and redemptive as that of the ethics of Nicholas Berdyaev, Communist turned Christian. As for me, I can see no self-sufficient philosophical alternative to the nihilism of positivism; therefore, if philosophers are not to betray contemporary culture with respect to ethical studies they will have to keep in touch with the religious dimensions of thought. It appears that Bertrand Russell had no less than a nostalgic concern for so doing whether he admitted it or not.

* * * *

The more direct purpose of this discourse has been fulfilled; however, it would be well to supplement it with a pro-empirical ethical reply to Russell's ethics. Russell attempts technically to invalidate ethics as associated with emotions and desires rather than with facts. But is this as empirically valid as it appears to be? Are not human desires facts? Cannot emotions at least point to facts? Are they not "responses of a physiological and neurological creature to its environment"?[30] Is not Russell in danger of separating the mind from the body in this respect, so as to make emotion the total opposite of reason?[31] Existentially, it can be argued that both reason and emotion belong to a total person, and emotion is not altogether non-cognitive as in the case of persons, for instance, who know they respect each other or know they are mutually in love.

Furthermore, are desires strictly emotive? Can we not scientifically estimate the outcome or consequences of people's desires? Desires not only have perceivable cause but perceivable and anticipated effects. Can not these be appraised scientifically by hypostatizing them for further investigation by respecting as objective the same kinds of teleological factors that Russell sometimes employs in his applied ethics? Can they not be tested in the crucibles of social experience? What point would there be for some people including Russell to try to persuade others of public policies, if there were no reason to believe that the majority would benefit thereby, objectively. Does not this imply a respectable empirical reference? or a place for reason, existentially?

Unless the empirical reference of applied ethics is broadened beyond positivism's delimited criteria no social science with recommended theories of social good are either true or false and, as intellectual disciplines, might better close shop. But cannot social values, like anything else, be tested by experiment, either in fact or in thought? If so are they not more than subjective in that judgments about their truth or falsity can be made teleologically? If not, "then," as Wilber M. Urban put it, "all attempts of the social sciences to make pronouncements about values are either irrelevant or impudent" and all they tell us about what we should strive for economically, socially or politically is "sheer illusion."[32]

Bertrand Russell's ethical inconsistency points to the insufficiency of a positivistic philosophy, for it simply fails to open the door to the tenability of ethical claims. The very fact that Russell held to a dichotomy between his positivistic epistemology and his ethical interests reflects the insufficiency of a positivistic philosophy. In order to bring his epistemology and ethics together with a semblance of feasibility Russell needs to broaden his perspective of man so that both scientific criteria and ethical values and norms can function from within a man's concrete existence. The most apt such adjustment would be an existentialist perspective of man, for it is holistic as it reckons with man's varied capacities and functions from within the rational and empirical to the volitional and emotional dimensions of human personality. Without such an adjustment Russell's position remains an untenable dichotomy that disallows a combination of scientific and ethical thought. But with such an existentialist adjustment Russell's philosophy could embrace both a scientific outlook and epistemology and an ethical epistemology, if not of a Kantian variety whose tenability would be suspect then of a utilitarian type on the grounds that it would be basically empirical. The holistic adjustment could allow for such a double-pronged perspective.

Notes

1. A.J. Ayer, Language, Truth and Logic.
2. B. Russell, Religion and Science, selection in Value and Obligation, edited by R.B. Brandt, p. 377.
3. B. Russell, Power, p. 247.
4. B. Russell, Religion and Science, loc cit, p. 380.
5. G.E. Moore, "The Indefinability of the Good," from Great Traditions in Ethics, 1953, New York, edited by Albert, Denise and Peterfreund, pp. 304-322.
6. Cf. "Bertrand Russell," Encyclopedia of Morals, ed. V. Ferm, p. 512f.
7. B. Russell, Religion and Science, loc cit, p. 380.
8. Cf. Paul A. Schilpp, The Philosophy of Bertrand Russell, p. 723. Cf. Religion and Science, loc cit, p. 380.
9. David Hume, An Inquiry Concerning the Principles of Morals, Library of Liberal Arts, ed. by Hendel, Liberal Arts Press, New York, 1957.
10. B. Russell, Religion and Science, loc cit, p. 379f. Cf. Schilpp, loc cit, p. 720.
11. Cf. C.E.M. Joad, Critique of Logical Positivism, pp. 118-123.
12. Russell, Religion and Science, loc cit, p. 380f.
13. Ibid, p. 382.
14. Russell, A History of Western Philosophy, p. 779.
15. William S. Sahakian, Systems of Ethics and Value Theory, p. 428f.
16. Russell, Religion and Science, loc cit, pp. 382-384.
17. Sahakian, op cit. Quotation corrected by writer from Russell, A History of Western Philosophy, p. 834. Cf. Joad, op cit, p. 122f.
18. Schilpp, The Philosophy of Bertrand Russell, "Reply to Criticisms," p. 720.
19. Cited by Leo R. Ward, Ethics, p. 20.
20. Russell, "An Appeal to the Intellectuals of Europe," from Justice in War Time, selection in Ethical Choice, ed. by Beck and Orr, p. 190-198, also Russell, Power, op cit, p. 271.
21. Russell in Schilpp, op cit, p. 573ff.
22. Emerson, "Self Reliance," Essays, p. 47.
23. Schilpp, loc cit, p. 720.
24. Ibid.
25. B. Russell, The Scientific Outlook, p. 269.
26. Etcetera, American Friends Service Committee, College Program, March, 1960, p. 4.
27. Russell, The Impact of Science on Society, p. 59.
28. Cf. Eric Fromm, The Art of Loving and other works.
29. Cf. Nicholas Berdyaev, Slavery and Freedom and other works.
30. Evelyn Shirk, The Ethical Dimension, p. 142.
31. Ibid, pp. 143-145.

32. Wilbur M. Urban, "Science and Value," Ethics, Vol 51, 1941, pp. 296-305. Selection in The Examined Life, ed. by Troy W. Organ.
33. Charles L. Stevenson, "The Nature of Ethical Disagreement," Great Traditions in Ethics, ed. by Albert, Denise and Peterfreund, Am. Book Co., New York, 1953, pp. 341-349.

CHAPTER VIII

ETHICS AND PRAGMATISM

    19.   The Ethics of John Dewey

    20.   The Ethics of Erich Fromm

The Sketch of John Dewey

John Dewey (1859-1952) was a reputable philosopher who was identified with pragmatism, though he preferred to be called an Instrumentalist. Born in Vermont, he strongly favored democracy both in politics and education. He was a "down to earth" philosopher and educator who related all thought to social experience. For Dewey philosophy and educational psychology were a working team. He was greatly influenced by evolutionary thought. He had a long career and taught at the University of Michigan, University of Minnesota, University of Chicago and Columbia University. He was of profound influence upon the school teachers of America stressing experimental methods in what he regarded as progressive education. His early work <u>The School and Society</u> was translated into twelve languages, <u>Democracy and Education</u> into nine. Dewey places logic and ethics together in his works: <u>Reconstruction to Philosophy</u> (1920) and <u>A Common Faith</u> (1934); also <u>Quest for Certainty</u> (1928) and other works. Ethically, Dewey links morals with the methods of science. He relates beliefs about the world to values for living. Morals must be related to a changing world, hence beliefs must shift away from permanent principles to adaptible views allied with practical problem-solving. Ideas must lead to satisfactory life adjustments, truth being relative rather than absolute.

The Ethics of John Dewey

John Dewey was a pragmatist who preferred to be called an instrumentalist, because for him ideas were instruments of life adjustment. Ideas are products of experience and help persons adapt to their natural and social environments. In fact all education is designed for such adjustment.

Dewey's instrumentalism is based upon the changing experiences men have in a changing world. This is much in contrast to the idealism of classical philosophy, which embraced an immutable realm of eternal ideals. Dewey broke away from the rational idealism of Hegel with its metaphysical monism and rudiments in Plato's philosophy. Instead of embracing rational first principles Dewey stressed that all learning is from experience and we cannot transcend the world of pluralism and change. In this respect Dewey is an empiricist in the train of Locke and Hume.

As an empiricist Dewey appeals to the scientific method including experiments in education. As such he stresses education as a science rather than an art. Methodology takes precedence over substance, since it is a matter of experience. The keynote aim of man as a problem - solving organism is adaptation to his natural, social and economic environments. Hence, there must be a shift away from all metaphysical theories to scientific methods based on the trial and error of experience. All social progress is held to be a product of experimental adjustments in nature and society. Under the influence of William James' doctrine of meliorism Dewey sees the world as neither good nor bad in itself but capable of improvements.

Pro-evolutionary in outlook, Dewey believes in temporalism and futurism. The world is in the making as are people and is moving into the future. All experience and learning must look toward the future, since nothing is fixed or permanent, in contrast to classical and medieval thought. As it bites into the future and away from the past one's experience caters to relativism in all things including moral judgment. With little or no respect for principles that bespeak permanencies and the systematic perspectives of life Dewey stresses vocational education over liberal education. This places things practical over things theoretical. Similarily, morals are a product of trial and error on a social scale.

Ethically, Dewey had an empirical version of the theory of self-realization. Yet he tried not to accept the hedonistic motif of the British empiricists and utilitarians. His version of the drive for self-realization was different from that of Plato and Aristotle, since it did not look to rational universals but to experience in a social context. He developed a psychological analysis of human motivation and the judgment of values in such a way as to keep society's welfare paramount and above self-interest. In this respect men are more than egoistic and formulate their moral norms and improve upon them empirically. Values are largely the result of seeing their social utility in experience. There are no absolutes except as men project them as instrumental, pragmatic ends or goals, mores or laws through democratic agreements. Human nature is accepted as the only universal, since it is what all men have in common, but it is not conceived as a Platonic universal but as an empirical phenomenon that men share.

Self-realization is the product of right action, not just contemplation, the kind of action that is "faithful to relations to others." One becomes a fuller self in social relationships when akin to the aims and needs of other people. Yet Dewey holds that it is dangerous to make one's own self-realization his conscious aim, lest self-centeredness set in. Dewey comes close to saying that social service is essential to true self-realization. Self-fulfillment is the result of morally right conduct in a social context, but it is not one's direct aim, lest self-centeredness be self-stultifying and arrest one's growth.

For Dewey the self must be viewed dynamically as involved in a changing process of becoming. The self is in the laws of changing experience in a changng world to the extent that even moral values change as they experimentally grow out of the social conditions of life. Yet Dewey does not condone an "anything goes" attitude or moral license, for always the self is in a social matrix that calls for one's respect for others.

The idea of a moral "good" springs from the natural needs, desires and aspirations of people, Dewey believes. Since people live together, social demands are placed upon them. Though ultimate or metaphysical principles are rejected by Dewey, he sees society providing the individual with norms, which he must respect. It is through social interplay that concepts of duty, rights and laws arise. The good, then, is what meets social approbation democratically while socially transcending personal desires and preferences. Here Dewey is anti- hedonistic, since society's welfare comes before the individual's concerns. Yet, ethically, Dewey is still aligned with David Hume who saw morals to be a matter of social sentiment.

Morals are seen by Dewey to pertain to any activity involving alternatives for better or worse. Only deliberate action involving choice is moral, yet moral judgment is experimental and subject to revision. It is not a matter of inner motive nor is it a fixed achievement for it is a "continuing process" that spells a growth of conduct. Morals, then, constitute education, says Dewey. The only good in our central is the "end" of our growth by which progress is measured. All else is accidental. The claim for fixed ideals belongs to a "dream world," says Dewey. Rather moral growth is a "constant arriving" that gives meaning to present experience. It is not a dogma of fixed ends in the future but is open-ended vistas and new tasks. These are not based on a remote life of reason with the rationalists but on continuous "external achievement."[1]

As for social action it is commendable whenever it widens the horizons of others and fosters their happiness through "a command of their own powers." It is sensitive to what should be the case over against what is the case yet is a product of experience, since it concerns human nature. Better social relations await the growth of a scientific social philosophy.[2]

Gradually, social standards are thought to arise which are quite stable. How does Dewey account for their stability? His appeal is to the stability of human nature. Dewey states: "The fundamental conceptions of morals are, therefore, neither aritrary nor artificial. They are not imposed upon human nature from without but develop out of its own operations and needs."[3] Morals are then strictly natural developments to Dewey and based on neither theoretical or religious principles but empirical findings through natural desires. A moral norm is linked with neither an objective ideal nor a Kantian imperative but a socially approved desire. In this context a duty is based on social sentiment and not on an inner moral authority or sensitivity. Monogamy, for instance, would be seen strictly as the best form of social adjustment and not something based on an objective mandate or ideal. In other societies, polygamy might be viewed as best. Hence, the relativism in Dewey's ethics.

Dewey rejects philosophical idealisms and lacks a typical form of religion based on revealed truths or principles. For him God is the sum total of man's self-projected ideals or goals, and both religious supernaturalism and religious institutionalisms are rejected as superfluous. Religion is humanist self-improvement and whatever works for social progress. The religious critic can legitimately say that Dewey makes God in his own image.

Pragmatic ethics has been closely related to the Utilitarian, since both are preeminently empirical, practical and teleological. John Dewey as a pragmatist was much concerned about bringing about "value in a world of fact." As an empiricist he saw the human mind discovering values through experience within a social context. Morals and values were to him not transcendent, eternal ideals, as for Plato, or belonging to a metaphysical hierarchy, with Aristotle, but matters of concrete choices in daily life, especially those choices of tested means to achieving desirable ends. Whenever an end is clearly perceived, Dewey maintained, a value judgment could be made scientifically or in terms of successfully terminated acts of previous experience. But before the act is done intelligence, which is also a product of experience, sorts out the various possibilities and appraises the foreseen consequences, teleologically.[4] In so doing it differentiates desires from what is desirable. The latter is an appraisal of desired results of acts in view of the best means and conditions for attaining them. The desirable results are not absolute ideals or a priori values but products of experience. Social conditions and consequences are important in the distinction between the "is" and the "should be" or "ought."[5] Dewey so much as makes the "ought" a sub-class of the "is" in a way that makes it not only a factual matter but makes it prescriptive. This allows it to affect conduct or regulate desires. In this way Dewey seems to overcome "the naturalistic fallacy" contended by G. E. Moore in <u>Principia Ethica</u> that no "ought" can spring from an "is."[6] The extent to which this is tenable helps offset the claims for emotivism by Ayer and Russell. Value to Dewey is practical or very much within "a world of fact" by being based on satisfactory results in making life adjustments to one's natural and social environment. Means and ends or end results are made to jibe when dealing with concrete problems. Science can be helpful, Dewey contended, by sorting out standards based on experience-based value judgments.

Though Dewey is somewhat utilitarian he is more than utilitarian, as Samuel E. Stumpf reminds us, because he not only links the desireable with human desires but says that the sciences can show how to best satisfy desires. They can improve the links between means and ends. A desire must be submitted to the critical powers of an intelligence influenced by scientific thoughts as it looks to consequences based on the satisfaction of desires. A value, then, is not simply the satisfaction of desires but the satisfactory solution of the problems related to or implied by desires. In this way John Dewey says experience provides ethical ends toward which human behavior should move.[7] In contending this Dewey is an empiricist who avoids the ethical pitfalls of positivism.

There is a special ethical question, however, that must be re-raised from the empirical point-of-view: Can an "ought" be derived from an "is"? Can ethical responsibility arise from empirical matters of fact? As inferred above, G. E. Moore earlier in this century denied the possibility and looked to an intuition of the "good" as the sole alternative. When the logical positivists like Ayer and Russell came along they denied both elements i.e. both the empirical grounds as well as the intuitive or a priori basis for ethics. Robert V. Hannaford has re-raised the question and has contended that if <u>ought</u> implies 'can' or 'must', then 'can' or 'must' often leads to ought. He asserts that arguments based on empirical claims about actions can provide an objective basis for moral commitment. This is because such assertions can lead to norms of action concerning conditions and freedoms that ought to be preserved in a community. Hannaford states, "It is clear that empirical accounts of behavior can be used in deciding questions of value when one is employing hypothetical value judgments."[8] Such value judgments imply that if certain goals are to be achieved certain conditions or means must be met as based on empirical observations and experiment, and those means or conditions should be defended. Norms of action will be arrived at socially for directing subsequent actions. Here Hannaford is not unlike Dewey.

But a special ethical insight comes to the surface at this point. Hannaford says, "If we want to engage in any activity that involves other people..we must defend and preserve the persons with whom we must act."[8] Implied here is the worth of persons and the protection, too, of those conditions or means which make for community life. This, in turn, points to a moral <u>ought</u> or value judgment from within an empirical <u>is</u> judgment; it opens up norms or principles of value seen to be derived from factual assertions. On such a basis prescriptive norms, standards and laws are far more than emotive. They involve obligations of persons to other persons.[10] As John Roger Searle points out, an empirical assertion like "I promise to pay him" carries within it social institutional understandings akin to what Kant called constitutive principles. The same for the commitment to marriage or even to play a game of baseball. Each is empirical and yet implies rules of obligation, since the empirical element is within the social setting, the constitutive rules of which imply moral "oughts" from within the factual "is's" of xperience. The facts per se involve moral commitments. A promise is descriptive but also evaluative.[11] It has social implicaions. Thus a broader empirical perspective yields ethical considerations in ways that positivism's more restrictive perspective does not.

The question arises, however, whether Dewey's socially endorsed "ought" is really a moral "ought." It seems Dewey is guilty of what G. E. Moore called the "naturalistic fallacy" of projecting an "ought" from an empirical "is" of desire. A. C. Garnett, however, is not sure that such a criticism is justified, for he claims that Dewey argues the "is" and the "ought" are related, the "ought" being a sub-class of the "is," which is to say that not only is it empirically factual but directive or prescriptive.[12] But this can be counter-argued with the question: Is a socially projected law necessarily or indigenously moral? The civil rights movement has been based upon the objection that some laws are immoral. Similarly, laws once condoning slavery were not necessarily moral. Reformers would be wrong if all laws based on social sentiment were legitimate.

Dewey asserts that something may be deemed desireable or satisfactory while a matter of attitude to secure or perpetuate a form of conduct. Thus value judgments are more than empirical desires, since the attitudes involved affect conduct. They can also be "judgments about that which should regulate the formation of our desires, affections and enjoyments."[13] But, critically, how can this be so? How can norms arrived at from desires regulate desires? Is not this round-robin logic? Furthermore, does not Dewey open up a relativism in ethics, since morals are allowed to change. How does one judge changing morality amidst changing morality? By what can it be judged with finality?

For Dewey morals and values are both matters of fact and matters of judgment about how we should regulate our conduct and the desires basic thereto. They are both indicative and imperative, ("is" and "ought"), and they predict consequences for ongoing life. But Dewey does not distinguish between morality and prudence. This being the case it is questionable whether Dewey has a sound basis for the professed imperative element in his ethical theory. The prescriptive "ought" remains confused with the empirical "is" of desire; their identification is asserted but not well demonstrated. Again, critically speaking, socially endorsed mores or laws may be immoral.

Self-realization is linked with a type of "ought," but the question may be reiterated whether it is a truly moral ought. Dewey allows for no fixed ultimate principle but only for social harmony as the condition of self-realization. The closest to a fixed principle that Dewey comes to is that one's habits conform by human nature to society's demands as based on human nature's desires. Good conduct is relative to social demands or sentiment.

In general, then, Dewey's ethics caters to moral relativism, for society's demands can very well be based on whimsical to superficial desires. Witness the deterioration of sex mores and morals in our present culture. Even Dewey's appeal to fair-mindedness and social justice begs the question. Society's demands remain but working hpotheses for the sake of social utility, but often they are unprincipled. The chief issue for the individual becomes this: Why should one be fair or just when it does not seem to enhance one's self-realization? On what grounds can it be said that society is right in its demands? Again, socially endorsed laws are not always moral as was the case in Montgomery. Dewey's social reference is well taken as an important aspect of a sound ethic but it has little basis, for it has no reference point beyond the relativism of human desires. He fails to show why it would be wrong to betray the social group's preferences save for self-realization as a social product. The hedonism and egocentricism which Dewey tries to overcome are still basic problems. Also, from the standpoint of why the social group makes its demands for justice Dewey is weak. It is because he lacks an ultimate frame of reference beyond human nature's relativistic desires. In other words, Dewey does not recognise any principles of self-realization which could become universal on their own. He has no absolute criterion of what he calls "right," i.e. no reference point beyond social sentiment, only a hypothetical claim that often works but has no undergirding or intrinsic value. The overall consequence of this is moral relativism.

Erich Fromm has seen the weakness in Dewey's ethics and tries to amend it by an appeal to love as a universal principle basic to self-realization. Thus egoism is overcome and presumably, relativism also. Society, then, is given a basis for its social desires and demands related to fairness. Love is thought to provide an inner motivation that sheer social sentiment does not.[14]

Another weakness in Dewey's ethics is his loss of existential particularity on the part of man in favor of a general human nature, which, though not Platonic in nature, obfuscates the individuality of the individual. The individual is really subordinated to a human nature identified with society and its sentiments. This is a form of universalism that obscures the "me" of everyday existence; it is a social universalism on the grounds that all men are presumed to have like or similar desires. This does much to hide the individual or subordinate him to what Kierkegaard in his way speaks of as "the crowd" and Heidegger in his way as "das Man." The individuality of "a man" is lost sight of in favor of an opaque mankind. One of the most serious consequences of this is the loss of the uniqueness of the self, and another is the loss of the distinctiveness of the reformer. Much like man in Hobbes' ethics man is made subservient to society almost as man in Marxism is made subservient to the state. The reformer is not allowed to be head and shoulders above his society, for Dewey keeps him like all men necessitated by social sentiment. The logic of this is that social progress cannot be made, since there are no reformers to change the social sentiment. It is not enough for Dewey simply to say that societies change. There must be a sound basis for the change, even as there must be some form of absolutes by which to judge whether or not the changes are progressive.

Notes

1. John Dewey, "Morals and Conduct" from Human Nature and Conduct, 1922, in The World's Great Thinkers, The Social Philosophers, pp.449-458.
2. Ibid, pp.460-463, 479.
3. John Dewey and James H. Tufts, Ethics, rev. ed., New York: Henry Holt and Co., 1932, Pt. II by Dewey, p.343f.
4. John Dewey, The Logic of Inquiry, p.218. Standards are derived from experience but are also subject experimentally to revision in view of conditions and consequences. They are like language in that both are matters of custom, while they change with situations. Cf. Human Nature and Conduct, I, p.5. But this view rejects intrinsic values and absolute norms and ideals. Cf. The Quest for Certainty, Chap. X, esp. p.257ff, 262. Values are what people enjoy or what satisfy them, especially in view of consequences. But Dewey hardly does justice to the difference between "is" and "ought." The latter would imply an intrinsic value or end. Critically, scientific method can describe but hardly produce norms.
5. John Dewey, "Theory of Valuations" in Contemporary Philosophic Problems, ed. by Krikorian and Edel, p.503-514.
6. John Dewey, Quest for Certainty, pp.260-265.
7. Samuel E. Stumpf, Philosophy: History and Problems, p.412ff.
8. Robert V. Hannaford, "You Ought to Derive 'Ought' from 'Is'," in Ethics In Perspective, ed. K. J. and Paula R. Struhl, N.Y.: Random House, 1975, pp.135-141 (p.137).
9. Ibid, p.138.
10. Ibid, p.140.
11. John Rogers Searle, "How to Derive 'Ought' from 'Is'" in Moral Philosophy, ed. by A. G. Oldenquist, 2nd ed., Boston, Houghton-Mifflin Co., 1978, pp.358-370.
12. A. C. Garnett, Ethics, pp.238, 240.
13. John Dewey, The Quest for Certainty, 1929, pp.260-265.
14. Cf. the next Chapter.

The Sketch of Erich Fromm

Erich Fromm (1900-1980) was born in Frankfurt, Germany, and received his Ph.D. from the University of Heidelberg in 1922. He became a psychoanalyst and general critic and writer. After training in psychoanalysis in Germany he moved in 1933 to the United States, where he practiced privately in New York City and taught in several American colleges. Before he died in 1980 he had moved to Switzerland. Fromm's views modified those of Freud with a stronger social reference while addressing what he saw to be the individual's need of self-fulfillment. He questioned Freud's strong emphasis upon sexual motivations. Akin to Karl Marx, in social theory he stressed that men are not conditioned by instinct so much as by culture. Though sexual drives are often a problem, neuroses also are caused by social pressures. In 1941 he wrote **Escape From Freedom**. Alternative views to personal and social alienation were expressed in such books as **Man For Himself** (1947), **The Sane Society** (1955), **The Art of Loving** (1956) and other works. In contrast to socially endorsed 'character types' he stressed self-realization through Agápe or self-giving love, a theme with marked ethical implications.

The Ethics of Erich Fromm

Erich Fromm seeks to base ethics on the nature of man in such a way as to combine psychoanalysis with a philosophy confident in human reason much in the spirit of the Enlightenment. In so doing he resists the realism of the times which often makes man appear helpless in his relativism, on the one hand, while rejecting the idea that religion is the only recourse, on the other. Man, he argues, cannot live without values and norms, but they will have to be found through man's own reason and human nature alone.

As a psychoanalyst Fromm keeps the study of ethics a psychological matter, but rightly criticizes psychoanalysis for having separated itself from ethical and other philosophical cosiderations.[1] While increasing our knowledge of man, it has not contributed to the knowledge of how man ought to live. It did not look at man in his totality, which includes the need to find an answer to the question of the meaning of one's existence plus norms by which to live. Fromm says there must be a return to the humanistic level of manhood with its implicit ethics. In stressing this he says such a study need not succumb to ethical relativisms, as in the case of John Dewey, positivism and atheistic existentialism, since he finds "the sources of norms for ethical conduct" in human nature itself. In this respect Fromm is somewhat Kantian. The violation of norms results in mental and emotional disintegration. Virtue and vice are to Fromm matters of character. For one thing, self-love need not be viewed as the negation but the affirmation of the individual. "If man is to have confidence in values," says Fromm, "he must know himself and the capacity of his nature for goodness and productiveness."[2] This belongs to Fromms' central thesis and implies a resolute willingness to be "for oneself." The latter reminds us of Sartre's *pour soi* basic to subjectivity.

Opposed to all forms of authoritarian ethics, Fromm favors what he calls humanistic ethics in which "man himself is the norm giver and the subject of the norms..." Something good or bad is to be understood in terms of its usefulness to "me." Man's own welfare is central rather than anything transcendent, be it state, church or God. But a social reference is included in what Fromm deems favorable to man -- in fact with such optimism that Fromm thinks that to love one's neighbor is something inherent in man's nature and power. Such love is natural. The aim of life is the unfolding of man's powers and nature much like the self-realization ethics of Dewey. What is good or virtuous must be seen in this light, whereas evil is the crippling of these powers. Evil is largely environmental.[3]

Human nature, to Fromm, is neither a fixed entity nor something so malleable to social forces as to make man a puppet. Yet the empirical study of man, he thinks, can give us a kind of model of human nature. When man is studied psychologically in terms of his dynamic wholeness as a rational and free, autonomous creature even an ethics may be articulated. Here psychoanalysis is superior to other psychologies such as the behavioristic type, which fail to deal with the total self or personality. It includes reason as well as the irrational strivings of the Freudian unconscious mind.[4]

Man has his existential tensions and dichotomies, but he is capable of facing and resolving them by reason qualified by love, says Fromm. In fact there is no meaning to life except in what man gives himself in the unfolding of his powers in so called "productive living." His strivings need not be interpreted as a nostalgia for something transcendent, since they are indigenous to the human situation. Devotion to an end or ideal is not necessarily a theistic matter but characteristic of man's "need for a system of orientation and devotion." All men are "idealists," in a Dewey-like sense, but they strive for different views of the ideals. The lack of visions of the "better" man and society in this century have had the effect, however, of paralyzing man's faith in himself and the future.[5] There has been too much "realism" in the picture of man, causing a less productive outlook or less self-realization and thus a faulty locking to authorities for alternative answers, Fromm thinks.

Fromm states, "It is a paradox of human existence that man must simultaneously seek for closeness (relations with others) and for independence..." The answer lies in the "productive living" fostered by love expressed through care, responsibility, knowledge and respect-not as a mere passion but as activity. Everyone is capable of love, but it may be difficult to realize. In order to love others one must have a self-love or self-respect also.[6] Self-love is not selfishness, however. With a "good egocentricism" Fromm says man is an end in himself. Even one's conscience is a calling back to oneself, a voice of one's true self to become what he potentially is, including the essence of his moral experience. "Humanistic conscience" is an expression of self-interest and personal integrity. It makes for happiness as a "concomitant of productive living." Fromm is confident enough about this humanistic conscience to say, "No power transcending man can make a moral claim upon him. Man is responsible to himself for gaining or losing his life."[7]

Humanistic ethics makes man the sole source and judge of his values. But as such it does not find pleasure a guiding principle of actions. Thus Fromm is anti-hedonistic. The hedonistic view is too subjective and relativistic.[8] Faith in oneself, however, is a prime essential, an attitude and character trait which enables one to face reality without illusions. The lack of such "rational faith" may be a neurotic lack of integration of the total personality. Such rational faith makes for "productive living" or the fulfillment of one's potentialities. Human ethics implies there are moral powers in man, for he is not evil but inherently good. He becomes evil only if conditions for growth or development are lacking, i.e. good is inhibited by circumstances or environment. Evil, then, is a privation of the good. Even mental illness is a matter of suppression based on environmental forces operating against a person. A neurosis is the result of forces which block the development of one's inherent powers. Humanistic ethics views neurosis and any failure to achieve maturity and personal integration as a moral failure due to unsolved moral conflicts, says Fromm, often due to one's environmental pressures.

The will of man is an expression of his character. When allied with productiveness it leads one to trust his reason and to love others and himself. Reason and conscience are basic capacities which one is responsible for using and developing, yet they are not completely free and undetermined, since they are products of our empirically conditional self. When a person does an evil thing we can understand something of why and how he did it, but we must also judge him for what he did and is. There is still room for moral judgment, thinks Fromm. But at this point Fromm is weak, since his ethics has a circular reference point in the self, a type that recognizes shortcomings in men's conduct but without an objective frame of reference for making moral judgment possible. It is difficult to avoid relativism here, since the moral orientation is centered in the self. Fromm seems to see the problem of relativism but does little to offset it.[10]

Ethical norms need not be absolute, says Fromm. They can be "socially immanent" to a given culture or society and its maintenance. In case of the latter, the individual's interests are bound up with that of his society, so he must accept its ethical norms. Experience has shown men, however, that there are a few universal principles essential to most societies, if not all, such as "Thou shalt not kill." and "Love thy neighbor as thy self." The conflict between universal ethics and the socially immanent ethics has lessened in later generations, thinks Fromm. Though humanistic here, Fromm improves upon Dewey by seeing love as the motivation behind social norms and giving them a basis so that an empirical "is" or desire is also an altruistic "ought."[11]

Erich Fromm's concern for human self-realization has much in common with that of John Dewey. Both are naturalistic, empirical and humanistic views of self-fulfillment in a social context. But, commendably, Fromm seeks to be less relativistic than Dewey through giving the individual and society a basic principle to live by, viz the love motive as essential to "productive living" in the social context. This also helps overcome Dewey's psychological egoism through a benevolence and altruism held to be implicit in human nature. What Fromm calls "productive living" is a form of self-realization through agape, which integrates the self and makes for mental and social health.

Of the two humanistic thinkers, Fromm and Dewey, it is Fromm who is the more altruistic. He sees how a socially conditioned conscience such as held by Dewey needs to be qualified by a love-based motif. The qualification makes for what Fromm calls "productive love" basic to integrity. With it comes an impartial concern for human welfare and a norm that is essential to true self-realization. Dewey's ethics is more of a product of social coercion, mores and laws, which is more external to man's nature than Fromm's inward motivation and conscience. To Fromm conscience is more of an inner moral sentiment than it is to Dewey. Fromm sees how man's moral experience includes distinctions enabling persons to develop universal norms which uphold the impartiality Dewey sees to be important but for which he found no basis in man. Dewey rests social ethics only on what is a matter of natural desires. Fromm at best tries to overcome such egocentricity by a productive love that is out-going toward others. In this respect Fromm's self-realization ethics is more mature, since it is linked with the objectives beyond the self. In other words, his altruism is less egocentric being one of impartial concern for others. As self-realization it is therefore more conducive to mental and social health.

But, negatively speaking, Fromm paints a very optimistic picture of man, refusing to face up to the realistic aspects of human nature and what causes human tensions in self and society. At times he admits man is a battlefield between the rational and the irrational, the conscious and the unconscious, but he never concedes to a serious deficiency or any egotistical competitiveness to the good in man's make-up. Even Kant, despite his basic optimism about "duty", saw a "perverse will" and "evil propensity" in man.[12]

When it comes to the love of neighbor Fromm finds it so simple, easy and natural that one almost wonders whether there could be any virtue in love. How can a man, especially a neurotic person, surmount his selfishness or egocentric predicament? is the question we must ask. Surely sacrificial love (agape) cannot be turned on like a TV switch. Fromm speaks as though there were no basic problem in human make-up to overcome, hence no need to human re-motivation. Agape is treated as a natural motivation. This is questionable as a true picture of man.

Whence the agape? is the underlying issue. Were it as natural to come by as Fromm depicts, this world should be next door to paradise. How do we possess agape as an inner motive, and how do we actualize it in the face of a corrupt society? Fromm sees an impartial concern for human welfare to be a natural norm of conduct essential to self-realization. But if it were so natural why must we have so many laws and guidelines to help put it into practice? Fromm obviously has borrowed the principle of agape from Christianity but has tried to humanize it as "doing what comes naturally." Fromm's plagiarism is another form of what Renaissance humanism did when it borrowed from religion the dignity of man. Christianity is much more realistic when it sees Agape as a matter of a re-motivated good will and re-orientated selfhood based on a truth from beyond man's rationalistic and empirical strivings. Here Kierkegaard is more shrewd. Agape is not humanistically asserted but redemptively received, i.e. a faith-conditioned love motive, not a natural bent.

Fromm threatens to reduce agape to a means rather than an end, i.e. a means to one's self-realization. While altruistic in practice it appears to be egoistic in concern or motive. This tends to sterilize genuine agape by keeping the self at the center rather than others. As a form of self-gratification Fromm's type of love remains not true Agape, but eros or philia at best. True Agape is total self-giving with no thought of personal reward or benefit, something Fromm obscures.

Basically, Fromm is almost hedonistic because of his egocentric form of self-realization. He does not intend such but the question is: How can pleasure-seeking or self gratification be avoided? Though he disliked total relativism he has no absolute to offset it. The love to which he looks is strictly a self-sufficient, psychological self-assertion that merely copies Christian ethics without having any undergirding metaphysical principle or basis. This reduces Agape to a self-concocted means without linkage to an inspirational end.

Furthermore, it is dubious that Fromm as an empiricist can embrace Agape epistemologically without an existentialist, holistic view of man, a view that allows for the tenability of Agape through a Kierkegaardian, faith-conditioned encounter with the Absolute revealed through Christ to be Agape personified. Without such an underlying adjustment Fromm's place for love is strictly the application of a borrowed concept, a kind of ethically parasitical notion with no motivational undergirding or motif. Though there can be empirical applications of Agape there can be no genuine inspiration for it without the existential encounter. St. Paul's "Hymn of Agape" in I Corinthians 13 is far more than a humanistic copy of a Christly love; it is a faith-conditioned inspiration and experience.

For such to be the case one's interpretation of man must be more than empirically humanistic; it must be religious.

So, like Renaissance humanists who borrowed the dignity of man from religion, Erich Fromm has borrowed Agape-love from the Christian revelation while stripping it of its underlying motivation based on faith. This he has done by stressing that man is himself the norm giver. Through wishful thinking Fromm has inferred between the lines that man can himself concoct Agape, a position which overlooks the divine nature and inspiration behind Agape, on the one hand, and which stresses the self-sufficiency of man and his ethics, on the other. Such optimism is supported by the failure to acknowledge whatever Kant saw to be the evil in man, an "evil propensity" that competes with man's ethical sensitivity. In addition Kant was shrewd enough as a philosopher to open the door to man's need of divine transcendence and Grace. As sufficient as he viewed man morally, he saw man as not fully self-sufficient but in view of a re-motivation from beyond whereby he could fulfill his ethical potentialities in the face of his evil propensities. Fromm is much in need of something similar in order that man's love ethic might remain true self-giving and not merely a modified self-gratification. But for such a re-motivation to be made possible it would appear that Fromm would need an existentialist interpretation of man whereby not only man's dichotomy would be recognized but man's capitulation to the Divine Absolute in Kierkegaardian manner would be allowed for. Actually, Fromm's favorable attitude toward religion[13] should not make this an impossibility. It would only require a more holistic view of man, on the one hand, and a view of man amenable to a faith seen relevent to his concrete existence, on the other.

Notes

1. Erich Fromm, Man For Himself, p.16ff.
2. Ibid, p.29ff.
3. Ibid, p.30ff, 34, 36.
4. Ibid, pp.35-46.
5. Ibid, pp.17, 49-55, 89-92, 96-107. Cf. Fromm, The Art of Loving, pp.6ff, 70ff; 40ff.
6. Ibid, pp.124-137; 137-145.
7. Ibid, pp.162-175.
8. Ibid, pp.24f, 177f, 193f.
9. Ibid, p.47ff.
10. Cf. Ibid, pp.15-17, 24, 30f, 42-45, 58, 201-203, 250.
11. Ibid, 34, 41, 37-39. Cf. Fromm, The Sane Society, for expansio of the social implications relative to psychoanalysis.
12. I. Kant, Religion Within The Bounds of Reason, see my essay on Kant and evil in Religious Issues in Philosophy Today.
13. Erich Fromm, Psychoanalysis and Religion. Fromm sees the two disciplines united in man's spiritual quest.

CHAPTER IX

ETHICS AND EXISTENTIALISM

    21.   The Ethics of Søren Kierkegaard

    22.   The Ethics of Friedrich Nietzsche

    23.   The Ethics of Jean-Paul Sartre

    24.   The Ethics of Joseph Fletcher

The Sketch of Søren Kierkegaard

Søren Kierkegaard (1813-1855) was a religious philosopher of Denmark who is the titular founder of existentialism. His father's departures from Christian decorum bothered son Søren very much. Kierkegaard studied philosophy at the University of Copenhagen becoming a reactionist against the strongly prevalent philosophy of Hegel. The abstract idealism of Hegel, Kierkegaard believed, was much too depersonalizing as it lost sight of the individual of concrete existence in favor of man as an abstract concept. Personal beliefs and ethical convictions were obscured in the rational monism of Hegel. Kierkegaard also reacted against the institutionalism of the state Church of Denmark of his time and the tendency to make Christianity conform rationally to Hegelianism. His writings have an autobiographical approach and often use paradox and irony. Man and God, Søren Kierkegaard contended, are separated by a gulf. Faith is not rational but rests on the incarnation of Christ which to a naked reason is "absurd." Among his writings are <u>Either/Or</u>, <u>The Sickness Unto Death</u>, and <u>Fear and Trembling</u>. Kierkegaard has greatly influenced twentieth-century thought in literature, philosophy and theology.

The Ethics of Søren Kierkegaard

Kierkegaard of Denmark in the last century was the titular father of existentialism. As such he not only recovered a genuine individualism of the self but led the revolt against rationalism, especially that of Hegel, whose monistic metaphysics of reason depersonalized the individual by treating man as an abstract concept. Hegel put universalism ahead of particularity; Kierkegaard did the opposite. Kierkegaard said graphically that Hegel depicts man in a castle of reason though he really lives in a shack of existence.[1] In this respect Hegel projects a cosmic system of reason while losing sight of the thinker as an individual; he speaks of 'man' but not 'me.'

Like Nietzsche in the next generation, Kierkegaard saw how both rational and empirical theories betrayed men in their anxiety, especially, Kierkegaard felt, in the face of an unknown infinite, which neither metaphysical nor scientific explanations could justify. Decision is seen to be the seat of a human existence steeped in anxious inquiries and concerns. Reason fails to do justice to such an existence. Abstract universals are too often allowed to displace concrete particulars and rational theories made to obscure or obviate decisions. Truth is concrete inwardness or "subjectivity" said Kierkegaard.[2] It is not objectively self-contained or universally manifest but must be relevant to the knowing subject-self. Thus inwardness precedes outwardness, even as freedom and decision precede system and theory. Also will is more basic to existence than reason as reflected in the fact that very often choices must be made even when rationalistic ideals or codes are missing or do not address one's situation. "To exist is to choose," said Kierkegaard.[3]

Akin to a depersonalizing philosophy is a depersonalizing religion. What a monistic rationalism is to philosophy institutionalism is to religion.[4] Nothing churchly, said Kierkegaard, should stand between a man and God. Yet there is an abyss between finite, sinful man and his creator God. The eventual result of this awareness is the anguish of despair, for a man cannot measure up to divine expectations. Yet not to experience this anguish is for a man to miss the meaning of life opened up by "the Moment" of encounter with the Absolute on its own terms. Despair makes for a self-honesty which is the negative condition of the positive encounter. It leads to "the leap of faith" when one faces the paradoxes of existence and capitulates to the Absolute on its own terms.[5] Faith is a "total-self commitment," a commitment of the whole self, which Kierkegaard also spoke of as "the absolute relation to the Absolute."[6]

For Kierkegaard Christ is the revelation or key to how the abyss is crossed from the 'other' side or how what is absurd and paradoxical to reason is given the answer to life's meaning through faith. The incarnate Christ is God coming to man and cannot be explained or defended by reason.[7] Kierkegaard sees the leap of faith as an either/or situation topping off the many either/or confrontations of daily existence, since life is replete with choices and decisions. A person is either committed to God or in rebellion, either accepting the Absolute or settling for all the relativistic opinions and judgments of life.

Kierkegaard believed that the central issue in life was that of being an individual.[8] The next basic issue was: What does it mean to be a Christian? Ontologically, abstract being is not of concern to Kierkegaard but the particularity of the human being in existence is his main concern. Two things obscure the individual of existence, Hegelian rationalism and religious institutionalism. Kierkegaard scorns the idea that Christianity can be congruent to an objective ontology of reason, for the Incarnation is a paradox relevant not to pure reason but to the subject-self who is committed to it by faith, not reason.[9] Similarly the virtues of faith, hope and love are absurd to a self-sufficient reason.

The conventional church-goer is an enemy of true Christianity due to his form of social conformism, which is bad; for all conformism stunts true selfhood. "The crowd is untruth," said Kierkegaard.[10] Much of institutionalized religion and its rituals are depersonalized religion, though they need not be. This weakness is a failure to vivify the transcendence of God along with the abyss between man and God, a qualitative disjunction between the divine Absolute and all ethical and social standards projected by men.[11]

Since God is the eternal Absolute, divine truth is neither innate to man nor attained by reason. Only by his faith-conditioned encounter with the Absolute can man come to know a truly meaningful existence and destiny. Conditioned by despair makes it parallel to the Socratic ignorance, the religious corollary of which is repentance. Thus Kierkegaard challenged the sufficiency of a speculative reason by appealing to the particularity of the individual and to nonconformity as well as to a religious credo absurdum or transrationality.[12] True self-transcendence lay in faith as the "absolute relation to the Absolute."[13]

Kierkegaard's ethics is different in that instead of being identified with a finalized ontological structure it is a dialectical scheme belonging to the individual self.[14] Not dealing with man in the abstract, it deals with man as a concrete individual. Only the subjective self exists, for he alone can choose; man in the abstract sense does not exist or choose. "Not to choose," said Søren Kierkegaard putting the individual on the spot, "is still a choice."[15]

If one does not decide, the world will decide for him. "Truth is subjectivity" or what is inwardly relevant to "me." "If you love the truth," said Søren Kierkegaard, "you will suffer (sacrifice) for it."[16] Suffering is to be preferred to sin, he said.

Sin is a broken relation with eternity, and eternity not only supercedes time but qualifies it with meaning on a faith-conditioned basis. Human reason is finite and its findings are qualitatively inferior to what is infinitely eternal. God is the eternal Absolute who transcends time, history, finitude and human existence. Divine transcendence is not to be viewed spatially but as qualitatively superior to all that is temporal and finite including reason. To be out of relation to the transcendent Absolute is to be in a sinful state. The only good in human existence is a good will inspired by faith's association with the Eternal. Ethically, at this point it is necessary to note the contrast between good will as conceived by Kant and Kierkegaard. For Kant good will is basically innate and rationally natural; for Kierkegaard it is divinely inspired. Here Kierkegaard has a superior answer to the duplicity of good and evil in man, especially in view of Kant's admission that man's will is not only good but "perverse" and lined with man's "evil propensity." In short Søren Kierkegaard has a redemptive answer that Kant only viewed philosophically from afar.[17]

Since the love ethic based on good will as stressed by Kierkegaard is realizable only in relation to eternity, humanistic critics accuse him of being pessimistic. But Søren Kierkegaard sees this love ethic opened up by a faith-conditioned good will as something existentially possible in this life through the Moment of encounter. It is essential to what he meant by modifying Socrates' "Know thyself" by "Choose thyself."[18] Self-realization is a natural and worthy pursuit, but it is not fulfilled through a finite reason but a willful faith-commitment. By it potentialities, including good will and love, are transformed into actualities.

Human existence is steeped in anxieties leading to the <u>Angst</u> or dread of being one's self and dread of not being one's self. The "masks" of conformity must be removed. Life is replete with choices, many being paradoxically necessary though free. One is continuously confronted by either/or situations, which cannot be evaded.[19] In his famous two-volume work <u>Either/Or</u> Kierkegaard enunciated a strong dialectics between an individual's ethical and aesthetic natures. It is a polemic against speculative idealisms, especially that of Hegel, for whom all things in opposition are blended into a synthesis of pure reason. Søren Kierkegaard detested Hegel's both/and dialectics in favor of the either/or dialectics of decision. Hegel saw truth as an objective, monistic whole. Kierkegaard saw it as subjective, decisive and particular.[20]

An element of pessimism or, better, ethical realism enters Kierkegaard's picture of man, since he asserts that while faced with either/or alternatives we invariably make wrong choices -- apart from "the Moment" -- and even masquerade ourselves and hide from life enigmatically. Existence is as irrational, then, as it is rational, if not more so. A moral decision with ideal or right results is often an impossibility, thinks Søren Kierkegaard, because we have no absolute rational ideals or standards to live by, while truth is still a matter of subjective inwardness. There is no objective security about morality. Thus under inspiration from Abraham's existential election to sacrifice his son, Kierkegaard spoke of "the teleological suspension of the ethical." The sole value of an act is the edification of the subject-self, i.e. it is a matter of pathos for 'me.'[21] Since one's existence is subjective, one must see himself immersed in it while also having existential possibilities. The completely objective thinker is a fool. Often he is on the level of the aesthete, a mere observer or Platonic spectator on the balcony.[22] The true ethical thinker must come "out of the balcony into the arena." said Søren Kierkegaard. While the arena is a more basic level of existence, in another sense it is a higher level, because one is involved subjectively in what he thinks and chooses. It is "every man's duty to reveal himself" or to attain an ethical victory over his own concealments, role-playing, conformism, melancholy and despair.

How is this ethical victory realized? It is through "existential inwardness" based on decision, which places will over reason.[23] Whereas the aesthetic thinker seeks a better way of life through intellectual schematisms of either rational philosophy, science or indecisive pleasure (that of the playboy or seducer), the ethical thinker seeks to realize himself through one's real selfhood or what Heidegger refers to as "authentic existence." This to Søren Kierkegaard is a matter of inwardness and personal pathos.[24] Through despair or the recognition of one's finitude by a kind of self-psychoanalysis one sees and admits his concealments or phoniness. The victory comes about when a person really wants to find his true self by freely choosing himself. While despair is an admission that one cannot lift himself by his own bootstraps of finitude, it is a moment of self-honesty and decision, which also means that one acknowledges his need of divine assistance.[25] Nietzsche said this life is a "mendacious swindle." Kierkegaard does not deny it, but unlike Nietzsche, he does not resign himself to it, but, rather, faces up to one's moral failures so that through despair one will also become aware of the religious dimension of his existence through the positive side of a negative despair, vis. the "leap of faith." By this "total-self commitment" one stops living in aesthetic neutrality and concealment. In "the fear and trembling" accompanying one's inner sensitivity to "the abyss," as one morally fall's short of the infinite Absolute, the despair through self-honesty leads to the intense either/or of decision to live life on the highest level, that of faith that spells communion with the eternal-in-time.[26]

Thus human existence is not only replete with many choices day-in-and-day out but the intensive choice, the either/or of living on either the aesthetic level or ethical level. Yet there are regrets on either level. A person's enigmatic nature is one of anxiety, even though he always chooses what he thinks is good. The underlying problem is the manner in which the good is pursued. Quite in keeping with Socrates and Plato, Kierkegaard says people are not so depraved as to desire evil, but they often are blind and lack the moral stamina to live ethically, especially in view of the Christian ethics of love.

But it is through decision that a finite personality is made infinite in quality, being given faithwise a good will whereby one can realize his possibilities in existence. Moral freedom or a self-transcending will is basic to choosing one's true self, which constitutes the higher freedom in the light of the eternal much like the "freedom major" expressed by Augustine.[27] Objective distinctions between good and evil do not exist or are irrelevant, for they are strictly subjective. Søren Kierkegaard states, "The good is for the fact that I will it, and apart from my willing it, it has no existence....It is so also with evil..." Men are evil as well as good, some more than others; however, they need not be resigned to evil, for they can come to despair of their existential inconsistencies and moral failings and repent and repress the evil allowing the good to hold sway inwardly. Søren Kierkegaard says, "Choosing oneself is identical with repenting oneself."

The ethical individual's strength lies in his willingness to be transparent to himself -- to "know thyself" as Socrates put it, which means to be acquainted with one's motives and to be psychologically naked before oneself, others and God. The aesthetic person has not come to this. The ethical person has begun to; he knows himself because, as Søren Kierkegaard stresses, he has chosen himself. "Choose thyself" Søren Kierkegaard says, - Choose your real or ideal self with its possibilities. The ethical person has duties residing in his inner self; duty expresses his very nature. If duty were objective or external to a person rather than within him, no distinction between good and evil would exist. A person is ethically mature when he senses duty and takes on responsibilities. The multifarious duties really boil down to one, vis. "duty in earnest." It is everyone's duty to have a vocation or calling, and one's life task should be to do what he is capable of doing -- to actualize his talents, possibilities and duties.[28] Søren Kierkegaard provocatively says this: "It is very dangerous to go into eternity with possibilities which one has prevented from becoming realities. A possibility is a hint from

God. One must follow it." It is essential to one's inner duty to become self-revealed to oneself and others.

Kierkegaard spoke of a "purity of heart" linked with the good will inspired by faith in the eternal. "Purity of heart," he said, "is to will one thing, viz. the willing of the good in truth."[29] In other words, one's choices must be single-minded. This purity of heart is conditioned by repentence and "the Moment" of encounter. It is a costly motivation, the cost of complete commitment to the good and to one's dutiful relationship with sacrificial suffering accompanying one's love of truth. It belongs to a right relationship with God. Purity of heart is a solitary experience based on one thing, willing the good.[30] Only as the individual is reconciled to God can he realize this oneness of purpose and resolve. If one wills or seeks the good for the sake of some reward or out of fear of some kind of punishment he will be remiss due to a double-mindedness and mixed motives. Commitment, sacrifice and loyalty are the conditions, if not the prices, involved in willing one thing, the good. By them one lives as a genuine individual giving account of himself. Often it is a lonely existence, yet a calling to be one's true self. Good means must be consistent with such a good end, for ultimately there is but one good end - the Eternal Good of God. Such is purity of heart.

Contrary to Nietzsche and Jean-Paul Sartre, man does not make his own meaning, thinks Kierkegaard, but is accorded meaning. As Friedrich Gogarten has reminded us, is not meaning, like honor, something accorded us by another? Also, contrary to Nietzsche and Sartre, the absolute is not a rationally projected concept vulnerable to tearing down as readily as it can be built up but is the qualitatively different Ultimate, which supercedes all finite conceptualizations. Only by orientation in such an Ultimate can the self transcend itself, find meaning and realize true selfhood, for only in the existential Moment does one find a relevant truth to which he can give himself unstintedly. Anything less would be either self-defeat or idolatry.

Paul Tillich is in fundamental agreement with Kierkegaard. For him the revelatory encounter with the Absolute or Ultimate is the answer to every man's "ultimate concern" and the realization of true being or "new being." Such a self-transcendence reintroduces the self to the "ground of (his) being" from which his existence has been psychologically and spiritually estranged. The new perspective gives the self "the courage to be," says Tillich, the courage to be one's true self, unmasked and creatively fulfilling.

Psychiatrist Earl Loomis recognizes in a way that psychiatrist Eric Fromm does not that we must face up to the despairing and neurotically estranged "self in hell." Not to do so is to fail to realize the "self in communion" -- the transcended self who can now give himself to others. Only by a Kierkegaardian "curing of the split condition" can man transcend himself and extend agape, a self-giving love, to others, thinks Loomis. The spirit of tjhis is much in keeping with Kierkegaard's book Purity of Heart.

Kierkegaard provocatively insists that commitment to the will of God can even override or supercede the demands of ethics. All rational casuistry is deficient, because it is static in its finitude and fails to be obeisant directly to the Absolute. It places rules into the divine-human relationship that fail to allow for exceptions and that fall short of the divine command that on a faith-conditioned basis needs no alien interpretation. In this respect ethics is only a reflective preparation that needs to be surpassed by a commitment of faith that makes for a freedom of obedience and love, a freedom to respect yet to rise above the ethical by commitment to the Absolute.

Notes

1. Søren Kierkegaard, Journals, p.98. Cf. Hegel, The Phenomenoloty of Mind, p.798.
2. Kierkegaard, Concluding Unscientific Postscript, pp.182, 306. Journals, 44ff, 144, Søren Kierkegaard, Training in Christianity, pp.87, 91, Cf. Martin Heidegger, Existence and Being, p.331.
3. Søren Kierkegaard, Either/Or, Vol. II, pp.177, 191; Concluding Unscientific Postscript, pp.182, 306.
4. Søren Kierkegaard, The Journals, 185f, 197ff, 205, 209ff, 212, 231ff, 253f.
5. Søren Kierkegaard, Concluding Unscientific Postscript, pp.49f, 52f, 62, 66, 115f, 202, 309-350, 440, 498-502; For Self-Examination, pp.44-46; Concept of Dread, p.81f. Stages on Life's Way, third stage, Religiousness 'B', p.399-403.
6. Søren Kierkegaard, Journals, pp.63-73, 129; Fear and Trembling, pp.66-73. Re "the knight of faith," see p.86; Concluding Unscientific Postscript, pp.84, 95, 176, 183. Re. "paradoxes" see pp.176, 310, 350 and Journals, pp.58, 122, 139.
7. Søren Kierkegaard, On Authority and Revelation, p.57ff; Sickness Unto Death, p.149, 230; Attack Upon Christendom, p.144; Journals, pp.98, 129.
8. Søren Kierkegaard, Concluding Unscientific Postscript, p.85.
9. Ibid, pp.95, 176, 183.
10. Søren Kierkegaard, Journals, pp.121, 123ff, 133ff, 187, 191.
11. Ibid, pp.98, 172f, 219. Cf. Training in Christianity, pp.45, 67, 95, 31, 98, Cf. Concluding Unscientific Postscript, p.409; Journals, pp.98, 219.
12. Søren Kierkegaard, Journals, p.139; Sickness Unto Death; Stages on Life's Way, p.399-405; Edifying Discourses, p.15; Concluding Unscientific Postscript, pp.91, 94f; Cf. Attack Upon Christendom, pp.162-165.
13. Cf. note no. 6 above.
14. Søren Kierkegaard, Concluding Unscientific Postscript, pp.107, 178, 217, 213, 275, 437.
15. Søren Kierkegaard, Either/Or, Vol. II, p.216.
16. Søren Kierkegaard, Training in Christianity, pp.201f, 195; Journals, pp.151, 167.
17. Kant had place for both transcendence and grace in his Religion Within the Bounds of Reason.
18. Søren Kierkegaard, Either/Or, Vol. II, p.216, Cf. p.177, 181.
19. Søren Kierkegaard, Journals, pp.53, 59, 68, 67-69. Cf. Concept of Dread, p.35f, 75, 78; Fear and Trembling; Sickness Unto Death, Pt. I, p.146ff, For Self-Examination, pp.35-74; Concluding Unscientific Postscript, p.505-508.
20. Cf. note No. 1 above.
21. Søren Kierkegaard, Fear and Trembling, pp.33, 64, 67. Cf. Journals, p.120; Cf. The Point of View, pp.29, 33, 35.

22. Søren Kierkegaard, Concluding Unscientific Postscript, p.85.
23. Cf. note No. 2 above.
24. Søren Kierkegaard, Either/Or, Vol. II, p.279.
25. Søren Kierkegaard, Edifying Discourses, p.15.
26. Søren Kierkegaard, Fear and Trembling, theme.
27. Søren Kierkegaard, Stages on Life's Way, 3rd stage, "Religiousness 'B'."
28. Søren Kierkegaard, Concluding Unscientific Postscript, p.309; Journals, p.117.
29. Søren Kierkegaard, Purity of Heart, thesis, pp.58, 79.
30. Ibid.

The Sketch of Friedrich Nietzsche

Friedrich Nietzsche (1844-1900) was born in Prussia of Germany and educated at the universities of Bonn and Leipzig. His basic profession was as a teacher of philology while also a classical scholar and philosopher stressing human existence. He was the son of a Lutheran minister who died at an early age, which led to the son being raised by his mother and two aunts and later cared for by his sister when be became ill. Nietzsche's writings include <u>The Birth of Tragedy</u>, <u>Thus Spake Zarathustra</u>, <u>Beyond Good and Evil</u>, and <u>Toward a Geneology of Morals</u>. Appealing to power Nietzsche attacked Christianity as too tender even as he attacked democracy in general and feminism and socialism in particular. Stressing his "God is dead" doctrine he appealed to people to be strong, virile and powerful over one another. Those who would subscribe to such would be a superior people (Übermensch or Superman) who would prove more noble. After teaching ten years at the University of Basil in Switzerland he retired due to ill health but continued his writings. Eventually he broke down mentally and never recovered.

The Ethics of Friedrich Nietzsche

Usually regarded as an existentialist because of his down-to-earth individualism, Friedrich Nietzsche is often regarded, too, as a radical thinker. One interpreter of his views labels him a "mad prophet" due to his heated attacks on all forms of systematic idealisms in philosophy and religion, also his repudiation of so much that is conventional in society. Yet, despite his reactionary type of thought, Nietzsche is also constructive and provocative in many of his aphoristic assertions.

Nietzsche broke away from his Christian background and resisted much that was indigenous to the pro-Christian culture of Europe. To him European civilization was weak and decadent due to its idealism. Rejecting such thought Nietzsche held that all truth is relative in a changing world, much like the pragmatists of the following generation. From his youth Nietzsche envied military prowess and glamour and he accepted the soldier as his hero. Belonging to the era of Napoleon III, he envied the power that militarism portrayed. Also in keeping with the rise of Darwinism he liked the idea of the survival of the fittest. The two factors seemed to coalesce in favor of the evolutionary struggle as a struggle for power much in keeping with a nature "red in tooth and claw." For Nietzsche, then, any form of idealism or Christian ethics would have to be at odds with nature. European culture would have to be wrong being based on schemes that looked back to four Jews: Jesus, Peter, Paul and Mary.

True progress, Nietzsche believed, could be realized only by imitating nature's processes as well as in combating them, the underlying phenomenon being one of force against force, i.e. power-seeking. This would allow for neither an acquiescence to nature nor a form of benevolent conduct but a struggle both within and against nature. Why? It is nature's way. Progress, then, is not an inevitable move toward an end but a power struggle of one set of forces versus another. A Darwinian view of nature, this is also basic to the nature of man in his social conduct. In short, man is a microcosm who is against the macrocosm to which he belongs.

European morality, if continued, Nietzsche maintained, would lead to the collapse of Western civilization. To avert such a disaster the interim would call for a general reversal to an emphasis upon strength. The Judaeo-Christian love ethics would have to be offset by an emphasis upon power-seeking.[1] Realistically, this would in no way foster altruistic interests. In fact, for Nietzsche there is a kind of camouflaged will-to-power even behind all morality and love. Instinctively men seek power, and it is most intelligent of them to conform to such a drive. Strong men have strong wills. The true ethics, then, is biological in nature. Thus the Judaeo-Christian ethics must be reversed along with Greek rationalism. Pride must replace humility, and aloofness must replace sympathy and charity. Nietzsche calls this reversal "the transvaluation of values,"[2] yet he asserts that the common run of people are not equal to it, only the intelligentsia, the aristocracy, who are truly free.

In his book <u>The Genealogy of Morals</u> Nietzsche traces society's perversion of natural impulse back to St. Paul. Christian morality, he says, is the perversion of every wholesome instinct, because it caters to mercy and pity. The under-privileged Jews began "the slave revolt in morals" daring to invert the aristocratic Roman equation of the good with what is noble, powerful beautiful and happy. The counterpart of the latter gave blessing to the poor, powerless and weak and sickly. Such an effeminate morality enhanced the position of the really cursed people, said Nietzsche. In contrast an ethics of masculine aristocracy is to be hailed with the nobleman applauded over the commoner.[3] Democracy has favored the ignoble commoner so that the weak can subdue the strong, who put the premium on struggle and warfare. Contemporaruy society has come to reflect this "slave morality" of the weak masses. "Faith, hope and love thrive where man has grown tame." Conscience has come to overrule instincts. Nietzsche actually went so far as to say, "No act of violence, rape, exploitation, is intrinsically 'unjust,' since life itself is violent, rapacious, exploitive, and destructive..." Any legal system demoralizes life.

Nietzsche carried his argument to its logical conclusion. The Church would have to be jolted into the realization of what kind of world this is. Society in general is based on moral pretentiousness. Most people do not really believe the ethics they hold from either Jesus or the Greek philosophers and should stop bluffing. Beneath their cosmetic morality is a disguised belief in competition and "the will to power." Nietzsche even believed that war is the "mother of great virtues" bringing forth what is noblest in men. In the face of these contentions Nietzsche overtly identified himself with the "Anti-Christ."[4] Since Europeans are not living up to their professed moral principles, it were better that they drop them. On the positive side, Nietzsche was making a provocative denunciation of hypocrisy while appealing to an honest search for power.

A people who would consistently seek power, Nietzsche believed, would become a superior people. They would become Übermensch or Superman, free spirits flexing their strength and admiring their unusual worth and mastery of nature. True morality condones and promotes this sense of power, thinks Nietzsche, for it is doing what comes naturally from within the cruel contest of nature's forces. The true morality accepts and affirms life as it is. Thus Nietzsche castigates any and all who preach or teach a love ethic, for it is a denial of life as it is in nature. Philosophers are also wrong who stress that man is a rational animal. Instead of exalting reason, Nietzsche stresses existentially the preeminence of will, for to him it is basic to the will-to-power.[5]

A strong-willed people are ready for a "master morality," to wipe away the "slave morality," thinks Nietzsche. In a society of masters the moral distinction between good and evil disappears. Superman lives beyond good and evil. In such a master race each person cultivates self-mastry by both psychical and physical power. He tries to do as he pleases, and he has duties only to his equals. Enemies are a wholesome outlet for his emotions. Whereas the commoners are all liars, the aristocrats are honest in their power-seeking and creating of their own values.[6] Unlike democracy and Christian ethics, the "inequality of rights" is stressed. Rights must be earned, not taken for granted.

Nietzsche blames Christianity for denouncing his life-affirming values such as free sex, the lust to rule and selfishness. It is due mainly to the Christian contempt for the body and the concept of sin fostered by a priestly religion.[7]

Thus a transvaluation of values is called for, true happiness being the attainment of power in whatever form. "God is dead" said Nietzsche in Thus Spake Zarathustra "We have killed him," said one of the characters implying that belief in God is irrational.[8] In fact, all metaphysics is inane.

As a proponent of a new cultural revolt Nietzsche looked to the Renaissance as an earlier attempt to relinquish religious values in favor of human self-sufficiency. To him the transvaluation of values would make for a more noble individuality among men. Nietzsche blamed German idealists, especially Kant and Hegel, for stopping the Renaissance trends toward a freer, rebellious type of man.[9] He also blamed Luther for re-raising the doctrine of original sin and stopping the Renaissance philosophy of human self-sufficiency and for renewing the Church, which the Renaissance humanism had begun to undermine upon resisting much in medieval Scholasticism.[10] Nietzsche also broke with his friend Richard Wagner, whose music, he believed, was still Christian in its sensitivity to sin and man's need of salvation.[11] The Christian ethic in general was deemed "sickly," and a poison that tends to sterilize man of his virility as a power-seeker. It is a "slave-morality," said Nietzsche, which undermines the "master-morality."[12] The latter belongs to the noble elite of society, who determine the real values; if they help the unfortunate it is not out of sympathy but the superabundance of power and the arousal of fear. The very distinction of good and evil is the "invention of slaves" who, motivated by resentment, call evil what the aristocrats-in-power honor most.[13] The slave mentality denies the value of the egoism of these masters. Similarly, Nietzsche condemns the ideals of peace and social equality.[14] Competition is accepted as conducive to power. Suffering adds to the nobility of the aristocrats, who, unlike the masses can appreciate it.[15] Moral philosophers deny true life.[16] True philosophers avoid egalitarianism in favor of aristocratic individualism with its true freedom. The latter alone keeps people fit to live by the true philosophy of power;[17] they live dangerously but creatively.[18]

The European hypocrisy attacked by Nietzsche is such that while professing altruistic, benevolent and sacrificial principles people actually practice mendaciously a different code in politics and commerce.[19] The really "good" ideals, according to Nietzsche, originated with the Aryans and Goths who saw themselves better than the peasants and barbarians. As lordly castes they concocted values in their own interests while seeking to dominate others. Their "true" morality was one of power based on an instinctive, irrational perspective contrary to any rationally projected idealism, which places reason above instinct. The result is the "enslavement" of many people under their own "slave morality," which seeks to undermine the powerful by an appeal to love and pity.

Socrates, thinks Nietzsche, helped turn the tables in favor of the slave morality by representing the weakened herd, which was revolting against its masters. Socrates established a rational outlook that offset the instincts and which, to Nietzsche, spelled decadence.[20] But an earlier revolt began with the Jews, who, too, developed idealistic values designed, he says, to curtail their Roman masters and get revenge in a clever indirect manner. Christianity superceded this campaign in a climax focused on Jesus' love ethics and bringing of salvation to the underprivileged. The result of this trend was the derogation of those in power.[21]

Though Nietzsche hails Renaissance man as a rebel against forces that challenge his sufficiency he also shows his disgust with man, the worm, who lets himself be dominated by others. The doctrine of original sin, he thinks, has contributed to this self-depreciation.[22] This competes with Superman, so modern man must be surpassed as he develops the arts of retaliation. Revolutions are not good if they favor the masses. Aristocrats must be catered to, a kind of people who are hard on themselves, a point in common with Kierkegaard from a different standpoint.

With his sudden flashes of insight Nietzsche was not all wrong, even to those who differ with him. He was right in protesting the inconsistent bourgeois moralism of his day. The conventional goodness of avoiding harm to oneself and others was a threat to true greatness, true individualism and nobility. Unless his sister-in-law has misled us, Nietzsche claimed anti-Semitism was a "mendacious race swindle." He definitely felt totalitarian systems were wrong for regimenting individuals. Despite extolling power he scorned the embodiment of it in Bismark's policy of "blood and iron." No single nationalism has embodied power properly, he felt. A United States of Europe, he said, would be advisable, though by military conquest and not by socialistic structure. Yet democracy is too effiminate as a "leveller" of people.[23] Influenced by Schopenhauer, Nietzsche stressed the will of man over reason and was opposed to a Marxian economic determinism. He preferred a Platonic "soldier state" in which the rulers are philosopher-statesmen. He felt that there was a place for pleasure and art and freedom of thought, while being against asceticism and puritanism. Humility, he felt, is only a puritanical covering for the unwillingness to enjoy the world.

Critically, however, Nietzsche failed to see how the lust for power may be the outcome of fear and meaninglessness. He failed to see that his aristocracy may lead to a stagnant hereditary situation.[24] He failed to see that the Renaissance was not led by men of aristocracy but by men like Voltaire and Erasmus who were middle-class humanists. Nietzsche became the philosopher whose views gave most immediate support to the Third Reich as Hitler adapted his doctrine of Superman while holding the Jews and French to be degenerates; however, Nietzsche would not have condoned the Nazi subservience of the individual to the state.

Philosophically, Nietzsche's thought was a type of skepticism marked by the assumption that truth is relative and cannot be a coherent scheme. Here he is pro-existentialist. Human existence is unsystematic and strongly centered in free will. The true philosopher, he thinks, does not discover values but makes his own, much like the view of Jean-Paul Sartre. In asserting "God is dead" Nietzsche makes a sweeping denial of all eternal, unchanging universals or ideals. His nihilistic position supports what many regard as the hopeless and meaningless aspects of the present age. The undergirding will-to-power has a variety of guises, however, sometimes as sheer domination, sometimes as a form of integrity or areté, sometimes as a hubris of self-glorification, sometimes a self-overcoming. Basically, however, it subordinates reason to will.

Nietzsche was existential in that he so much as said, "Be yourself." And you are unique.[26] It can be contended, however, that Nietzsche is an incomplete existentialist, for he fails to stay by the holistic view of the self. What of man's will to benevolence? What is the end or ultimate purpose even of the will-to-power? Nietzsche seems to dislike power in the hands of the commoners as when in a state of revolution. Natural urges are held to be perfectly right. Thus Nietzsche fails to see the value of the spiritual regeneration of human nature as taught in the Bible; a re-motivated will is foreign to him. While he recognized a form of existential self-transcendence and self-fulfillment, it was entirely egocentric in form and practice failing to have a place for self-sacrifice. He did not like the idea of the elite having to relate or conform to the majority in a levelling democracy. Logically speaking, he was against education for the masses, and he was against socialism as another form of social levelling. Though Nietzsche has sought the meaning of life he has really not found the answer, as Karl Heim has observed.[27]

Giving priority to the individual's will was basic to Nietzsche's pro-existential thought. In this respect he had much in common with Kierkegaard and subsequent existentialists. But he also has something in common here with Kant's place for will, despite his rejection of Kant's idealistic ethics of duty. But Nietzsche's view of the will is different. "Conscious will is but the expression of the unconscious ...judgments emanating from our muscles...," he states, implying not so much a naked free will as a will linked with power-seeking. In this respect Nietzsche, unlike Kant, refuses to elevate reason over will. He uses the Greek gods, Dionysus and Apollo, to express the relationship of will to reason. Dionysus, a more impulsive and passionate, is the symbol of a less disciplined will to power.[28] Apollo, representing reason, becomes an instrument of the will to power, supporting, but not subduing, the Dionysian impulsive element, which to Nietzsche is basic.[29] Then, too, Nietzsche fails to see what Kant saw to be the evil propensity in man. The natural, impulsive man was assumed to be good. Lacking anything comparable to the I-thou relationship stressed by Buber, Nietzsche leaves man a loner and a rebel at that.[30] He fails to see what the self owes to other selves in being an individual and stultifies the otherwise social dimensions and potentialities of man.

As already suggested, Nietzsche had provocative insights and was not all wrong, especially in attacking bourgeois hypocracies. Despite some of the rather negative views expressed above, Nietzsche is to be credited with something quite positive. It is his affirmation of life. Much in contrast to the idealistic systems of philosophy and the Judaeo-Christian perspective, which in his opinion were negations of life, Nietzsche affirms life in this world as a temporal existence to be taken seriously. The old morality was too other-worldly and held men down and looking away from mundane existence, he felt, especially the doctrine of original sin held by Christian orthodoxy. His "God is dead" aphorism was meant to suggest a nihiliam based on the collapse of the old metaphysics and ethics. Even so, Nietzsche believed that men need values, those of a life-affirming type. His Übermensch, Superman or Overman theory intended this, as it stresses a master morality based on power-seeking. As such it is meant to be a creative, aesthetic view of life which is held to be the highest level thereof. Individualistically, it is a self-seeking and disciplined level, which cretively combines passion and reason. As such it is both passionately Dionysian and rationally Apollinarian.

As an affirmation of the self, Nietzsche's philosophy sees self-fulfillment belonging strictly to this temporal life with no place for religious views of the afterlife lest self-affirmation of life be missed. However, Nietzsche is in error, for he utterly fails to see the life-affirming nature of the religiously regenerated man. He sees only the negative side of Christianity and not how this leads to the positive side of redeemed manhood as a fulfilled selfhood. In this respect Nietzsche had much to learn from Kierkegaard's existentialism, which saw self-sufficient men coming to despair, which as the negative stage of existence opens up the positive stage through the existential encounter with the divine Absolute making for good will and "purity of heart."

Another positive feature of Nietzsche's philosophy is that his ethics is not merely a set of principles or theories. It is a matter of performance, not only of willing but doing. "If Nietzsche often seems to come up empty-handed and obscurely calls for 'the creation of new values,' it is because he finds himself rejecting principles without a set of practices to fall back on."[31] This at least was a demand that we evaluate our values to see what role they play in society. But his opposition to Christianity as too other-worldly is countermanded today by Christian movements which are this-worldly in appealing to the "secularizatin" (not secularism) of things sacred. In attacking bourgeois morality Nietzsche was trying to appeal to excellence and the fulfillment of a people's potential through creativity and a revised, though questionable, set of values. At its best, this implied an ethics of life-affirming character rather than elitist projections. It is for the few, not the many. As Walter Kaufmann has put it, Nietzsche "challenges the reader not so much to agree or disagree as to grow."[32]

Notes

1. Friedrich Nietzsche, The Will to Power, sects. 200, 201, 204, 249; Nietzsche, Beyond Good and Evil, no. 62, 259.
2. The Will to Power, nos. 1007, 1009, 1014.
3. Ibid, no. 54, 59.
4. Ibid, no. 249; Beyond Good and Evil, 162; Will to Power, 3rd essay, 24.
5. Friedrich Nietzsche, The Genealogy of Morals, 1st essay.
6. Ibid, 1st essay, 2, 7, 8; third essay 10.
7. Ibid, 1st essay, 6; third essay, 9; "The Gay Science" ed. by Kaufmann, ed. Existentialism From Doestoevsky to Sartre, p.105.
8. Friedrich Nietzsche, Thus Spake Zarathustra, pp.6, 104, 105.
9. Geneology of Morals, 2nd essay, 3.
10. Ibid, 2nd essay, 1.
11. Ibid, 3rd essay, 2.
12. The Will to Power, 59.
13. Beyond Good and Evil, 260; Genealogy of Morals, 3rd essay, 4, 10, 11, 24.
14. Ibid, 259.
15. Friedrich Nietzsche, Ecce Homo, 2; Beyond Good and Evil, 44.
16. The Will to Power, 428, 434, 461.
17. Beyond Good and Evil, 230.
18. Genealogy of Morals, Preface, 4; 1st essay 2, 4, 5, 7; 2nd essay, 16.
19. The Will to Power, 200, 201, 204, 244; Beyond Good and Evil, 62.
20. Ecce Homo, 1, 2; Genealogy of Morals, 1st essay, 1; 3rd essay, 6.
21. Ibid, 1, 2; Genealogy of Morals, 4th essay, 9.
22. Genealogy of Morals, 2nd essay 10; 3rd essay 5, 4th essay, 8.
23. Beyond Good and Evil, 43, 44.
24. Philip Wheelright, A Critical Introduction to Ethics, pp.90, 85ff.
25. F. Nietzsche, "Concerning My Work as an Author," Existentialism from Doestovsky to Sartre, ed. by Walter Kaufmann, p.93ff.
26. F. Nietzsche, "Live Dangerously," Ibid (loc cit), p.101.
27. Karl Heim, Christian Faith and Natural Science, p.17.
28. Genealogy of Morals, Preface, 2; Ecce Homo, 1, 2.
29. Ecce Home, 1, 2.
30. Albert Camus, The Rebel, in which the author creatively amplifies the meaning of "rebel."
31. Robert C. Solomon, "A More Severe Morality," Nietzsche As An Affirmative Thinker, ed. by Y. Yovel, Martinas NW Huff Publishers, 1986, p.8.
32. Walter Kaufmann, Introduction, The Portable Nietzsche, Viking Press, New York, 1968, p.19.

The Sketch of Jean-Paul Sartre

Jean-Paul Sartre (1905-1980) was born in Paris and educated at the Ecole Normale Supérieure. Even in his youth he showed the ability to express himself literarily. He is most known for his short stories and plays but also for his philosophical works including his tome <u>Being and Nothingness</u> and <u>Existentialism and Humanism</u>, his most noted work. His most noted play is entitled <u>No Exit</u>. Other works include a play <u>The Flies</u> and a novel, <u>Nausea</u>. They tend to accentuate the absurdity of human existence. After 1939 Sartre became a leader of French intellectual life. He stressed that the individual must "make himself" or find his own meaning and essence. He is perfectly free and responsible for his existence. During World War II Sartre served in the French army and the French underground or Resistance against Germany. Strong on the belief in moral freedom he was pro-democratic with some later leanings toward a socialist economy. In 1964 he refused to accept the Nobel Prize in literature due to his political philosophy.

The Ethics of Jean-Paul Sartre

Though most noted as a literary existentialist, who wrote plays and short stories, Jean-Paul Sartre was also a philosopher of renown. Basically, he was a critical realist of sorts with much in common with Kant's phenomenalism while also having a strong bent toward the phenomenology of Husserl.

For Sartre most knowledge is relative and all idealism rejected. In his literary works he stressed the absurdity of human existence and the world in general. As he said in his play, No exit, "Hell is other people." Yet Sartre was not a materialist, and he did not accept scientific reductionism any more than rationalism. Man was to him of nature but not abandoned to nature, for he was transcendent of nature. Man is pour soi (for itself), not merely en soi (in itself).[1] He is conscious subject, not object; subject is more than natural process, more than a thing or object. One of the marked features of pour soi is moral freedom of choice; another is self-transcendence in the form of self-examination and self-questioning. These factors are important to ethical considerations.

Basic to the subject-self is consciousness, which is both self-consciousness as well as what is aware of the outside world. Consciousness is primary, lest the objects around us be of no consequence. At this point Sartre is phenomenological. Furthermore, this conscious and free subject-self is the core of existence. "Existence precedes essence," said Sartre.[2] This implies that man's particularity is more basic than any universality, just as subjectivity supercedes objectivity and thatness is prior to whatness.[3] This is much like Heidegger's "a man" over "man" (der Mann versus das Man).

Sartre looked somewhat to Descartes, because of his basic Cogito and because he said, "Conquer yourself rather than the world."[4] Self-assertion and choice are central to the individuality of the existing self. Hence, concrete human being is primary as the seat of existence in contrast to the abstract essence of the rationalistic view of man. In fact, to Sartre there is no universal human nature. He said, "You make yourself." "You draw your own portrait."[5] Yet at times when addressing ethical issues Sartre almost betrays this principle when he says, "Choose for all mankind."[6] What he seems to mean, however, is that in making our decisions we should ethically keep in mind the welfare of others.

Sartre assumes the freedom, worth and dignity of men. Yet these factors center in man, the individual. "You make yourself," Sartre stresses, implying that one's destiny is realizable only from within one's existence.[7] Whatever "whatness" or essence you may have is strictly a personal attainment, not a ready-made universal to subscribe to idealistically. Self-reliance and decision are absolutely necessary to the genuine selfhood of existence. There is no metaphysical security of any kind. Ethically, there are no universals, so one is strictly alone in the world. There are no ideals, Sartre stresses, since there is no God to think them.[8] So upon rejecting idealism Sartre rejects God, for though he agrees with Kierkegaard's rejection of the God of the Scholastics,[9] he misses what Kierkegaard saw at this point, viz that God is the Absolute beyond all finite or relative conceptualizations. Thus to Sartre there is neither universal humanity nor an ideal man to emulate or identify with.[10] Each individual must make the most of his finitude. In fact, to rely on another person's advise or an institution's authority is not a genuine choice or decision.[11] At the same time, one should not simply rest his case in "the quietism of despair,"[12] for no choice is still a choice.[13]

Yet, for Sartre human life has its possibilities due to its freedom. All forms of determinism, whether scientific, rationalistic or religious, are to be rejected while free will, choice and self-assertion in the face of alternatives are to be unleashed upon making oneself or realizing one's possibilities. Yet one is on his own, alone and lonely at that, in the face of an outer world that threatens one's individuality.[14] Social conformity is bad, for, as Kierkegaard said, "the crowd is untruth," and the role-playing "masks must come off."

Decision is the center of human existence. Though social forces work upon us, philosophically it is wrong to settle for necessitative or deterministic views of existence. They never dissolve human freedom. Too often sociological arguments in favor of either heredity or environment by-pass the role of moral freedom. Often appeals thereto are forms of excuse-making. What Sartre calls the "paradox of freedom" is that freedom is necessary to be a responsible moral person, and it is essential to human dignity saving man from being either a beast or an object. Man, says Sartre, is "condemned to be free"[15] which means that whether one likes it or not he is free and responsible. Also, a free person encounters various forms of resistance, yet resistance itself implies its opposite, which is freedom. Peer pressures, for instance, are thrust upon a free personality under their constraints. Such freedom under constraints is all the more reason why the individual is so often a lonely and tragic figure. Massive forces threaten to undo his freedom while assuming it. Even so, Sartre stresses that we should never blame deterministic forces like heredity and environment or peer pressures for what we become. To do so is to reduce reponsibility and true selfhood.

Yet Sartre allows for the moral relativism of the self. It is not only due to freedom in given circumstances but a relatively conditioned conscience. Conscience is deemed a very important aspect of the self-transcendence of the self and must be respected despite its relative conditioning, because it is a basic aspect of the self to which one's free will must subscribe if integrity is to be maintained and dignity or self-respect realized. Despite its relativism, Sartre tries to respect the role of conscience about as much as Kant did with his duty-based universalism. Though every man's conscience is different, it is inwardly an authoritative feature of the self and not to be ignored. It is one of the basic marks of self-transcendence and subjectivity. One must respect his conscience to be true to himself. But, critically speaking, it can be contended that Sartre's view of conscience is parasitical in that a conscience is influenced by other men's philosophies and religions. The Sartrean man's conscience is not self-sufficient but dependent, then, upon the moral views of others. Then, too, Sartre must be seen to be wrong for condemning the coward,[16] whose conscience may be just as legitimate as anyone elses on Sartre's terms.

Sartre's moral relativism is all the more acute in view of his rejection of God, ideals and universals.[17] He is pro-Nietzscheon here, for Nietzsche said, "God is dead." "We have killed him," said one of Nietzsche's characters, meaning that rationalistic proofs of God are unacceptable. Yet Sartre is not happy about his atheism with its lack of an absolute ideal or universal.[18] Every man, then, is his own absolute, if not his own God. Surrounded by an absurd world, all for him is chance or accident in a completely pluralistic world lacking any form of system -- except for what one makes of himself, which is no accident. Nominalism and relativism take over in a non-metaphysical view of things. Sartre rules out any and all forms of rationally objective ontology. All we can rely on is our own subjective being based on a pour soi that makes itself in its finitude.

Such an existence in such a world implies no purpose, goal or end to life; it is absurdly meaningless and tragic with no form of destiny in view beyond a self-made existence. The only purpose in life is self-made purpose. Values are not objective but strictly man-made.[20] Thus Sartre is utterly humanistic in the sense that men experience only things relative to their consciousness, there being no unseen or hidden essence behind them and no ideals to pursue, contrary to both Plato and Kant. Sartre, then, is epistemologically skeptical about all ontological theories based on reason. Yet Sartre says, much in keeping with Husserl's phenomenology, that we intuit things as they are i.e. their essences beyond the empirical perception thereof. Settling for what he calls a "phenomenological ontology" Sartre states that our concrete existence (particular being) is the one thing we really know, i.e. the "me" of our particularity, which we intuitively discern.

Such an ontology is not capable in itself of unveiling ethical principles. Its indicatives do not give rise to moral imperatives. But by virtue of the fact that this phenomonological ontology makes for the "for-itself" conscious subject it gives occasion to values, which "haunt" subjectivity. Even existential psychoanalysis entails moral issues, since "it releases to us the ethical meaning of various human projects." In this context Sartre states, "Man makes himself man in order to be God, and selfness considered from this point of view can appear to be an egoism."[21] Human existence is an egoism, because it is a passion of self-interest, yet existential psychoanalysis helps reveal to a person that he is the moral agent, the "being by whom values exist."[22]

Sartre has a holistic view of the self in that a person is an existential whole not reducible to his parts.[23] Here Sartre is against scientific reductionism represented, for instance, in behavioristic psychology while also being anti-Greek, since the Greek philosophers stressed man's reason almost as though it were the only significant feature of man. Sartre holds this view quite like most existentialists. In fact this holistic view of man is one of the most distinctive emphases of existentialist philosophy, being something overlooked by practically every other brand of philosophy.

Man is also beyond good and evil in the senses observed by most historical philosophy. Good and evil are relative to the present situation and not reducible to a code. Sartre blames religion for clinging to the Platonic immutable view of the Good, thus making for passé legalisms. Sartre says man makes his own good or evil in relation to his freedom and degree of self-integrity. Again, man makes his own values and is his own absolute.[24] Yet men need each other, for they are social beings and can make for community. Fundamental to this accomplishment is mutual respect. We must respect each other, says Sartre, for as selves we are all in the same condition. Critically, however, it can be said that Sartre's ethics is such that he provides no distinctive grounds for respecting each other and choosing for all mankind. Why did he not join Nietzsche in the appeal to power-seeking? Self-realization, Sartre stressed, is from within the social milieu and includes service to one's fellows. But here Sartre is weak having no undergirding love ethic making repect for others truly feasible. He says every man should carry "the weight of the whole world on his shoulders" in that is is responsible for it.[25] But on what basis? is the underlying question, especially in the face of Sartre's assertion that it is immoral to rely on the ideals of the past.

The self's goal in his concrete existence is a more ideal self, a heightened consciousness of being free and responsible. Like the avid golfer's pursuit, this is an endless quest. Though men may fail, they can retain their integrity amidst failure as they pursue the fulfillment of their possibilities looking to the future with a sense of responsibility for it.[26]

Despite the self's solitude in its choices and decisions, the self can know a "solidarity" with others, as Sartre learned through the war effort of the '40s. With it came an awareness of the interdependence of human destinies. At these points Sartre's earlier individualism was modified socially. He even came to accept the socialist economics as the best, though he rejected Communist materialism. Also, Communism, he saw, fails to protect the uniqueness of the individual giving him minimal significance only as he is subservient to the state. To Sartre Communism is too compulsory and dogmatic, and, to the contrary, he sees that man is more than a product of socio-economic forces. Man is a project in the making and is responsible for his dignity.

Many of Sartre's interpreters, as William Barrett has observed, think Sartre's brand of existentialism is too bleak and discouraging, so they turn to religion, often religious existentialism. In either case the going is hard, as it should be, suggests Barrett.[27] Often a coming to understand and appreciate Kierkegaard's encounter with the Absolute beyond all our relativisms becomes the pivot of the turning point, whereupon the interpreter becomes amenable to the thinking of religious existentialists like Berdyaev, Marcel, Buber, Tillich, Jaspers and/or Barth, not to overlook the psychoanalist Viktor Frankl.

Notes

1. Jean-Paul Sartre, Being and Nothingness, p.617ff.
2. Ibid, Pt. Chapter I. Cf. Sartre, Existentialism and Humanism, pp.26, 28f. Cf. Sartre, Existentialism and Human Emotions, pp.13, 16.
3. Being and Nothingness, Pt. II, Chapter I.
4. Sartre, Existentialism and Humanism, p.39. Cf. Sartre, Existentialism and Human Emotions, p.29f.
5. Sartre, Existentialism and Humanism, p.42.
6. Ibid, p.29f. Cf. Existentialism and Human Emotions, pp.16, 18.
7. Existentialism and Human Emotions, p.17.
8. Ibid, p.22.
9. Sartre, Being and Nothingness, p.xxviii
10. Existentialism and Humanism, p.48.
11. Existentialism and Humanism, pp.35, 37, 42. Cf. Existentialism and Human Emotions, p.24.
12. Ibid, pp.23, 25. Cf. Existentialism and Humanism, pp.23, 24, 41, 44. Cf. Existentialism and Human Emotions, p.4.
13. Ibid, p.48. Cf. p.50.
14. Existentialism and Human Emotions, p.23.
15. Existentialism and Humanism, p.34. Cf. Existentialism and Human Emotions, p.23.
16. Ibid, p.43.
17. Sartre, Existentialism, pp.16-20. Cf. Existentialism and Humanism, p.23, 34, 36.
18. Being and Nothingness, p.624. Existentialism and Humanism, pp.23, 33, 56.
19. Existentialism and Humanism, p.54.
20. Existentialism and Human Emotions, the theme of this book.
21. Being and Nothingness, p.626. Cf. Existentialism and Human Emotions, p.91f. Cf. pp.60, 68.
22. Ibid, p.627.
23. Existentialism and Human Emotions, p.68.
24. Existentialism and Humanism, p.54f.
25. Being and Nothingness, pp.553f. Cf. p.489.
26. Existentialism and Human Emotions, p.23f.
27. William Barrett, Irrational Man, p.263.

The Sketch of Joseph Fletcher

Joseph F. Fletcher was born in 1905 in Newark, N.J. and in 1925 received an A.B. degree from West Virginia University, in 1929 a B.D. from Berkeley Divinity School and in 1932 an S.T.D. from the University of London. He was ordained in the Protestant Episcopal Church in 1929 and became Dean of the Graduate School of Applied Religion in Cincinnati, 1936-1944, and Dean of St. Paul's Cathedral in Cincinnati. He became professor of pastoral theology and Christian ethics at Episcopal Theological School, Cambridge, Mass., 1944-1970. From 1970-77 he was professor of medical ethics at the University of Virginia. Earlier he held visiting positions abroad in the West Indies and Japan. In 1964-65 Fletcher was a lecturer at Harvard Divinity School and a visiting fellow at Cambridge University, 1967-1968. Among his several books are <u>The Church and Industry</u>, 1930, <u>Morals and Medicine</u>, 1954, <u>The New Morality</u>, 1966, and his most influential book, <u>Situation Ethics</u>, 1966. He has been a writer for a number of journals in theology and medicine. His greatest impact lay in his endeavors to correlate medical and religious ethics with respect for both morel absolutes and life situations.

The Ethics of Joseph Fletcher

For over two decades the so-called "situation ethics" of Joseph Fletcher has been gaining prominence in the United States and the United Kingdom. It is also known as "the new morality." Basically, it is a combination of the Christian ethics of love and respect for the relativistic situations in which people often find themselves. Also it is the mid-point of two extremes, the one legalism, authoritarianism and/or codified morals; the other freedom from all norms apart from the existential moment of spontaneous decision. The mid-point is situation ethics wherein both poles are respected.[1]

Legalism has been common in Roman Catholic morality as well as some forms of Protestant pietism. The opposite view that is more free from absolute norms is recognized especially in the atheistic existentialism of Jean-Paul Sartre, who leaves the individual on his own to trust his relativistic conscience. Theology has at times drawn close to relativism in antinomianism or freedom from law. Whereas the first type of ethics is more fixed or binding, the latter accentuates the nature of authentic choice more than the rightness of an act, i.e. it wants the individual to be personally conscientious, whatever his decision, and not necessarily to act on the basis of pre-established objective norms, laws or codes that may not directly apply to the situation. Fletcher is quite amenable to the latter in the sense that there are times one must modify his principles in terms of what is right in the concrete situation.[2]

Situation ethics does respect the major ethical ideals or principles inherited from the past but is also sensitive to the need to make exceptions, especially when agápe or sacrificial love demands it, since the only universal good is love. This allows Joseph Fletcher to contend that an act is right or wrong according to the situation. If love serves a situation better than an absolute ideal or law does, then love should prevail. The main reason for this is that love is always directed to persons rather than to abstract principles aloof from life situations.[3]

Fletcher respects the existential self and the Nietzschean idea of the priority of the will of a person. In another sense he is Kierkegaardian for rejecting the sufficiency of abstract ideals. In yet another sense he is Augustinian, since love is the basis of virtue. As for the two extreme types of ethics, authoritarianism versus relativism or antinomianism, Fletcher sees paradoxically a measure of truth in both extremes. Legalists are correct in holding rules as rules of moral wisdom, which guide us, whereas their opponents, the relativists, are right in seeing the uniqueness of every situation of choice. But Fletcher rejects the idea that idealistic rules or codes are universal while also rejecting the idea that values rise solely out of relativistic human relations. While laws are not absolute, they do help us discover values when viewed in relation to the situations i.e. they may shed light on situations.[4]

In the main Fletcher believes that only as a person has a Godward reference will moral decisions be pure. The love of God and the love that is inspired, faithwise, in a person is essential to the highest moral motive and act. But the love of God as such is not an abstract notion or ideal, nor is it merely a sentimental emotion. It is a loving concern, a sacrificial spirit, first identified as God, who is Christly Agápe, and, second, identified with the loving response men make to God's love and, outwardly, toward their fellow men.[5] Certain conditions must be present, however, such as: 1. an awareness of the facts of the concrete situation, 2. a sensitivity to the consequences of a choice, and 3. a willingness to accept guidance from traditional norms.

While legalism may be too rigid or detached from a person's situation, the opposite extreme of antinomianism or total relativism may be as bad or worse, since it is almost unprincipled, usually, being inclined toward libertine and agnostic forms of action. Jean-Paul Sartre, for instance, says there are no generally valid principles or universals. There is no systematic fabric of existence for generalizing moral norms. Every situation is particular. There is neither norm nor norm-giver. "There are no universals, since no God to think them," says Sartre. No imperatives or "oughts" can rise from the indicative facts of existence. Here he is much like the positivists and avoids "the naturalistic fallacy," since the "ought" is not derived from the "is."[6]

Fletcher pleads for an ethics which is reducible to neither legalism nor relativism. Situation ethics is a middle-of-the road position. First, the love of God, while not abstract, is a norm of a sort; it implies sacrificial acts, and as a norm it is not antinomian. At the same time it sees how the moral principles of either philosophy or theology are not objective, absolute ideals, contrary to traditional legalisms. Yet both poles of emphasis help illuminate the concrete situation in which divine love is expressed. Ethical maxims or norms are still respected, then, but also they are sometimes compromised in a situation where love is better served. Agápe must have priority as the only universal. Not even the Ten Commandments are universal regardless of circumstances. There are times when you must do wrong to do right, so to speak, i.e. times when lying or stealing may be right. He tells the story of early settlers in Jefferson County at Long Run, Kentucky. It was a community of mostly Baptists. During an Indian raid the community was split between the lying and non-lying Baptists, when asked whether there were more children. The situation made the difference.

Situation ethics reminds liberal religious believers that morality, like the Sabbath, was made for man, not man for morality. Fletcher refuses to absolutize any normative principle lest it be idolatrous. At the same time he tries not to relativise the absolute so as to sterilize it. Men ought to live by the law of love, then, not the love of law.

Rules have their place, but they are not inviolable. Fletcher speaks illustratively of this saying good baseball and football have rules of good performance, such as: "on fourth down you must punt," but there are times when such rules may be broken, and the best players may know when. Greek thinking is more absolutistic; Biblical thinking of the prophetic type is more particular. The one is more contemplative or rational, the other more action-centered.

Situation ethics in general sees the uniqueness of situations and that they must be considered on their merits. Unless a moral judgment benefits persons it is either wrong or meaningless. This kind of ethics is highly individualistic, and some critics would say it does too little to take into consideration the social context or community. Perhaps so.

A more important criticism, it would seem, is that love is sometimes blind - even agápe love -- unless the individual who chooses to love is guided clearly and consistently by certain respected norms such as justice or righteousness. Most of the time this writer agrees with Fletcher in theory, but sometimes he is exasperated with some of Fletcher's illustrations of love-in-action, especially where matters of sex are germane to the case in point. Sometimes Fletcher allows <u>eros</u> to run nearly rampant in the name of agápe, as though the latter were unprincipled and he had forgotten his own respect for traditional maxims. This amounts to saying that Fletcher becomes too permissive at times.

In spite of Fletcher's emphasis upon love there are times when he leaves us wondering what it means to love. Also, if situation ethics should become typical practice in our society, would it not threaten the very legal structure, for no man's testimony would be dependable. Furthermore, there is no plan in the New Testament that says the Law of God is to be suspended by love but rather fulfilled. Love needs law to guide it. The situation ethicist recognizes the ambiguity of situations and what ought to be done but the tendency is to justify himself. For example, to have an abortion out of loving concern for every body's interest is not an evil act but a good one. Acting out of love makes it right. Harman Smith of Duke would say there may be times when abortion is the lesser of two evils, but it does entail wrong-doing and the wrong-doing must be faced, not effaced. Similarly, when a sniper shoots at a policeman and the latter shoots back, killing the sniper, the wrongness of the act must be faced as belonging paradoxically to the rightness of the act. Neither absoluteness nor relativism points to the whole truth.

Critically speaking, the cardinal factor to keep in mind respecting the situational approach to the ethics of Agápe is that, in keeping with the spirit of Jesus' example and teachings, the love motive is one of being hard on yourself while easy on others. Another important factor is that if it is to be consistently Christian, the new morality must be one of spiritual freedom but not permissive license. Though sensitive to concrete, complex situations and averse to forms of legalistic piety or idealistic puritanism, one who is motivated by Agápe does not resort to sheer antinomianism. He acts responsibly in love, but is not enslaved to a code, for he sees how love supersedes all law. A third factor is that the existential perspective of Agápe is a faith-commitment and not a public morality based on a neutral theory of rational universals. It must be consistently God-centered, hence, neither a rational nor empirical product based upon either reason, human nature or social experience. It is neither a universal ideal nor a utilitarian or pragmatic goal. Genuine moments of Agápe must be existentially motivated or intensified by personal faith in the revealed Logos of Love. Yet, fourthly, such moments always have a social reference, for love of this kind is never merely an idea and never functions in an egocentric vacuum but is born of an I-Thou relationship of a vertical, Godward kind, that it might express itself in outgoing I-thou relationships of a horizontal, social kind. The horizontal is the dimension of a love response to the vertical divine initiative, uniquely clarified by Christ. Nicholas Berdyaev has elucidated the social and cultural implications of this through his brilliant distinctions between legalistic ethics, redemptive ethics and creative ethics. Redemptive ethics proves most creative and value-producing as men relate their faith to their work and their world.

The true Agápe motif does not make for a public ethic. This is because it is solely a faith-conditioned ethic of individuals, while known socially by the <u>koinonia</u> or fellowship of those redeemed similarly by the unique love of God in Christ. Such a fellowship respects the revelations of divine law epitomized in the Decalogue and the more positive Sermon on the Mount as guidelines of Christian conduct, but not as definite to the point of being final in every instance or binding beyond consecrated imagination. Jesus himself set the spiritual precedent for this, when he said, "Man is not made for the sabbath, but the sabath is made for man." When David stole the bread from the Holy of Holies, he broke a religious law, but a higher divine law of love vindicated him. When Jesus met the woman about to be stoned for adultery, he squelched the legalistic Pharisees with: "He that is without sin, let him cast the first stone." "Judge not that ye be not judged," he taught. "Love thy neighbor as thyself."

Such an ethical outlook comes neither naturally nor easily.[8] It belongs to the "narrow way," not the narrow-minded way but the difficult way. It "relativizes" the Absolute but does not absolutize the relative. Yet, some interpreters of the new morality, who seek to keep Agápe paramount, push the motive beyond the limits of its Godward nature into the lanes of license, particularly when dealing with sex. The tendency is to over-accommodate home-sexuals, for example, as though they were perfectly normal in their physical and psychological adjustments, and much the same for pre-marital and extra-martial sex relations. When Joseph Fletcher illustrates such problems in his Situation Ethics he tends to confuse the true faith perspective of the Agápe motif with a secular perspective so as to vindicate the latter as though it were the former.[9] In so doing he often seems to justify what divine righteousness, scripturally understood, does not sanction, as though Agápe were a self-styled, unbridled kind of Eros with no guidelines of behavior.[10] Thus Fletcher tends to confuse, if not secularize, the nature and character of Christian responsibility, almost as though Agápe were neither a distinctively Christian motivation nor responsible for righteous principles.

Today our society is a "sex suffused" culture in which a moral revolution is one of the most insidious of problems. If the Christian ethics of Agápe is to be an inspiration in life, it must not become so relativistic as to over-accommodate the "sex-ploitation" of human responsibility. Historically, such would be the shift from legalism to license, from one extreme to another. Whenever sex is endorsed as a form of human expression without answering to some form of repression, it can hardly be in tune with Agápe. For example, sometimes soldiers expect sexual liberties on the pretext of someone owing them something for serving their country. Neither the banal expectation nor the superficial accommodation is indigenous to a God-centered Agápe, either in the form of vertical inspiration or horizontal response. Trial marriage, common law marriage, and free love are hardly expressive of genuine Agápe but ways of making men laws unto themselves. It must be remembered that Agápe is a transforming ethic, not a conforming one, a re-motivating love, not merely an emulating type. As such it is always compassionate and imaginative as well as serviceable to others, while never unprincipled.

Jesus said, "Love fulfills the law," even surpasses it in going the second mile in dealing with others. Going the second mile, however, is not by-passing the first! Thus, Agápe-love is not less than the fundamental law of God's righteousness but is that and more. Though legalism tends to betray the primacy of the Spirit of Love, Agápe is no warrant for sheer lawlessness or license. It always respects what God expects. A faith-conditioned Agápe does not seek or condone excuses for committing adultery, for instance, or automatically vindicate a person who violates the Decalogue, yet it is understanding, humble, patient, kind and compassionate. Though Fletcher is right in reminding us that there are times when Christians seem to be outdone ethically by some people in secular settings or by persons not God-centered in their choices, this is no warrant for inferring that true Agápe is manifested in some sinful situations as much or more than in moments of true faith response. Often Fletcher is extreme in asserting the ethical relativism of "the new morality" to the point of condoning what is a stronger Eros motivation than Agápe. This is too much like looking to one's situation for the answers of life's questions, rather than to the Christly focal point of faith, which re-orientates both the situation and the answer. Granted, the Christian often must concede a relativistic, critical situation, he still looks beyond himself to a revealed Absolute for inspiration, guidance and motivation. Thus, his paradoxical situation is qualified by his convictions, not merely his impulses; his spirit-inspired faith and not merely his sensate feet!

Contrary to Fletcher, the woman who gives herself to a man to allay his erotic impulses and related anxieties is hardly expressing a self-giving Agápe. She may be as self-centered as he. True Agápe is prompted by God, for Agápe is "of God." God is not a schizophrenic, whose laws of righteousness are alien to His law of love (I John 5:23). Even forgiveness would be almost of no account, if righteousness were not indigenous to the character of the God who wills to love and does so expendably. Fletcher tends to forget this. His nearly secularized version of Agápe is the dangerous aspect of situation ethics or the new morality. It pre-supposes that a Christly love is any form of concern for other people, while overlooking the hedonistic self-entanglements and Hobbesian biases of the individual, which often limit love to another type of Eros. Eros is any form of self-gratifying love and ranges from sex to success to the Greek love of wisdom --even to heavenly rewards. Fletcher seems to intend to say that a Christ-committed person becomes his own moralist. This is in the spirit of Augustine when he said, "Love God and do what you like." But Fletcher's explications seem to depict his intention differently, as though he were saying any man is his own moralist. Augustine could say what he did, because he viewed a person's love of God to entail loving what God loves. Often Fletcher's secular illustrations tend to by-pass this difference.

Apart from such weaknesses, Fletcher's situation ethics is a respectable attempt to articulate an existential perspective of Christian ethics in such a way as to avoid the extremes of legalism, on the one hand, and antinomianism,* on the other. What is needed to qualify its dangerous aspects is what I call a "balanced existentialism," one which recognizes that even the encounter with the divine Word is from within an existence which is phenomenalistically empirical. One way to see this is that the New Testament exponents of love were by no means suddenly extricated from divine righteousness, even though modified in interpretation.

Though frequently Christians cannot escape the existential relativism in which they are involved, even in reflecting Agápe, they need not apply it as though it were unprincipled. Their ethics must[11] supersede both a graceless moralism and a normless relativism. Existentially, a prayerful faith-encounter with God and an outgoing love are the inside and outside of the same thing. Paul speaks of "faith working thru love." (Galatians 5:6). Both aspects of Agápe look to the Unconditioned Spirit to qualify one's conditioned moments of existence. To do this is neither to justify lesser motivations nor to confuse them with the highest; it is to be involved, nevertheless, in the both/and paradox of looking to the Absolute through the existence-colored glasses of one's concrete situation. Even in the hymn of Agápe, Paul said, "We see through a glass darkly." Admittedly a venturesome risk of error at times, what does this imply basically but a trustful relationship between persons? It consistently puts persons before law and the spirit ahead of the letter. This is because it regards the Person of God as central.

There may be times when what one clings to as an ideal may have to be suspended. Abraham's experience of being asked by God to sacrifice his son Isaac was a "teleological suspension of the ethical," as Kierkegaard indicated,[12] but here the teleological reference was not an egocentrically pragmatic interest but the divine Absolute itself! Similarly as Dietrich Bonhoeffer stressed, the "cost of discipleship is often a "religionless Christianity," i.e., contrary to "the cheap grace" of limited doctrine, institutional conformity, religious patterns, creeds, dogma, ritual, law,[13] or custom, quite like Paul's rejection of circumcision and legalism. The Agápe motif is always personal and means that the individual responds directly to the Spirit of God. As Bishop Robinson has said, however, a person is not necessarily anti-Christian merely because he cannot subscribe to certain definite forms of Christianity.[14] To drop some pre-established interpretations is not necessarily to forsake the substance of the Gospel but might imply a purer expression of it, if Agápe is paramount. Ethically, birth control and complex instances of abortion and civil disobedience may be parallel cases in point. One who

---

*disregard for moral laws.

rebels against an unjust civic law, which men selfishly refuse to change, may actually be in a higher right as he looks to the higher law.[15] At points like this the contemporary Church is often cowardly and hypocritical.

Both Fletcher and Robinson fall short, however, because of neglect of divine righteousness, apart from which neither Love nor Grace can be fully understood. Though a Christian may be sensitive to another's anxieties and may desire to be of help, he is not justified in "playing God." He does not re-write the divine law of righteousness at a moment's notice, as though adultery, for example, were a dispensable matter due to the "situation."[16] To cite an instance, a young man of Christian convictions understood something of a married woman's inner plight over her inability to have a baby due to her husband's sterility. On one ocasion she initiated the opportunity for mutual satisfaction, but he politely refused -- not out of a lack of Agápe but because of it. Agápe was allowed to remotivate Eros. Otherwise, not only divine law would have been spurned altogether, but providence would have been taken into their own hands. Fletcher overlooks these dimensions of Christian ethics and faith, apart from which Eros is apt to dominate life's choices, rather than a true, God-centered Agápe. Consequently, expediencies are really condoned and the centrality of God's involvement in the existential decision is obscured.

However, one strength of "situational ethics" is that it questions the finality of any code of conduct, on the one hand, or any catalog of sins, on the other. Are there not times when divorce is the lesser of two evils? A supernatural view, long defended ecclesiastically by an ontological theory, has contended that marriage cannot be dissolved. But the true spiritual meaning, existentially, is that it should not be, the "I-thou" relation within the "I-Thou" relation being paramount. "What God has joined together let not man put asunder," said Jesus. Obviously, persons play a moral role here from within a spiritual bond -- one which it is possible to break -- lest there be no need for the exhortation.[17]

Another strength of situational ethics is that it shifts ethical standards of judgment from the impersonally objective plane to the personally subjective, i.e. from "out there" to "in here." This is akin to Jeremiah's yearning that the law of God "be written on our hearts." Human responsiveness is genuinely operative through existential relevance, not artificially by legalistic imposition. This may be the only true way in which we can combine autonomy and theonomy, so that in the faith-conditioned "New Being"[18] Agápe can function with consistency of spirit; anything less may not spring from a vital I-Thou relationship of faith. Also, it may be the only way persons can be trusted to respect others as persons and be truly sensitive to their needs. On such a basis relativistic, moral situations can be dealt with as such without prescriptive laws and ideals being manipulated as foregone conclusions or pre-fabricated categories and codes of conduct. By this a more genuine compassion is fostered with enough consecrated imagination to overcome puritanical Phariseeism and the judging of others.

But, for situation ethics or the new morality to be consistently Christian, perhaps it must be more specifically enunciated as meant only for the "remnant" of (existentially) faith-committed people[19] who are encountered by the Living Word, reclaimed by the Kerygma and thereby made amenable to the Didache[20] to which Jesus gave precedent as "the narrow way." It is a way of high expectations, not low ones, because of the nature of Agápe as the Spirit basic to the very character of God and the principles of His Kingdom. In this light, Jesus' teachings are not universally binding, like a philosophical idealism meant to guarantee a public morality, but are personal injunctions expressive of the redemptive and transforming faith-perspective of the Koinonia.[21] Universal ideals imply little or no decisiveness, for they leave open no situational alternatives or crises, whereas personal faith-relations amidst individual situations do so. Furthermore, love is not something we have but do, not something we possess but which possesses us. "But what of all the other people in the world?" you might ask. They are of the social "loaf" of society to which Jesus referred and must be influenced by the "leaven" and "salt" of the minority who have made the faith-commitment to love; the many will then seek to emulate the few.

* * * * * * * * *

Instead of appending a conclusion that attempts to epitomize the central issues of the leading chapters, the author suggests a re-reading of the Introduction with, no doubt, more critical acuity and perhaps more understanding than the first reading warranted. This will call for an application of several of the main insights of the respective thinkers discussed and likely in a comparative manner. It is hoped that the reader will recognise repeatedly the relevance of the basic issues to his other fields of study and endeavor.

Notes

1. Joseph Fletcher, Situation Ethics, Chapter I.
2. Ibid, p.13, 18f.
3. Ibid, p.31ff. 45.
4. Ibid, p.43f, 52, 104, 111.
5. Ibid, pp.15, 33, 49, 69, 79, 82, 89, 95, 104ff, 148.
6. Ibid, pp.25, 52, 60, 147, 18f.
7. Nicholas Berdyaev, The Divine and the Human; Slavery and Freedom.
8. The "natural" is closer to the psychological egoism implicit in the ethics of hedonists and their modern equivalents from Thomas Hobbes to Bentham and Mill.
9. Cf. Situation Ethics, several of his illustrations.
10. Cf. Anders Nygren Agape and Eros, Parts I, II and III for probably the finest study of the distinction between Agape and Eros ever to have been rendered. This I say despite my preference for modifying his extreme dualism thereof.
11. Cf. Paul Tillich, Morality and Beyond in which he argues for this very point.
12. Søren Kierkegaard, Fear and Trembling, pp.64-67.
13. Bonhoeffer, The Cost of Discipleship, p.45ff, 661ff.
14. Robinson, Honest to God, Chapter I.
15. Cf. Martin Luther King's "Letter from Birmingham City Jail," The Range of Ethics, eds. Titus and Keeton, p.288.
16. Yet this point is not unmindful of a legitimately compassionate attitute toward some persons caught in the dilemma of choosing between immorality and life itself, such as represented by the woman who bought her freedom from a concentration camp by sexual concession to a guard. Cf. V. Frankl, Man's Search for Meaning.
17. Cf. Robinson, op cit, pp.107ff, 111.
18. Cf. Paul Tillich. The Protestant Era, p.44f, p.53, 56f, 173. Cf. his work The New Being. This point-of-view was anticipated by Emil Brunner's work The Divine Imperative.
19. The N.T. "proclamation" of God revealed in Christ.
20. The moral principles and teachings of the N.T.
21. The N.T. church as a "fellowhship" of believers in Christ.

Name Index

Antisthenes, xii
Aquinas, Thomas, 53ff
Aristotle, xi, 13ff, 35, 53f, 106, 115, 169f
Arminius, James, 50
Ayer, A. J., 147ff, 157, 172

Barrett, Wm., 47
Bentham, Jeremy, xiii, 13ff, 119, 121
Berdyaev, Nicholas, 161, 224
Bonhoeffer, Dietrich, 227
Buber, Martin, 208

Cynics, xii, 35f

Descartes, René, 65, 85
Dewey, John, xiv, 10, 80, 97, 129, 167ff, 179, 181f
Diogenes, xii

Emerson, Ralph W., 160
Epictetus, 33ff
Epicurus, xi, xiv, 25ff

Fletcher, Joseph, 219ff
Freud, Sigmund, 177, 180
Fromm, Erich, p.161, 175, 177ff, 196

Garnett, A. C., 22, 123, 151, 173
Gogarten, Friedrich, p.146

Hannaford, Robert V., 172f
Hegel, G. F. W., 189, 191, 205
Heidegger, Martin, 175
Heim, Karl, 208
Heraclitus, p.5
Hobbes, Thos., 63ff, 93, 115, 117, 139, 145, 175
Hume, David, 10, 77ff, 93, 97, 115, 122, 150, 158, 169f
Husserl, Edmund, 213
Hutcheson, Francis, 113, 115

James, Wm., xiv, 169
Jefferson, Thos., 115
Joad, C. E. M., 150

Kant, Immanuel, xiii, 35, 93, 95, 97, 101ff, 115, 123, 132f, 141, 151,
    162, 182, 184, 193, 205, 208, 215
Kaufmann, Walter, 209

Kierkegaard, Søren, 22, 35, 51, 175, 183f, 189ff, 208, 217, 221, 227

Locke, John, 10, 71, 77, 115, 141, 169
Loomis, Earl, 196f
Luther, Martin, 205

Marcus, Aurelius, 35
Mill, John S., xiii, 119ff
Moore, G. E., 15, 123, 127ff, 141, 149, 150, 153, 157, 172
Morris, Bartram, 142

Newton, Isaac, 66
Nietzsche, Friedrich, 191, 194, 196, 201ff, 215, 221

Paul, St., 9, 28, 38, 45, 183, 208, 227
Pelagias, 50
Plato, 3ff, 17, 22, 35, 53, 103, 106, 115, 169, 197f, 207, 215
Pritchard, H. A., 149

Rawls, John 131ff, 137ff
Robinson, John A. J., 227
Ross, W. D., 149
Rousseau, Jacques, 139
Russell, Bertrand, vi, 149, 152, 155ff, 172

Sahakian, Wm. S., 159
Santayana, George, 137
Sartre, Jean-Paul, 108, 179, 195, 207, 211ff, 221f
Shaefer, David L., 140
Shaftesbury, Earl T., 71ff, 140
Sidgwick, Henry, 123, 127, 129f, 141
Socrates, xii, 3, 5, 15, 121, 192, 195
Sophists, 10
Sorokin, Peterim, v, xiv
Spinoza, Benedict de, 85ff
Stevenson, Charles, 147ff, 152f
Stumpf, Samuel, 172

Tillich, Paul, 196

Urban, Wilber M, 162

Whitehead, Alfred N., 155

Zeno, 35

Bibliography

Albert, Denise and Peterfreund, editors, Great Traditions in Ethics, Fifth Ed., Belmont, Calif. Wadsworth Publishing Co., 1984.
Aquinas, Thomas, Summa Contra Gentiles, from Basic Writings, ed. by Pegis, New York: Random House, 1944.
Aquinas, Thomas, The Summa Theologica from Basic Writings, ed. by Pegis, New York: Random House, 1944.
Aristotle, The Basic Works of Aristotle edited by Richard McKeon, New York: Random House Inc., 1941.
Augustine, Aurelius, Confessions, London: Everyman's Library, J. M. Dent and Sos, Ltd., 1949.
Augustine, Aurelius, The Enchiridion on Faith, Hope and Love, ed. by Henry Paclucci, Chicago: Regnery Editions, Gateway Editions, 1961.
Augustine, Aurelius, Faith, Hope and Charity, trans. by L. A. Arand, Ancient Christian Writers, Westminster, Md.: The Newman Press, 1947.
Augustine, Aurelius, City of God, London: Evryman's Library, J. M. Dent and Sons Ltd., 1947.
Aurelius, Marcus, Meditations, First Book, London: Everyman's Library, J. M. Dent and Sons, 1949.
Ayer, Alfred Jules, Language, Truth and Logic, New York: Dover Pub. Co., 1965.
Barrett, William, Irrational Man, New York: Doubleday Anchor Book, Doubleday & Co., 1962.
Beck, R. N. and Orr, J. R., editors, Ethical Choice, New York: The Free Press, 1970.
Bentham, Jeremy, An Introduction to the Principles of Morals and Legislation from British Moralists, ed. by Selby-Bigge, Indianapolis: The Bobbs-Merrill Co., Inc., 1964.
Berdyaev, Nicholas, The Divine and the Human, London: Geoffrey Bles, 1949.
Berdyaev, Nicholas, Slavery and Freedom, New York: Chas. Scribner's Sons, 1944.
Bonhoeffer, Dietrich, The Cost of Discipleship, New York: MacMillan Co., 1962.
Brunner, Emil, The Divine Imperative, Philadelphia: Westminster Press, 1947.
Butler, Joseph, Sermons, including Dissertatin II from British Moralists ed. by Selby-Bigge, Indianapolis: The Bobbs-Merrill Co., Inc., 1964.
Camus, Albert, The Rebel, Vintage Books, New York: Random House, 1956.
Cooper, Anthony Ashley, Earl of Shaftesbury, An Inquiry Concerning Virtue or Merit from British Moralists ed. by L. A. Selby-Bigge. Library of Liberal Arts, Indianapolis: The Bobbs-Merrill Co., Inc. 1964.

Dewey, John, The Quest for Certainty, Capricorn Books, New York: G. P. Putnam's Sons, 1960.
Dewey, John (and) James H. Tufts, Ethics, rev. ed., Part II, New York: Henry Holt and Co., 1932.
Dewey, John, Human Nature and Conduct, New York: Modern Library, 1930.
Dewey, John, Logic, The Theory of Inquiry, New York: H. Holt & Co., 1938.
Dewey, John, "Theory of Valuations," in Contemporary Philosophic Problems ed. by Y. Krikarian and A. Edel, New York: Macmillan, 1959.
Dewey, John, "Morals and Conduct," from Human Nature and Conduct, 1922 in The World's Great Thinkers, The Social Philosophers, p.49ff. New York: Random House, 1947.
Emerson, Ralph Waldo, Essays, New York: Books Inc., 1938.
Epictetus, The Enchiridion, New York: Walter J. Black Pub., 1942.
Epictetus, The Discourses and Enchiridion, Classics Club, New York: Walter J. Black, Inc., 1944.
Epicurus, Letters, Principle Doctrines and Vatican Sayings. Indianapolis and New York: The Bobbs-Merrill Co., Inc. 1964.
Ferm, Vergilius, Encyclopedia of Morals, New York: Philosophical Library, 1956.
Fletcher, William, Situation Ethics, Philadelphia: Westminster Press, 1966.
Frankl, Viktor, Man's Search for Meaning, New York: Washington Square Press, 1965.
Fromm, Erich, Man For Himself, Connecticut: Fawcett Publ. Inc., A Premier Book, 1965.
Fromm, Erich, The Art of Loving, New York: Bantam Books, 1956.
Fromm, Erich, Psychoanalysis and Religion, New York: Bantam Books, 1967.
Fromm, Erich, The Sane Society, Connecticut: Fawcett Publ. Co., Inc., 1967.
Garnett, A. Campbell, Ethics, A Critical Introduction, New York: The Ronald Press Co., 1960.
Grean, Stanley, Shaftesbury's Philosophy of Religion and Ethics, Athens, Ohio: Ohio Univ. Press, 1967.
Hannaford, Robert V. "You Ought to Derive 'Ought' from 'Is'," in Ethics in Perspective, ed. by K. J. and Paula R. Struhl, New York: Random House, 1975.
Hegel, G. F. W., The Phenomenology of Mind, trans. J. B. Baillie, 3rd ed., New York: MacMillan Co., 19__.
Heidegger, Martin, Existence and Being, London: Vision Press Ltd., 1949.
Heim, Karl, Christian Faith and Natural Science, New York: Harper and Bros., 1953.
Hobbes, Thomas, Leviathan, London: J. M. Dent and Sons Ltd., 1953.

Hobbes, Thomas, Of Human Nature, from British Moralists, ed. by Selby-Bigge, Indianapolis: The Bobbs-Merrill Co., Inc., 1964.

Hume, David, An Inquiry Concerning the Principles of Morals, New York: Library of Liberal Arts, ed. by Hendel's Liberal Arts Press, 1957.

Joad, C. E. M., Critique of Logical Positivism, Chicago: Univ. of Chicago Press, 1950.

Kant, Immanuel, The Critique of Pure Reason, London: Goe, Bell and Sons, 1897.

Kant, Immanuel, The Critique of Practical Reason, and other writings, trans. & ed. by L. W. Beck, Chicago: Univ. of Chicago Press, 1949-50.

Kant, Immanuel, Foundations of the Metaphysics of Morals, and other writings, trans. and ed. by L. W. Beck, Chicago: Univ. of Chicago Press, 1949-50.

Kant, Immanuel, Religion Within the Limits of Reason Alone, Chicago: Open Court Pub. Co., 1934.

Kaufmann, Walter, editor, "The Gay Science," by F. Nietzsche (and) "Concerning My Work As An Author" (and) "Live Dangerously", Existentialism From Dostoevsky to Sartre, New York: Meridian Books Inc., 1956. Cf. Kaufmann; The Portable Nietzsche, Viking Press, N.Y., 1968.

Kierkegaard, Søren, The Journals of Kierkegaard, ed. by Bretall, New York: Harper and Bros., 1959.

Kierkegaard, Søren, Concluding Unscientific Postscript. Princeton, New Jersey: Princeton Univ. Press, 1944.

Kierkegaard, Søren, Training in Christianity, Princeton, New Jersey: Princeton Univ. Press, 1944.

Kierkegaard, Søren, Either/Or, Vol. II, Princeton, New Jersey: Princeton Univ. Press, 1944.

Kierkegaard, Søren, For Self Examination. Minneapolis: Augsburg Publ. House, 1959.

Kierkegaard, Søren, Concept of Dread, Princeton, New Jersey: Princeton Univ. Press, 1944.

Kierkegaard, Søren, Stages on Life's Way, Princeton, New Jersey: Princeton Univ. Press, 1958.

Kierkegaard, Søren, Fear and Trembling (and) Sickness Unto Death, New York: Doubleday & Co., 1955.

Kierkegaard, Søren, On Authority and Revelation. New York: Harper Torchbook, 1966.

Kierkegaard, Søren, Attach Upon Christendom. Boston: Beacon Press, 1944, 1956.

Kierkegaard, Søren, Purity of Heart, New York: Harper and Bros., 1938.

Kierkegaard, Søren, The Point of View. New York: Oxford Univ. Press, 1939.

Kierkegaard, Søren, Edifying Discourses. New York: Harper Bros., 1958.

McKeon, Richard, editor, Selections From Medieval Philosophers. New York, Chicago: Chas. Scribner's Sons, 1929.

Mill, John Stuart, Utilitarianism (and) On Liberty and Representative Government, New York: E. P. Dutton & Co., 1926.

Moore, G. E., Principia Ethica, Cambridge: Cambridge University Press, 1903, 1959.

Moore, G. E., Ethics. London: London & Oxford Univ. Press, 1912, 1971.

Morris, Bartram, "Rawls' Egalitarianism," Philosophic Research and Analysis. (Now: Contemporary Philosophy). Vol. V, no. 8, Winter, 1975.

Nietzsche, Friedrich, Thus Spake Zarathustra. London: J. M. Dent and Sons Ltd., 1946.

Nietzsche, Friedrich, The Will to Power. New York: MacMillan Co., 1924.

Nietzsche, Friedrich, Beyond Good and Evil. Penquin Books, Harmondsworth: 1973.

Nietzsche, Friedrich, The Genealogy of Morals (and) Ecce Homo, ed. by W. Kaufmann, Vintage Books, New York: Random House, 1967.

Nygren, Anders, Agape and Eros, Parts I, II, III. New York: The MacMillan Co., 1941.

Organ, Troy W., The Examined Life. Selection, "Science and Value" by Wilber M. Urban, Boston: Houghton Mifflin Co., 1956.

Plato, The Dialogues of Plato, trans. by Benjamin Jowett, New York: Liveright Publ. Co., (1893), 1927.

Plato, The Republic. Oxford: Clarendon Press, 1888.

Rawls, John, A Theory of Justice. Cambridge, Mass.: Harvard Univ. Press, 1971.

Robinson, John A. J., Honest to God. Philadelphia: Westminster Press, 1963.

Russell, Bertrand, Power, A New Social Analysis. New York: W. W. Norton, 1969.

Russell, Bertrand, The Scientific Outlook, Glencoe, Ill.: The Free Press, 1931.

Russell, Bertrand, The Impact of Science on Society. New York: Columbia Univ. Press, 1951.

Russell, Bertrand, A History of Western Philosohy. New York: Simon and Schuster, 1945.

Russell, Bertrand, "Religion and Science" from Value and Obligation, ed. by R. B. Brandt, New York: Harcourt, Brace and World, Inc., 1961.

Russell, Bertrand, "An Appeal to the Intellectuals of Europe" from Justice In War Time. Selectin in Ethical Choice, ed. by Beck and Orr. New York: The Free Press, 1970.

Russell, Bertrand, Statement in Etcetera, American Friends Service Committee, College Program, March, 1960, p.4.

Sahakian, William S., Systems of Etics and Value Theory, Paterson, New Jersey: Littlefield, Adams and Co., 1964.

Sartre, Jean-Paul, Being and Nothingness. New York: Philosophical Library, Inc., 1956.

Sartre, Jean-Paul, Existentialism and Humanism. Longon: Methuen and Co., Ltd., 1949.

Sartre, Jean-Paul, Existentialism, trans. Frechtman. New York: Philosophical Library Inc., 1941.

Sartre, Jean -Paul, Existentialism and Human Emotions. New York: Philosophical Library, 1957.

Schilpp. Paul A., The Philosophy of Bertrand Russell, 3rd ed. New York: Harper and Row, 1963.

Searle, John Rogers, "How to Derive 'Ought' from 'Is'," in Moral Philosophy, ed. by A. G. Oldenquist, 2nd ed. Boston: Houghton-Mifflin Co., 1978.

Selby-Bigge, L. A. editor, British Moralists (selections), Vols. I and II. Indianapolis: The Bobbs-Merrill Co., Inc. 1964.

Shaefer, David L. Justice or Tyranny, A critique of John Rawls 'A Theory of Justice.' Port Washington, New York: Kennikat Press, 1979.

Shirk, Evelyn, The Ethical Dimension, New York: Appleton-Crofts, 1965.

Spinoza, Baruch (Benedict), Ethics and De Intellectus Emendatione, trans. A. Boyle, London: J. M. Dent & Co., Inc. 1948.

Stevenson, Charles L. Facts and Values, New Haven: Yale Univ. Press, 1963, 1967.

Strodach, George K., The Philosophy of Epicurus. Evanston, Ill.,: Northwestern Univ. Press, 1963.

Stumpf, Samuel E., Philosophy: History and Problems. New York: McGraw-Hill Book Co., 1977.

Tillich, Paul, Morality and Beyond. New York: Harper and Row, 1963.

Tillich, Paul, The New Being. New York: Chas. Scribner's Sons, 1955.

Tillich, Paul, The Protestant Era. Chicago: Univ. of Chicago Press, 1959.

Titus, H. and Keeton, M., editors. The Range of Ethics. M. L. King, "Letter from Birmingham City Jail," New York: American Book Co., 1966.

Ward, Leo R., Ethics: A College Text. New York: Harper and Row, Publs., 1965.

Wheelwright, Philip, A Critical Introduction to Ethics, 3rd ed. New York: Odyssey Press, 1959.